W9-ARP-021

ARCTIC OCEAN

FINLAND
SWEDEN
POLAND   BELARUS
GANY
HUNGARY   UKRAINE
ROMANIA
ITALY   BULGARIA   GEORGIA
GREECE   TURKEY   TURKMENISTAN
TUNISIA   SYRIA
LEBANON   IRAQ   IRAN
ISRAEL   JORDAN
KUWAIT
LIBYA   EGYPT
QATAR
U.A.E.
SAUDI ARABIA
OMAN
CHAD   ERITREA   YEMEN
SUDAN   DJIBOUTI
ABIA   CENTRAL   SOMALIA
AFRICAN   ETHIOPIA
REPUBLIC
UGANDA
ON   RWANDA   KENYA
NGO   CONGO   BURUNDI
(DEM. REP.)
TANZANIA
ANGOLA
ZAMBIA
ZIMBABWE
NAMIBIA   MALAWI   MADAGASCAR
BOTSWANA   MOZAMBIQUE
SWAZILAND
SOUTH AFRICA   LESOTHO

RUSSIA

KAZAKHSTAN   MONGOLIA

UZBEKISTAN   KYRGYZSTAN

AFGHANISTAN   CHINA

PAKISTAN   NEPAL   BHUTAN

INDIA

MYANMAR   LAOS
BANGLADESH
THAILAND   VIETNAM

SRI LANKA   CAMBODIA

BRUNEI
MALAYSIA

NORTH KOREA
SOUTH KOREA
JAPAN

TAIWAN

PHILIPPINES

NORTH
PACIFIC
OCEAN

INDONESIA   PAPUA
NEW GUINEA

INDIAN
OCEAN

AUSTRALIA

NEW ZEALAND

Understanding God's World Series

Understanding God's World Series

Homelands Around the World

Grade 4

Teacher's Manual

Rod and Staff Publishers, Inc.
P.O. Box 3, Hwy. 172
Crockett, Kentucky 41413-0003
Telephone: (606) 522-4348

ACKNOWLEDGMENTS

We are indebted first of all to God who "hath made of one blood all nations of men for to dwell on all the face of the earth" (Acts 17:26). We are grateful that He has enabled the many who have worked on this project. Brother Bennie Hostetler and the sisters Mary Miller, Amy Herr, and Nancy Gnossa wrote the text. Others spent many hours reviewing the material, drawing the art work, and preparing the manuscript for publication.

We are also grateful for the permissions that were granted for use of photographs. See page 382 for credits.

The Publishers

2   3   4   5   6   7   8   —   22   21   20   19   18   17   16   15   14   13

CONTENTS

Introduction to the Teacher

"God that made the world and all things therein, . . . hath made of one blood all nations of men for to dwell on all the face of the earth, and hath determined the times before appointed, and the bounds of their habitation" (Acts 17:24, 26).

Homelands Around the World is both a storybook and a textbook. As a storybook, it portrays the lives of children in various lands and cultures. As a textbook, it explains some of the underlying reasons for differences in people's lives. The four main goals of *Homelands Around the World* are as follows.

1. To acquaint students with the way people live, work, and play in countries around the world, with special reference to the effect of climate on people's lives.

2. To establish a basic familiarity with the physical geography of the earth and with geographical terms.

3. To foster a wholesome attitude toward all people, no matter what their color or culture.

4. To develop skill in using maps and globes, the two most valuable tools of geography.

No book produced by man is ever the whole story. The pupil's text and this teacher's guide are designed to give the teacher something to teach and a method for teaching it; but they are not meant to replace or limit the teacher's own creativity, inspiration, and enthusiasm. The school board and parents can furnish books, financial support, and a schoolroom, but the final success of any course depends most heavily on you—the teacher.

Be a teacher who is sensitive to the needs of each student. Be a teacher who puts forth energy with a purpose. Haphazard lesson preparation and unplanned class discussions are of mediocre value at best, no matter how good the text might be. Remember that of all the experiences in a child's life, his experiences at school should be among the most beneficial.

LESSON FORMAT

In the teacher's guide, the **Lesson Aim** gives the main purpose of the lesson. The **Main Points** give the most important concepts, and they may also give additional information that is not in the pupil's text. This added material is enclosed in brackets.

Be sure you are familiar with the Main Points, for the exercises, reviews, and tests are based on them. The Main Points are listed in the same order that the concepts are presented in the pupil's lesson so that this section may be used as a guide during class discussion.

The class discussion is the time for the students to take part and for you as the teacher to see how well the students are comprehending the lesson. Then if you see a problem developing, you can deal with it in the beginning stages.

The **Related Points** give additional background material for a broader understanding of the lesson or simply as a matter of added interest. Material found under Related Points, or enclosed in brackets under Main Points, is not covered by the exercises, since it is not taught in the pupil's text.

Answers are given near each set of exercises, and a copy of each test with answers filled in is included in the back of this book. If an exercise asks for several answers, be sure students have two or more responses. Sometimes the instructions call for answers in complete sentences. However, answers are not given in complete sentences because a model answer would be just one of several possibilities. Rather, the items or main ideas that should be included in the student's answer are given. The teacher may judge whether the sentence is complete.

Testing Your Understanding has the written work, and *Further Study* provides questions to discuss in class.

The *Map Exercises* give practice in working with maps. Outline maps for tracing are found in the "Map Section," in the back of the book. These maps may be reproduced as needed in teaching this course.

Working with maps will be of considerable value to the students as they study the geography of each country. Encourage your pupils to make their maps neat and attractive by following the "Rules for Drawing Neat Maps" at the beginning of the Map Section. (These guidelines apply to hand-drawn maps. They do not apply to maps produced by publishers, who can distinguish map features by using different styles and sizes of type.)

A few chapters have an *Extra Activity* at the end. This activity is not an essential part of the course but is a supplementary project designed to broaden the pupil's understanding.

Beginning in Chapter 2, a part called *So Far This Year* gives a cumulative review of the main concepts studied to that point. These reviews can be done orally in class, or they can be given as the assignment after the chapter test (to be done for the day when the class starts the next chapter). *So Far This Year* is a set of basic, objective exercises that can be answered and checked quickly. Their purpose is not to make pupils dig, but simply to drill and review main facts they have studied.

May God bless you with wisdom and inspiration as you teach the lessons in this book.

Introduction

"And God saw that it was good" (Genesis 1:10).

In this book you will meet boys and girls from around the world. Some live in lands much the same as yours, but others live in places that are much warmer or much colder. This makes a difference in the foods they eat, the clothes they wear, the work they do, and the animals they see.

So come along and be a world traveler. You will travel to distant lands with your classmates and your teacher to see how children live in other countries. You will not need an airplane ticket; neither will you need to get on a ship. All you will need is your book, a good guide (your teacher), and some imagination. Then you will be able to see this beautiful world that God has made and has given us to use and enjoy.

In Genesis 1, we find these words over and over: "And God saw that it was good." As you go from one country to another in this book, you should be able to see that these words are really true. The world is indeed a good gift to us. It makes no difference what color our skin is. Neither does it matter what language we speak. In whatever country we might live, "God saw that it was good."

The trips you take will be imaginary, but they are very much like what would happen on a real trip. Are you ready to go? You have many places to see and many new friends to meet.

Front cover: Cattle graze on rolling green pastures on the island of Tasmania. Tasmania is an Australian state that lies off the southeast corner of the mainland of Australia.

UNIT ONE
Climates in Different Lands

CHAPTER 1

CLIMATE ZONES OF THE EARTH

"When it is evening, ye say, It will be fair weather: for the sky is red. And in the morning, It will be foul weather to day: for the sky is red and lowring" (Matthew 16:2, 3).

1. Climate Zones

Glossary Words

Antarctic Circle (ant AHRK tihk, ant AHR tihk) The imaginary line that marks the edge of the Southern Frigid Zone.

Arctic Circle (AHRK tihk, AHR tihk) The imaginary line that marks the edge of the Northern Frigid Zone.

axis (AK sihs) An imaginary line through the poles of the earth.

globe

continent A large landmass of the earth, such as Africa or North America.

equator (ee KWAY tur) An imaginary line running east and west around the middle of the earth and dividing the Northern Hemisphere from the Southern Hemisphere.

globe (GLOHB) A round model of the earth.

hemisphere (HEHM ih sfihr) Half of a sphere or globe.

Tropic of Cancer The imaginary line that marks the northern edge of the Tropical Zone.

Tropic of Capricorn (KAP rih kawrn) The imaginary line that marks the southern edge of the Tropical Zone.

Weather and Climate

Weather is the condition of the outside air. It includes temperature, sunlight, rain, and wind at a certain time and place. The weather can be very changeable. One day may have cool, rainy weather, and the next day may be sunny and warm. God planned these weather changes. He knew that the earth needs both rain and sunshine, heat and cold.

What is climate? It is the usual weather in an area. A place with a warm climate usually has warm weather, and a place with a cold climate usually has cold weather. The climate does not change as the weather does. We

LESSON AIM

To establish a foundation for the studies in this book by teaching what climate is, by acquainting the students with the five main climate zones, and by introducing the globe and some basic geographical terms.

MAIN POINTS

• **Weather and climate.** Weather is the day-to-day condition of the outside air. Climate is the usual weather in an area. Both weather and climate are under God's control.

[Have pictures ready to show in class—various weather conditions, tropical and Arctic lands, deserts, and so forth. The children will likely enjoy telling about a real trip they have taken to an area with a climate different from theirs.

Discuss the climate zone, general climate, and weather patterns in your area—temperature range, annual precipitation, and so forth. Talk about the severe weather your area might have over a year, such as thunderstorms, snowstorms, tornadoes, or hurricanes. This will help to show that weather and climate do affect us and sometimes even control us. A good illustration is areas that have snow. Here the people are compelled to have snow removal equipment, and they need snow tires and antifreeze for their cars.]

• **The globe.** Point out that a globe is a model of the earth. Use a globe to show the imaginary lines dividing the earth. Notice that the equator divides the earth into the Northern and Southern hemispheres. Point out the seven continents.

know the climate of an area by the weather it has over a long period of time.

God planned different climates for different parts of the earth. For example, the state of Florida has a warm climate. The weather in Florida is warm most of the year. So the houses do not need large furnaces, and they are not well insulated. But suppose we visit Maine, where the winters are much colder. There we would find that the houses are well insulated, and they have good heating systems. God gave Arizona a hot, dry climate. Many houses there have air conditioners so that people can stay cool.

Weather is very important. But climate is still more important because it affects the clothes we wear, the food we eat, and even the way our houses are built. Climate is one of the main reasons that people live differently in different lands.

The Earth and Climate

A *globe* is a small model of the earth. It shows where we could see land and water if we saw the earth from outer space. A globe looks like a ball. It is usually mounted on a rod (the *axis*) that is tilted to one side.

On a globe we can see the *equator*, an imaginary line running east and west around the middle of the earth. The equator divides the globe into two half balls, or *hemispheres*.

The top half of the globe is called the Northern Hemisphere. It has the *continents* of Europe, Asia, and North America, and the northern parts of Africa and South America. The bottom half of the globe is called the Southern Hemisphere. It includes the continents of Australia and Antarctica, and the southern parts of Africa and South America.

Northern and Southern Hemispheres

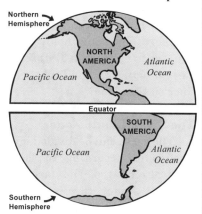

- **The five climate zones.** The imaginary lines on a globe are a convenient way of showing these main climate zones. [But make it clear that the boundaries of the climate zones are not as sharply defined as the lines suggest.]
- **Local climate variations.** Oceans and large lakes are a moderating influence on climate. [Warm or cold ocean currents also have strong effects.] A high altitude generally means a cooler climate, [and the sheltered side of a high mountain range is a rain shadow. These are but a few of the factors that create a wide array of local climate variations even within the same climate zone.]

RELATED POINTS

- **Tropics of Cancer and Capricorn.** You yourself should know the significance of these tropics and of the Arctic and Antarctic circles, but you need not explain the full details at this level. The Arctic and Antarctic circles could be mentioned as the limits of the midnight sun in summertime.

The Seven Continents

If you look closely at the globe on page 13, you will see other lines running east and west. Four of these lines are of special importance. One line near the top of the globe is called the *Arctic Circle*, and another line near the bottom is called the *Antarctic Circle*.

Two other lines are nearer the equator. The one above the equator is called the *Tropic of Cancer*. The one below the equator is called the *Tropic of Capricorn*. Can you find these lines on the globe?

The Five Climate Zones

The earth can be divided into five zones according to their general climates. They are the Tropical Zone, the Northern Frigid Zone, the Southern Frigid Zone, the Northern Temperate Zone, and the Southern Temperate Zone.

The Tropic of Cancer is at the northern edge of the Tropical Zone, and the Tropic of Capricorn is at the southern edge. The equator is in the center. So the Tropical Zone is like a belt around the earth's middle. In this region it is very warm year round. Follow the belt around the globe. Can you find Brazil and Nigeria? We will visit these lands in our travels.

The two frigid zones are the areas around the North Pole and the South Pole. These areas are very cold most of the year. The edge of the Northern Frigid Zone is the imaginary line called the Arctic Circle. This line crosses northern Asia and North America, and it goes across the southern tip of Greenland. All the lands from the Arctic Circle to the North Pole are in the Northern Frigid Zone.

The Antarctic Circle is the edge of the Southern Frigid Zone, and most of it is over water. The frozen continent of Antarctica is almost completely inside the Antarctic Circle. Can you find the frigid zones at the top and bottom of the globe?

Now it is easy to see where the two temperate zones are. The Northern Temperate Zone is the area between the Arctic Circle and the Tropic of Cancer. The Southern Temperate Zone is the area between the Antarctic Circle and the Tropic of Capricorn. Most lands in the temperate zones have the four seasons of spring, summer, autumn, and winter.

The Northern Temperate Zone is in the Northern Hemisphere. If you follow this zone around the globe, you will see that there are many countries in it. Do you see the United States, Canada, France, Germany, and Japan? All these countries and many others are in the Northern Temperate Zone.

What countries are in the Southern Temperate Zone? There are not as many as in the Northern Temperate Zone. But there are still a few, such as New Zealand, Argentina, and South Africa.

Climate Zones

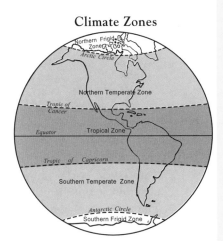

The five climate zones are like a cap on each pole of the earth and three bands around the middle.

Differences Within Climate Zones

Now you have studied the five general areas of climate. But you must understand that even within the same climate zone, God made some differences of climate. For example, Maine has a much colder climate than Florida, even though both are in the Northern

Temperate Zone. This is true because Florida is much closer to the equator than Maine is. Oceans, large lakes, and high mountains also make a difference in the climate of a place. You will learn more about these differences of climate as you study this book.

—————— Testing Your Understanding ——————

A. *Write the correct word(s) to complete each sentence.*

zone	hemisphere	Cancer
axis	continent	Capricorn
globe	equator	Antarctic Circle
climate	weather	Arctic Circle

1. The daily sunshine, rain, and temperature is called the ———.
2. The usual weather in an area is its ———.
3. A model of the earth that is handy for classroom use is called a ———.
4. The ——— is the imaginary line running east and west around the middle of the earth.
5. The rod on which a globe turns is called its ———.
6. A ——— is one of the seven large landmasses on the earth.
7. A half of the earth is called a ———.
8. The ——— marks the edge of the Northern Frigid Zone.
9. The Tropic of ——— is the northern boundary of the Tropical Zone.
10. The Tropic of ——— is the boundary between the Tropical Zone and the Southern Temperate Zone.
11. The ——— marks the edge of the Southern Frigid Zone.
12. Each climate ——— has differences of climate within it.

B. *Answer these questions.*

1. In which climate zone do you live?
2. Do you live in the Northern Hemisphere or the Southern Hemisphere?
3. Suppose you wanted to live in a land that is warm the year round. What imaginary line would you need to be close to?
4. Which continent has the coldest climate?

Lesson 1 Answers

  Testing Your Understanding

A. 1. weather
2. climate
3. globe
4. equator
5. axis
6. continent
7. hemisphere
8. Arctic Circle
9. Cancer
10. Capricorn
11. Antarctic Circle
12. zone

B. (Answers for 1 and 2 are correct for most North American students.)
1. in the Northern Temperate Zone
2. in the Northern Hemisphere
3. the equator (or the Tropic of Cancer or the Tropic of Capricorn)
4. Antarctica

Further Study

1. List three things that you can say about the weather today.
2. How does climate affect our lives?
3. Name two things that cause differences of climate even in the same climate zone.

Map Exercises

Write a word from the diagram below to match each description.

1. A large body of water surrounded by land.
2. A chain of mountains.
3. A large stream, usually flowing into a lake or an ocean.
4. A huge body of salt water.
5. An area of land completely surrounded by water.
6. An arm of land almost surrounded by water.
7. A stream or river that flows into a larger river.
8. A broad waterway between two areas of land.
9. A narrow stretch of water between two areas of land.
10. A large area of water partly surrounded by land.
11. An area of water partly surrounded by land, usually smaller than a gulf.
12. The land along an ocean or a sea.

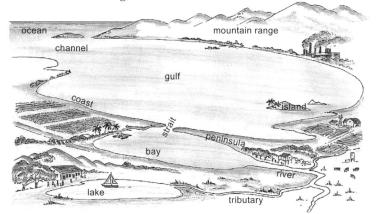

Further Study

1. (Sample answers) warm, sunny, calm, cool, cloudy, windy, rainy
2. Climate affects the kind of clothes we wear, the kind of food we eat, and the way our houses are built.
3. (Any two) distance from the equator, oceans or large lakes, high mountains

Map Exercises

1. lake
2. mountain range
3. river
4. ocean
5. island
6. peninsula
7. tributary
8. channel
9. strait
10. gulf
11. bay
12. coast

2. The Tropical Zone

Glossary Words

piranha

tile

fazenda (fuh ZEHN duh) 1. A large farm for raising crops such as coffee, sugar cane, or cotton. 2. A plantation in Brazil.

kapok (KAY pahk) A tree that produces a silk-cotton fiber.

mahogany (muh HAHG uh nee) A tree that has hard red wood.

national language The language chosen for the official business of a nation.

piranha (pih RAHN yuh) A savage flesh-eating fish with large, razor-sharp teeth.

port A city or town with a harbor where ships load and unload their cargoes.

tile A thin block of dried clay used as a shingle on a roof.

Life in a Tropical Land

Maria is a fifth-grade girl who lives in the country of Brazil. This is the largest country in South America, and it is almost as large as the United States. To get to Maria's home from North America, we fly southeast across the Caribbean Sea, across the equator, to São Paulo (sown POW loo). São Paulo is the largest city in Brazil. From there we travel to a small village in the countryside.

Growing Coffee in Brazil

Maria's family lives in a small stone house with a *tile* roof of red clay. Around the house are rows and rows of tall bushes with glossy leaves and white blossoms. "Those are coffee trees," Maria explains when we ask about them. "We get our living from them. My father and older brother work for the landowner of this *fazenda*."

"There are about two thousand workers on this fazenda," says

LESSON AIM

To give a brief overview of Brazil, a land in the Tropical Zone, for the purpose of later comparison with lands in other climate zones.

MAIN POINTS

- **Brazil is the largest South American country.** It spans the Tropical Zone from the equator to the Tropic of Capricorn.

- **Brazil has warm temperatures throughout the year.** Coffee is just one example of the many tropical crops that can be raised there. Only the very southern part of Brazil has any frost or snow. [Remind students that in the Southern Hemisphere, southern parts of countries are usually the coolest.]

- **Tropical seasons are the rainy season and the dry season.** [Contrast this with the four seasons most North Americans enjoy. The four seasons of the temperate zones will be studied in the next lesson.]

- **Rain forests cover northern Brazil.** The rain forests do not have seasons, but are warm and wet all year. Some trees that grow there are Brazil nut, kapok, mahogany, and rubber trees.

- **The Amazon River flows through northern Brazil.** It is the largest river in the world. [The Nile River is slightly longer than the Amazon, but the Amazon has the greatest volume of flow.] Large ships can sail up the Amazon to ports far inland.

- **Most of the people in Brazil live near the Atlantic Ocean.** Brasília, the capital, was built inland to encourage settlement of the interior. Portuguese is the national language.

Brazil

Maria's brother, Lopez (LOH pehz). "Each family that works for the owner has a certain piece of land and a certain number of coffee trees to care for all year long. Then at harvesttime each family gets a share of the profits."

"When do you harvest the coffee?" we ask.

"The berries will soon begin to grow where the blossoms are,"

Lopez answers. "It will be about seven months until they are ripe. During that time we pull weeds, stir up the soil, and spray the trees for insects and diseases. We pick the berries by hand when they are bright red.

"The berries are washed, and then a machine takes the pulp off the two beans that are inside each berry. We spread the coffee beans

RELATED POINTS

- **Animals of the Tropics.** The interest block and the text mention a few of the tropical animals living in Brazil. Further research could be done in encyclopedias or other books.

- **Rain forest versus jungle.** A tropical rain forest has such a dense canopy of foliage that only about one percent of the sunlight reaches the forest floor. Hence there is little undergrowth, and it is easy to walk through a rain forest.

    A jungle has a thinner canopy of leaves, so more sunlight comes through to the ground. Here the plant growth is so thick that it is difficult to pass through. Jungle growth occurs at the edge of broad rivers and in old clearings in a tropical rain forest.

Coffee branch and berries

Coffee growers and their workers spend much time carefully picking the ripe berries.

on big concrete floors to dry in the sunshine for two or three weeks. When they are dry enough, we send them to coffee buyers who prepare the coffee for market. Coffee is the main drink in Brazil. It is sold to countries around the world too. Almost one third of all the coffee in the world is raised in Brazil."

"Doesn't it rain on the coffee when you are drying it?" someone asks.

"By that time we will be in the dry season. We cover the beans with canvas at night to keep off the dew, but we do not need to worry about rain. Coffee trees need a rainy season and a dry season to thrive. The Lord sends plenty of rain during the time that the berries are growing. We get about 60 inches of rain each year. Coffee also needs a warm climate. If it should ever freeze here, the trees would die."

Tropical Rain Forest

"Does it ever freeze in Brazil?"

"Yes, it does. The very southern part of Brazil reaches into the Southern Temperate Zone. Some places there have frost or a little snow in the winter. But most of the country is warm the year round."

"It gets warmer as you go north," explains Maria. "Brazil reaches to the equator too. In the north there is a great tropical rain forest. There is no wet season and dry season there. The rain forest is hot and wet all year long. It may receive 160 inches of rainfall a year. That would be like having 3 inches of rain every week, all year long."

"Does anyone live in the rain forest?" someone asks.

"Some Indian tribes live there," Lopez explains. "They have houses built of wild cane plants and palm leaves. More people are moving in to clear forestland for raising crops."

"What kind of trees grow there?"

"Have you ever eaten Brazil nuts? They grow on giant trees in the rain forest. **Kapok**, or silk-cotton trees, grow there too. Fibers that cover the kapok seeds are used in mattresses and life preservers. Rubber trees give sap that is made into rubber. Lumber from **mahogany** trees makes beautiful furniture. God made thousands of different kinds of trees to grow in the rain forest!"

The Amazon River flows slowly through a tropical rain forest. Many people regularly use the Amazon as a river road to travel from place to place.

"And thousands of beautiful birds, insects, and butterflies!" exclaims Maria. "Lots of monkeys live in the trees. Great snakes and other animals live there too."

The Amazon River

"Your picture of the tropical rain forest is not complete without the *Rio Amazonas*," Maria continues.

"You would call it the Amazon River," explains Lopez. "*Rio* means 'river.'"

"The Amazon River is the biggest river in the world," says Maria. "It flows through the tropical rain forests in the northern part of Brazil. Ships can sail up the river more than 2,000 miles.

"We have an uncle who lives near Belém (buh LEHM) at the mouth of the Amazon River. He says it is dangerous to swim in that water. There are many alligators, flesh-eating fish called **piranhas**, and electric eels that can paralyze a man with their shock. But the Amazon is very valuable to our country because **ports** far from the ocean can use it to ship their goods to other countries."

These men are preparing for a busy market day in a Brazilian city.

Brazilians raise cattle and crops in the beautiful rolling hills of southern Brazil.

The People of Brazil

"There are some cities along the Amazon," says Lopez. "But by far, most of the people in Brazil live around the edge of the country near the Atlantic Ocean. It is easier to travel there, and the sea breezes make the climate more comfortable."

"Brasília (brah SEEL yuh) is not near the ocean though," Maria reminds us. "Brasília is our capital. It was built hundreds of miles inland to encourage people to settle in the interior rather than just along the coast. The plan seems to be working, for Brasília is growing."

We ask about the language we have heard many people speaking in Brazil. "Is it Spanish?"

"No," Maria replies. "It is Portuguese, which is our *national language*. The Portuguese ruled Brazil from 1500 to 1822. In fact, the Portuguese named Brazil for the red wood called brazilwood that they found in our country. They also named several of our coastal cities, like Rio de Janeiro (REE oh day zhuh NAIR oh). That city is a major port on the Atlantic Ocean."

At the end of our visit, we thank Maria and Lopez for telling us so many interesting things about their country.

"It was a pleasure," says Maria. "You are always welcome to come again to visit warm, beautiful Brazil."

Tropical Animals

The **ocelot** (AHS uh laht) looks like a small leopard or tiger. It lives on the ground, but it is a good climber, and it often hunts in forest trees. Ocelots eat small animals.

The **toucan** (TOO kan) is a large bird with a huge, brightly colored bill. Its food is fruit. When a toucan sleeps, it turns its head around and lays its bill down the middle of its back. Then it folds its tail up over its head.

The **marmoset** (MAHR muh seht) is a very small kind of monkey. Marmosets live in treetops and eat insects, spiders, and fruit. They sleep in holes in the trees.

A **macaw** (muh KAW) is a large parrot with beautiful feathers of blue, yellow-red, and green. Some kinds grow to be 39 inches long.

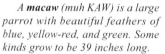

The **anteater** has a coarse fur coat and a great bushy tail. Its head and nose are tube-shaped. It rips open ant nests with its strong front claws and licks up the ants with a long, sticky tongue.

───────── **Testing Your Understanding** ─────────

A. *Write* true *or* false *for each sentence. Copy each false sentence, and change one word in it to make it true.*

   1. Brazil is the largest country in South America.
   2. Most of Brazil is in the Tropical Zone.
   3. Some places in the northern part of Brazil have frost.
   4. Coffee beans are harvested in the dry season.
   5. The tropical rain forest is cool and wet all year.
   6. A fazenda is a city or town where ships load and unload their goods.
   7. *Rio* means "grand."
   8. The Amazon River is the largest river in the world.
   9. The national language of Brazil is Spanish.
  10. The capital of Brazil is Brasília.

B. *Write the letters of the correct answers.*

   1. What two lines cross Brazil?
     a. Arctic Circle
     b. equator
     c. Antarctic Circle
     d. Tropic of Capricorn
   2. What two seasons does a tropical climate have?
     a. rainy season
     b. summer
     c. winter
     d. dry season
   3. What kind of tree is valuable for its sap?
     a. coffee
     b. rubber
     c. kapok
     d. mahogany
   4. How far up the Amazon River can ships sail?
     a. to Belém
     b. over 2,000 miles
     c. about 160 miles
     d. to the coffee fazendas

Lesson 2 Answers

  Testing Your Understanding

A. 1. true
  2. true
  3. false; Some places in the ~~northern~~ southern part of Brazil have frost.
  4. true
  5. false; The tropical rain forest is ~~cool~~ hot and wet all year.
  6. false; A ~~fazenda~~ port is a city or town where ships load and unload their goods.
  7. false; *Rio* means ~~"grand"~~ "river."
  8. true
  9. false; The national language of Brazil is ~~Spanish~~ Portuguese.
  10. true

B. 1. b. equator
    d. Tropic of Capricorn
  2. a. rainy season
    d. dry season
  3. b. rubber
  4. b. over 2,000 miles

5. c. The government wanted to encourage people to settle inland.

Further Study

1. No. Coffee trees need a dry season to thrive, and the tropical rain forest is wet all year.
2. (Possible answers) farm crops, Brazil nuts, kapok or products made with kapok, rubber, mahogany lumber or furniture

Map Exercises

1. south
2. east
3. a. north
   b. east
4. southeast
5. northwest

---

5. Why was Brasília built far inland?
   a. The climate is much cooler in central Brazil.
   b. It was not safe to have the capital near the sea.
   c. The government wanted to encourage people to settle inland.
   d. That area has the best farmland in Brazil.

Further Study

1. Do coffee trees grow in the tropical rain forests? How do you know?
2. What are some goods mentioned in this lesson that might be shipped from ports on the Amazon River?

Map Exercises

On the maps in this lesson, north is toward the top and south is toward the bottom. East is toward the right and west is toward the left. These are the four main directions on almost every map you will ever see.

The four main directions will help you remember the four in-between directions too. Northwest is toward the upper-left corner of most maps, and northeast is toward the upper-right corner. Southwest is toward the lower-left corner, and southeast is toward the lower-right corner.

Use the map of Brazil to answer the following questions.

1. Does most of Brazil lie north of the equator, or south of it?
2. In what main direction does the Amazon River flow?
3. (*a*) In what main direction would Maria travel to visit her uncle in Belém? (*b*) To visit Rio de Janeiro?
4. To go from Brasília to Rio de Janeiro, would you need to travel southeast or southwest?
5. On our imaginary trip from North America to Maria's home, we needed to travel southeast. In what direction do we need to travel to go from Brazil to North America?

3. The Temperate Zones

Glossary Words

a woodchuck hibernating

hibernate (HY bur nayt) Go into a deep sleep for the winter, as some animals do.

legend (LEHJ uhnd) An explanation of the symbols used on a map.

migrate (MY grayt) Travel from one area to another with the change of seasons, as many birds do.

temperate (TEHM pur iht, TEHM priht) Having a mild climate, neither very hot nor very cold.

A Land of Four Seasons

Today we will meet Kevin Harris on his parents' farm in Ohio. He has a visitor from Colombia in South America. On the map, find Colombia in the Tropical Zone and Ohio in the Northern Temperate Zone.

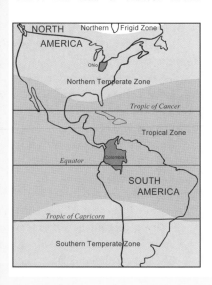

The *temperate* zones have many climates, but one thing is the same in most places of the temperate zones. They have the four seasons of spring, summer, autumn, and winter. In areas close to the frigid zones, the winters are very cold, with snow and bitter winds. Areas close to the Tropical Zone still have winter; but the closer a person goes to the equator, the warmer he finds the winters.

The four seasons strongly affect all living things—plants, animals, and people. God has

LESSON AIM

To give a brief overview of Ohio, a state in the Northern Temperate Zone, for the purpose of comparison with lands in other climate zones.

MAIN POINTS

- **Lands of the temperate zones have four seasons.** [Discuss the characteristics of each and the time of year they occur.

   Changing seasons are caused by the tilt of the earth's axis in relation to the sun. Actually it is the amount and slant of the sun's rays that make the difference. This concept can be demonstrated in a simple way by moving a globe around a point that represents the sun. One revolution represents one year and includes all four seasons.]

- **The temperate zones have many climates.** Winters range from mild to severe according to distance from the equator. [Local factors that affect climate could also be reviewed. See Main Points in Lesson 1.]

- **People and animals prepare for winter.** Crops are stored to feed the animals. Food is preserved for the family.

   Some animals hibernate during the winter. Some migrate to warmer lands. Others grow heavier coats, or store away extra food during the summer and fall.

- **Plants are affected by cold winters.** Plants do not grow during the winter in areas that have cold winters. Leaves change color and fall from the trees.

- **Snow and ice affect winter activities.** Different work needs to be done in winter, such as keeping roads and sidewalks safe. There is also opportunity for different games in winter.

26   Unit 1, Chapter 1   Climate Zones of the Earth

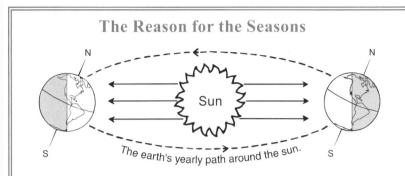

The Reason for the Seasons

The earth's yearly path around the sun.

The axis of the earth is tilted in relation to its orbit around the sun. When the earth is on one side of the sun, the North Pole is tilted toward the sun. Then the Northern Hemisphere has summer because it receives more sunlight and heat than the Southern Hemisphere. When the earth is on the other side of the sun, the North Pole is tilted away from the sun. Then the Northern Hemisphere receives less sunlight and heat, and it is winter.

promised that as long as the earth stands, the four seasons will continue (Genesis 8:22).

Preparing for Winter

It is a chilly Saturday in October. Luis Cano, Kevin's friend from Colombia in South America, has just arrived to spend the weekend with Kevin. Both boys wear light jackets as they do the chores. They have finished feeding the rabbits, hogs, and chickens when Luis says, "I cannot get used to your cold weather. My country is warm every month of the year."

Kevin smiles as he replies, "This is only fall. Wait until winter comes, when it is really cold. Then we have to wear heavy coats, gloves, and caps."

As the boys walk past the haymow, Luis stops and stares. "What a lot of hay! What do you do with all of it?"

"In winter no grass grows in the pasture, so we feed the animals hay. Over here in the granary, the bins are full of grain. The corncrib is full of corn. All these things are gathered to feed the animals through the winter."

"We have green pastures year

RELATED POINTS

- **Migration.** The migration of birds is a fascinating study. How can a bird fly hundreds or thousands of miles and then find its way back to the very same tree the next spring? Only God knows. The Arctic tern flies about 11,000 miles from its nesting grounds in the Arctic to a winter home in the Antarctic and back again each year.

- **Opposite seasons.** The Southern Temperate Zone has four seasons, but they are at opposite times of the year from seasons in the Northern Temperate Zone.

round," Luis said. "It would seem strange to have a season when things do not grow. That must take a lot of work and planning."

"It does, but that is such a normal part of our lives that it would seem strange to us to have it different. We plant a big garden in the spring. We enjoy eating the fresh vegetables, but we also store away much of the food for winter. My mother and sisters are canning and freezing fruits and vegetables through much of the summer and autumn."

Animals in Winter

"What happens to the wild animals in winter? Who prepares for them?" Luis asks.

"God does. It is God who provides for us too in giving us the things we gather for winter. But there are some very interesting ways that God provides for the wild animals in winter.

"Listen!" Kevin suddenly exclaims as the boys head toward the orchard. He had caught the sound of a faint honking in the sky. It soon grows louder, and the boys can see a flock of birds in a large V-shaped formation flying overhead. "Those are Canada geese," explains Kevin. "In the summer they live in the northern United States and Canada. They eat plants and grain. In winter they *migrate* to lands in the south where they can still find the

This farmer is harvesting hay. What farm animals eat hay during the winter?

Canada geese fly many miles to the south each winter.

food they need. Great flocks of these geese fly thousands of miles every year. That is God's way of providing for them in winter. Many songbirds, ducks, and buzzards migrate too."

As Luis and Kevin near the orchard, a fat, furry animal goes scurrying through the thick grass. The boys laugh at its heavy, waddling motions. "What was that?" asks Luis as the creature disappears into a clump of bushes.

"That was a ground hog, or woodchuck. He is another example of how God prepares animals for winter. He was out here eating fallen apples. The ground hog eats heavily in the autumn and builds up a supply of fat in his body. Then he goes to sleep. He **hibernates** through the winter, living on the fat stored in his body. Bats, frogs, skunks, and some other animals hibernate too."

The boys pick up some of the better apples on the ground and sit on the pasture fence to eat them. "Isn't it rather lifeless around here if so many animals move away or go to sleep for the winter?" Luis asks.

"Oh, no. Many animals stay around. Most of them grow heavier coats to keep out the cold. Squirrels, chipmunks, and mice store away grain and seeds in the summer and fall for a food supply. Birds live on nuts, rose hips, and seeds. Some animals such as rabbits eat twigs and bark. Others keep right on hunting the small animals they usually eat."

Work and Play in the Snow

The boys walk under the maple trees beside the lane, scuffing heaps of dry, crackly leaves with their feet. More leaves drift down from the branches overhead. "The leaves are really falling fast," Luis remarks.

"Yes. The colorful leaves were their prettiest a few weeks ago. It won't be long now till the trees and shrubs will be bare, the grass brown, and the snow flying."

"Do you go outside when it snows?"

"Oh, yes! We have many good times, playing in the snow. We make snowmen, throw snowballs, and go sledding. Snow makes some outside work too. We shovel it away from the doors and paths when it gets deep."

"What about the roads? Can you drive with snow on them?"

"The government has crews and equipment to plow the snow off the roads and spread cinders on them so that people can drive safely."

"Do you like wintertime?"

"I like all four seasons. There are special things about each one, and I look forward to the changes."

Testing Your Understanding

A. *Choose the best ending for each sentence. Write the complete sentences.*

1. Most lands in the temperate zones have
   a. a dry season and a rainy season.
   b. the four seasons of spring, summer, autumn, and winter.
   c. very cold weather in fall and spring.
2. Winters are very cold in areas of the temperate zones that are near the
   a. frigid zones.
   b. equator.
   c. Tropical Zone.

Lesson 3 Answers

Testing Your Understanding

A. 1. Most lands in the temperate zones have **[b]** the four seasons of spring, summer, autumn, and winter.
   2. Winters are very cold in areas of the temperate zones that are near the **[a]** frigid zones.

3. In the temperate zones, cattle need hay in the winter because **[a]** they cannot eat grass in the pastures.
4. Some animals prepare for winter by **[b]** storing a food supply during the summer and fall.
5. Two animals that hibernate during the winter are **[c]** the skunk and the woodchuck.
6. If a person lives in Kevin's area of the Northern Temperate Zone, he knows that autumn has arrived when **[a]** the leaves on the trees change to red, yellow, and brown.
7. A job that people do not have in Colombia is **[c]** cleaning snow off the roads.

3. In the temperate zones, cattle need hay in the winter because
   a. they cannot eat grass in the pastures.
   b. they have big appetites in cold weather.
   c. the trees lose their leaves.
4. Some animals prepare for winter by
   a. migrating to colder lands.
   b. storing a food supply during the summer and fall.
   c. growing a lighter coat of fur.
5. Two animals that hibernate during the winter are
   a. the rabbit and the bear.
   b. the mouse and the squirrel.
   c. the skunk and the woodchuck.
6. If a person lives in Kevin's area of the Northern Temperate Zone, he knows that autumn has arrived when
   a. the leaves on the trees change to red, yellow, and brown.
   b. snow and bitter winds come.
   c. daytime temperatures rise above 75 degrees.
7. A job that people do not have in Colombia is
   a. harvesting food from the garden.
   b. caring for animals.
   c. cleaning snow off the roads.

B. *Write the correct word(s) to complete each sentence. You will not use all the words.*

equator	hibernate	Tropic of Cancer
seasons	freeze	Tropic of Capricorn
migrate	Frigid Zone	Southern Temperate Zone
axis	Arctic Circle	Antarctic Circle

1. Where Luis lives, the climate is warm the year round because the ——— passes through his homeland.
2. Animals that ——— travel to a warmer place for the winter.
3. Animals that ——— go into a deep sleep for the winter.

B. 1. equator
   2. migrate
   3. hibernate

4. The seasons change because the —— of the earth is tilted in relation to its orbit around the sun.

5. The Northern Temperate Zone is between the —— and the ——.

6. The —— is between the Tropic of Capricorn and the Antarctic Circle.

Further Study

1. (a) If you had one lawn in Ohio and one in Brazil or Colombia, which lawn would you need to mow the most often in a year? (b) Why?

2. (a) What is some winter work at Kevin's home that Luis does not have at his home? (b) What is some summer work?

Map Exercises

Various symbols are used on maps to show different kinds of things. Some common map symbols are shown here. A map *legend* shows the meaning of each symbol used on a map.

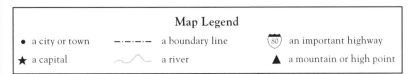

Map Legend		
● a city or town	–·–·–·– a boundary line	⑳ an important highway
★ a capital	∼∿∼ a river	▲ a mountain or high point

Use the map of Ohio on page 32 to answer the following questions.

1. What is the capital of Ohio?

2. (a) What large river forms the southern boundary of Ohio? (b) What river in southeastern Ohio is a tributary of this river?

3. What city in southwestern Ohio is found along the large river?

4. (a) What lake is north of Ohio? (b) What city is at the western end of this lake?

5. What is the highest point in Ohio?

4. axis
5. Tropic of Cancer, Arctic Circle
6. Southern Temperate Zone

Further Study

1. a. the lawn in Brazil or Colombia
   b. Grass grows the year around in that warm climate, while in Ohio the grass does not grow during the cold winter months.
2. a. shoveling snow, carrying wood or doing other chores related to heating a house, clearing roads of snow or ice
   b. preserving food for winter use, making hay

Map Exercises

1. Columbus
2. a. the Ohio River
   b. the Muskingum River
3. Cincinnati
4. a. Lake Erie
   b. Toledo
5. Campbell Hill (at 1,549 feet)

32   Unit 1, Chapter 1 Climate Zones of the Earth

Ohio

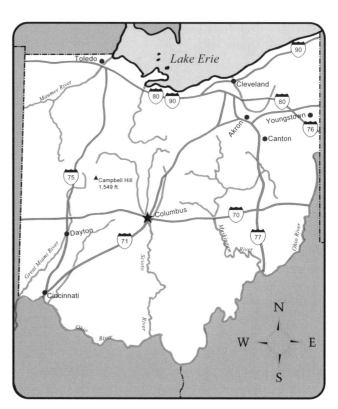

4. The Frigid Zones

Glossary Words

caribou (KAIR uh boo) Wild reindeer of North America.

frigid (FRIHJ ihd) Extremely cold.

igloo (IHG loo) A shelter built of ice or snow.

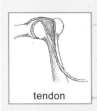

igloo

kayak (KY ak) A one-man Eskimo canoe made of a frame with skins stretched tightly over it.

lichens (LY kuhnz), Low mosslike plants.

northern lights Colored lights that shimmer across the sky at night in northern lands.

permafrost (PUR muh frawst) Deep underground soil that always remains frozen.

sledge A low, heavy sled often pulled by dogs, used to haul loads over ice and snow.

tendon

tendon (TEHN duhn) A tough fiber that connects a muscle to a bone.

tundra (TUHN druh) An arctic prairie too cold for trees to grow.

A Home on Baffin Island

Be sure you have your heavy coats, boots, and gloves. Today we are going to the Northern Frigid Zone, to Baffin Island of northern Canada. Find Baffin Island on the map on page 34. Most of it is north of the Arctic Circle. Benji, an Eskimo boy, lives with his family in a settlement called Arctic Bay on the northern part of the island.

What is the weather like in this northland? It may be cold and clear, or cold and cloudy, or cold and stormy—but almost always it is cold, and some days are colder than others. God gave the *frigid* zones a cold climate.

Animals of the Northland

It is early April. Benji and his father have just returned from

LESSON AIM

To give a brief overview of a region in northern Canada, in the Northern Frigid Zone, for the purpose of comparison with lands in other climate zones.

MAIN POINTS

- **Areas in the frigid zones have very cold climates.** [Discuss how the cold climate affects the clothing and the occupations of the Eskimos.]

- **Arctic summers are short. Most of the year is a long winter.** During the summer, the tundra thaws only on top, leaving permafrost underneath. Trees do not grow on the tundra.

- **Arctic animals are well suited for the cold environment.** Some have white fur during the winter and brown or gray fur during the summer. Eskimos trap and hunt animals for their meat, warm furs, and thick skins.

- **Waterways are frozen most of the year.** This limits water transportation and shipping. Hunters catch water animals through holes in the ice.

- **The Eskimo way of life has changed.** Boats bring in supplies from other parts of the world. Permanent villages with wooden or metal houses have replaced tents, earth houses, and igloos. Snowmobiles are taking over the work of dog teams.

- **The sun never sets during part of the summer and never rises during part of the winter.** [Have your students try to imagine what this would be like. Could they sleep if there was a full twenty-four hours of light each day? Would they like a month-long night? The moon, stars, and northern lights do provide some light during the long winter night. Also point out that the white snow reflects the available light and makes it somewhat brighter.]

Baffin Island

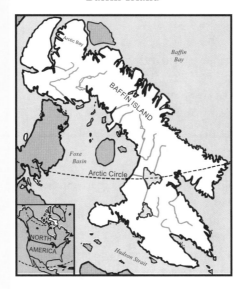

arctic fox is white only in the winter," he explains. "Its coat changes color in the summer months. When there is no snow on the ground, the fox is brown or gray. This helps it to hide on the *tundra*, where there are no trees and few bushes."

"What is the tundra?" someone asks.

"You might call the tundra a frozen prairie. It is too cold for trees to grow here. Grass, *lichens*, and stunted shrubs grow during our short summer. In the winter it is covered with snow and ice. In summer, the ground thaws just on the top. Summer is not long enough for the warmth to go

checking their traps. Benji happily carries a small white fox, and his father has a sack with several hares and another arctic fox.

Benji will help his father skin the animals and sell the furs. The meat is used for food or is fed to their dogs. In the past, Eskimos ate very little besides the meat of fish and animals that they hunted. Now they can buy many kinds of food and other things at the trading post.

We admire the snow-white fur of the fox Benji carries. "The

The caribou with the large antlers is a male. The one with the small antlers is a female. In the Arctic tundra, sometimes thousands of caribou wander in one herd.

very deep. The ground underneath is always frozen. We call it ***permafrost***. The permafrost does not let water drain through, so the tundra is swampy in the summer."

"What other animals live on the tundra?"

"The ***caribou*** is one important animal. It is a wild reindeer. Caribou eat grass and lichens, pawing through the snow to find their food. They wander about a lot, going farther south in winter. Our people used to hunt caribou for food, clothing, houses, and tools. Now there are hardly enough of the animals to support many people. We still hunt caribou and make good use of them, but we also get many supplies from the trading post."

"How do you get clothing, houses, and tools from animals?" someone asks.

"The skins are used for clothing and for tents. Caribou skin makes a very good suit for cold weather because it is warm and yet lightweight. Caribou tents were used in the summertime when there was no snow. In winter, people lived in earth houses or ***igloos***.

"Caribou bones and horns

This is a modern Eskimo village on Baffin Island. What things in this picture are different from the way Eskimos used to live?

were carved into tools such as fishhooks, spears, knives, and needles. ***Tendon*** strings were used for thread. People didn't have much of anything that they couldn't get right here. Now we live in a permanent village with houses of wood and metal. We have a trading post where we can buy supplies from other parts of the world."

Frozen Waters

"Some Arctic animals live in water," Benji says. "Fish, walruses, and seals are very important in providing food.

Would you like to go to the bay and see some walruses?"

Benji tells us that long ago the Eskimos used dogs to pull their ***sledges***, but he drives a snowmobile to take us to a bank where he expects to find some walruses. Out on the bay we see them, resting on a large, broken piece of ice. Their huge, bulky bodies have small flippers that help them to swim, and they have long tusks that stick out of their mouths.

"Most of the time, walruses stay in the water where they hunt their food. They will probably rest on that ice for the night," Benji

Years ago, dogs pulled the Eskimos' sledges. Today, many Eskimos travel on snowmobiles.

explains. "We sometimes hunt walruses for their meat. Their hides are very tough, and they make good tents or **kayaks**."

The water is full of great pieces of drifting ice. We wonder if the bay freezes solid enough to travel on the ice. "Oh, yes. The ice is breaking up now because warmer weather is coming. By July the bay will be clear enough for shipping. Boats will bring supplies to our village, and we will send away the furs from our winter trapping."

"Do you fish only in the summertime if the water is frozen so much of the year?"

"No, we fish in winter too. We fish through the ice," Benji answers. "We cut a hole in the ice and catch fish there. We also catch seals through the ice. Seals live in the water, but they breathe air. If they come to the surface at the same place every time when the ice is forming, it keeps a breathing hole open for them. When we hunt seals in winter, we look for these breathing holes in the ice and wait beside one until a seal comes for air."

Arctic Seasons

Darkness is falling as we return to Benji's village. The wind grows colder, and we are glad to get into the warm house. "I like the

Many flowers, grasses, and li-chens grow during the long days of the short Arctic summer.

The Kayak

The kayak is made by stretching skin over a canoe-shaped frame. The top of the kayak is completely covered, except for an opening large enough for a man. This opening is lined with a waterproof skin.

Eskimos wear waterproof coats when they ride in a kayak. They tie the lining of the kayak opening around themselves to seal themselves in the boat. This makes the boat watertight, even if it tips. The Eskimo can right the boat and continue on his way.

longer days," Benji says. "Just now the daylight and darkness are about equal. But the days are growing longer and longer. By mid-June there will be no night at all. Then for about a month and a half, the sun will go around in the sky once each day without setting. That's why the Arctic is sometimes called the Land of the Midnight Sun."

"Will you have warm weather then?" we ask.

"Yes, summer temperatures are usually between 40 degrees and 60 degrees Fahrenheit. You should see our land then. There is no snow for the months of July and August. The many hours of sunshine help grass and flowers to grow quickly, and the tundra is a beautiful sight!"

"You could come outside and see a beautiful sight right now," says Benji's father, who has just entered the house. "The **northern lights** are very bright this evening."

We jump up from the furry polar bear rug and put on our heavy coats, caps, and scarves again. Then we hurry out into the frosty darkness. But it isn't quite dark. Streaks of soft green and pink lights shimmer and flash across the sky. The sight is so strange and beautiful that we hardly know what to say. The heavens declare the glory of God, even in this frozen Arctic.

Back in the warm house, Benji breaks the silence. "I am so used to seeing the northern lights that often I hardly take notice of them," he says. "In our dark wintertime, the northern lights and the white snow give us a little light outdoors. You see, we have over a month in winter that the sun never rises—just as long as our summer day when it does not set."

"What do you do in the winter?" we ask.

"When I am not in school, Father teaches me things about hunting and fishing. This winter he helped me to build an igloo. I'm not very good at it yet, but I want to learn how to do it right. Father can build one by himself in a few hours. He thinks every man in the northland should know how to build a shelter and kill animals to feed himself."

Testing Your Understanding

A. *Write the correct word(s) for each definition. You will not use all the words.*

kayak   sledge   caribou   frigid zones
tundra   igloo   lichens   trading post
seal   tendon   permafrost   northern lights

1. A sled used to haul things, sometimes pulled by dogs.
2. An Eskimo house made from blocks of ice or snow.
3. The cold areas around the North Pole and the South Pole.
4. Colored lights that shimmer across the sky.
5. A frozen prairie where no trees grow.
6. A one-man Eskimo canoe covered with skin.
7. A place where supplies can be bought, sold, or traded.
8. An animal like the reindeer.
9. A water animal that keeps a breathing hole open through the ice.
10. Deep underground soil that is always frozen.

Lesson 4 Answers

Testing Your Understanding
A. 1. sledge
   2. igloo
   3. frigid zones
   4. northern lights
   5. tundra
   6. kayak
   7. trading post
   8. caribou
   9. seal
  10. permafrost

B. 1. trees
   2. ice
   3. month
   4. setting

B. *Write words to fill in the blanks.*

1. No ——— grow in Benji's land because it is too cold.
2. Boats cannot bring supplies to Baffin Island during much of the year because of the ——— on the water.
3. During the long winter night, the sun does not rise for over a ———.
4. During the long summer day, the sun goes around in the sky without ——— for a month and a half.

C.   **Old Ways**
   1. Sledges are pulled by dogs.
   3. The people eat only meat.
   6. The people live in igloos and tents.
   7. All the clothes are made from animal skins and furs.
       New Ways
   2. Sledges are pulled by snowmobiles.
   4. The people buy different kinds of food.
   5. The people live in wood and metal houses.
   8. People sell furs and use the money to buy clothing.

C. *Eskimos are changing their ways. Write the headings* Old Ways *and* New Ways *on your paper. Write these sentences under the correct headings.*

1. Sledges are pulled by dogs.
2. Sledges are pulled by snowmobiles.
3. The people eat only meat.
4. The people buy different kinds of food.
5. The people live in wood and metal houses.
6. The people live in igloos and tents.
7. All the clothes are made from animal skins and furs.
8. People sell furs and use the money to buy clothing.

       Further Study
   1. Yes. There was a polar bear rug in Benji's house. (That is also the climate and location where polar bears are naturally found.)
   2. (Answers may vary. A 50° room temperature would not be comfortable. A spring morning of 50° may be considered warm.)

Further Study

1. Do polar bears live in Benji's region? How do you know?
2. Do you think it is warm when the temperature is 50 degrees?

       Map Exercises
   Rules for Drawing Neat Maps should be copied neatly and accurately.

Map Exercises

In Chapter 2 you will begin making a notebook of maps for the countries you study in this book. Plan now to make maps that are neat, readable, and attractive. The Rules for Drawing Neat Maps, on page 325, will help you.

Give your map notebook a title such as *Homelands Around the World* or *My Trip in Geography*. Then find the map section and copy the rules given there on the first page of your notebook. Read them often, and follow them for every map you make.

5. Chapter 1 Review

— Testing Your Understanding —

A. *Number your paper from one to ten. Name the imaginary lines of the earth for numbers 1–5. Name the climate zones for numbers 6–10.*

equator	Southern Frigid Zone
Northern Frigid Zone	Northern Temperate Zone
Tropical Zone	Tropic of Capricorn
Tropic of Cancer	Southern Temperate Zone
Arctic Circle	Antarctic Circle

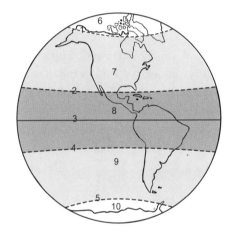

B. *Name the climate zone that fits each item.*

1. Rain forests.
2. Trees that shed their leaves and stop growing over winter.
3. No trees because of the cold.
4. Heavy fur clothing.
5. Houses without heaters.

Lesson 5 Answers

Testing Your Understanding

A. 1. Arctic Circle
   2. Tropic of Cancer
   3. equator
   4. Tropic of Capricorn
   5. Antarctic Circle
   6. Northern Frigid Zone
   7. Northern Temperate Zone
   8. Tropical Zone
   9. Southern Temperate Zone
   10. Southern Frigid Zone

B. 1. Tropical Zone
   2. Temperate Zone
   3. Frigid Zone
   4. Frigid Zone
   5. Tropical Zone

6. Frigid Zone
7. Temperate Zone
8. Tropical Zone
9. Tropical Zone
10. Temperate Zone
11. Frigid Zone
12. Frigid Zone

6. Midnight sun.
7. Spring, summer, autumn, and winter.
8. Wet season, dry season.
9. Coffee, rubber, kapok.
10. Many different climates.
11. Tundra, permafrost.
12. Waterways blocked with ice.

C. *Write the correct word for each meaning.*

weather	migrate	hibernate
climate	peninsula	tributary
hemisphere	Amazon	

1. Half of the earth.
2. The largest river in the world.
3. To go into deep sleep and live on fat stored in the body.
4. An arm of land almost surrounded by water.
5. The day-to-day sunshine, rain, wind, and temperature.
6. To travel to another place for part of the year.
7. A river that flows into a larger river.
8. The general temperature, rainfall, wind, and sunshine in an area.

C. 1. hemisphere
2. Amazon
3. hibernate
4. peninsula
5. weather
6. migrate
7. tributary
8. climate

Map Exercises

Use the map of Georgia on page 43 to answer the following questions.

1. In what direction does the Ogeechee River flow?
2. What is the capital of Georgia?
3. What is the highest mountain in Georgia?
4. What river forms part of the west boundary of Georgia?
5. What important highway runs from Macon to Savannah?

Map Exercises

1. southeast
2. Atlanta
3. Brasstown Bald
4. the Chattahoochee River
5. Route 16 (Interstate 16)

Review Study

1. Do you know the meaning of all the glossary words in Chapter 1?

Review Study

(Individual work. Review the words and terms orally. Have students point out the places on a globe.
Note: A chapter test follows each review lesson.)

Lesson 5   43

2. Do you know the meaning of the terms on the map diagram in Lesson 1?
3. Can you find Brazil, Ohio, and Baffin Island on the globe?

Georgia

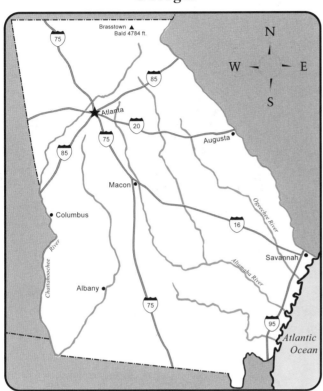

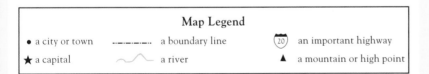

Map Legend

● a city or town	·····–··–·· a boundary line	⌢ an important highway
★ a capital	∿ a river	▲ a mountain or high point

UNIT TWO
Tropical Lands

Giraffes jog across an African savanna.

CHAPTER 2

NIGERIA, A WARM AFRICAN LAND

"O LORD, how manifold are thy works! in wisdom hast thou made them all: the earth is full of thy riches" (Psalm 104:24).

46   Unit 2, Chapter 2 Nigeria, a Warm African Land

6. A Visit to Antonia's Home

Glossary Words

cacao

thatch roof

cacao (kuh KAY oh, kuh KAH oh) A tropical tree whose beans are used to make chocolate.

compound An enclosed area containing two or more dwellings.

Muslim (MUHZ luhm) A follower of the Islam religion, which was started by Muhammad.

nomads (NOH madz) People who live in movable dwellings and move frequently from one place to another.

population (pahp yoo LAY shuhn) The number of people living at a certain place.

thatch (THACH) A roof or covering of reeds or straw so arranged that it sheds water.

tradition (truh DIHSH uhn) A customary belief or practice that is passed from parents to children.

A Home in Africa

Find the country of Brazil on a globe. Brazil is mostly south of the equator in the Tropical Zone. Cross the Atlantic Ocean to the continent of Africa. Find Nigeria in the Tropical Zone just north of the equator. What countries border Nigeria?

Nigeria is the largest country on the Gulf of Guinea (GIHN ee), and it has the largest *population* of any country in Africa. Most of the people of Nigeria are black or dark-skinned. Lagos (LAY gohs) is a busy port on the coast of the Gulf of Guinea. It is the largest city of Nigeria. Until a few years ago, Lagos was the capital of Nigeria, but Abuja is now the capital. About 75 miles north of Lagos is Ibadan (EE bah dahn),

LESSON AIM

To introduce the students to Nigeria, an African country in the Tropical Zone.

MAIN POINTS

- **Nigeria is on the continent of Africa in the Tropical Zone.** The Gulf of Guinea lies off the coast of Nigeria.

- **Nigeria has the largest population of any country in Africa.** Lagos is the largest city. Ibadan is the second largest city. Most of the people of Nigeria are black or dark-skinned. About half the people are Muslims.

- **Nigeria has a mixture of modern and traditional ways.** The traditional ways are followed more in the country villages than in the cities.

- **The Niger River and Benue River form a big Y in Nigeria, separating the country into the Yoruba, the Ibo, and the Hausa–Fulani tribal areas.** The languages of these tribes are the main languages used in Nigeria, but English is the official language.

RELATED POINTS

- **Countries around Nigeria.**

  Benin (beh NEEN) is a small French-speaking country with about two-thirds rural population. Over half of the people worship animals instead of God. This is a direct contrast to Nigeria, where most people have no special regard for animals.

  Cameroon (kam uh ROON), once divided between the British and the French, now produces many tons of bananas, its main export.

  In **Chad**—with the Sahara to the north and savannas to the south—about four-fifths of the people are farmers or herdsmen. Beans and cotton are its main exports.

  Niger (NY jur), like Chad, is a landlocked country of dry land inhabited mostly by nomadic herdsmen.

the second largest city in Nigeria. A few miles from Ibadan, we find the village of Adi (ah DEE), the home of Antonia.

Visitors From America

Antonia had been watching some boys play soccer and run foot races. Rising, she brushed off her long, colorful skirt. As she started walking toward home, she noticed the old gray taxi from Ibadan. Antonia knew the driver. She had seen his wife at a stand in the open market of Ibadan that morning. As the taxi turned, she saw the face of her father in the front window. The taxi was going to her home! Antonia hurried down the street to her family's **compound**.

Nigeria

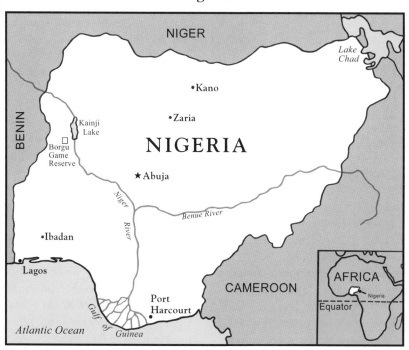

Many Nigerians wear brightly colored clothing.

Antonia's father stepped from the taxi with a white man, woman, and young girl. "This is Brother Parker with his wife and their daughter Clara from a church in America," he said. They all exchanged greetings, and then the grown-ups went into the house.

"We will soon have dinner," Antonia told her guest. "I walked to the market this morning and got tomatoes, peppers, and onions for Mother's chicken and rice stew."

"I've never had that kind of stew, but it sounds good," answered Clara. "We saw the market in Ibadan. So many things were out on the streets to sell! All kinds of food and tools and crafts and clothes."

Antonia noticed the shoes Clara was wearing. "Aren't your feet warm?" she asked.

"Yes, they are," admitted Clara, "but I can't go barefoot like you. My feet are too tender."

Antonia laughed. "Many girls wear sandals. I'll lend you mine."

Antonia's House

The girls walked through the opening in the fence of sticks that circled the compound, and Antonia led the way to the bedroom. "This is a new room for our compound," she explained. "Father made it with concrete blocks and put a tin roof on it. During the rainy season, this room is drier than the ones with mud walls and *thatch* roofs. Uncle Abuchi and his family live next to us, and Grandmother and

Grandfather live across the compound."

Antonia found a pair of sandals, and Clara put them on. "I was surprised to see so many people in Ibadan dressed like people in America," she said.

"Many people, especially in the cities, are changing their way of dress. But in the country villages, most people still keep the old *traditional* ways. Around here you will see many people with long, loose robes. Some men wear trousers and loose jackets. Those are comfortable clothes for a hot climate. Mother has dinner ready now. Let's go and eat."

The People of Nigeria

Brother Parker sat next to Chuli, Antonia's father, during the meal. "Is the church growing in Nigeria?" asked their visitor.

"It is growing, yes," answered Chuli. "But many, many people are not interested in the Gospel. About half the people of Nigeria are **Muslims**. They teach that there is one true God, whom they call Allah. But they do not believe that Jesus is God's Son. They call Jesus a prophet, yes, but they give more honor to Muhammad.

They say Muhammad was the last and greatest prophet of Allah. There are also many heathen religions in which people worship false gods.

This Nigerian market offers many fruits and vegetables. Many Nigerians do not have refrigerators to keep their foods fresh. They often buy fresh food each day from markets like this one.

In the foreground is a building with a thatch roof. The houses have tin roofs. These buildings are part of a small jungle village in Nigeria.

"I would like to take you to the church at Zaria," Chuli said. "In that area, most of the people are Muslims."

"What language do they speak?" asked Brother Parker.

"They speak your language," assured Chuli. "English is the official language of Nigeria, and it is taught in the schools, but most people use other languages. Hausa (HOW suh), Ibo (EE boh) and Yoruba (YAWR uh buh), are the three main languages used in our country. There are about 250 other languages used by small groups.

"The Niger River and its largest tributary, the Benue (BAYN way) River, make a large Y in the middle of the country. Those rivers are a kind of dividing place for the different groups of people in Nigeria. We are in the Yoruba section, the southwestern part of the country. Across the Niger River to the east, the Ibo people live. They are known for their energy and progress. Many of the Ibo have been a help to

The Main Groups of Nigerians

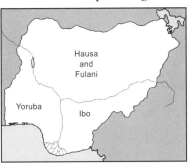

Nigeria in developing businesses and government.

"The northern part, in the top of the Y, is the land of the Hausa. Some people call it Hausa–Fulani (FOO lah nee), because the Fulani tribes also live in that section. The Hausa and Fulani people work well together. The Hausa are settled people that do a lot of farming. They are also noted for their crafts, such as pottery making and weaving.

"Many of the Fulani are **nomads**. They roam around to different grazing areas with their herds of cattle. After the harvest, the Fulani may graze their cattle on the stubble fields of the Hausa. The Hausa benefit from fertilizer on their fields and can get some dairy products. The Fulani appreciate the food for their cattle."

The two families planned a trip to Zaria for the next day. Chuli felt he could take the time off from his **cacao** farm, and he would rent a car to take them there. It would take most of a day to make the drive, and then another day to return after their visit ended.

--- **Testing Your Understanding** ---

A. *Name each of the following.*

1. The country where Antonia lives.
2. The continent where Antonia lives.
3. The climate zone where Antonia lives.
4. The gulf off the coast of Nigeria.
5. The two largest cities of Nigeria.
6. The two main rivers of Nigeria.
7. The religion of about half of Nigeria's people.
8. The official language of Nigeria.
9. Three other main languages of Nigeria.
10. Nigerian people who are nomads with herds of cattle.

B. *Answer these questions.*

1. Where did Antonia get the vegetables for her mother's stew?
2. What was most of Antonia's house made from?

Lesson 6 Answers

Testing Your Understanding
A. 1. Nigeria
   2. Africa
   3. Tropical Zone
   4. Gulf of Guinea
   5. Lagos and Ibadan
   6. Niger and Benue
   7. Muslim
   8. English
   9. Hausa, Yoruba, and Ibo
   10. Fulani

B. 1. from the market in Ibadan
   2. mud walls and thatch roofs

3. many heathen religions
4. farming, pottery making, and weaving

Further Study

1. Nigerians are black or dark-skinned. The visitors stood out as being different because of their white skin.
2. Antonia's family probably followed the traditional ways. She is described as wearing a long, colorful skirt, and her family did not live in the city.

Map Exercises

(Individual work. Check maps for accuracy and neatness.)

3. What religions are in Nigeria besides Muslim and Christian?
4. What are common occupations of the Hausa?

Further Study

1. Why does the lesson mention that the visitors were white-skinned?
2. Do you think Antonia and her family were modern or traditional people?

Map Exercises

1. Trace Map A in the map section in the back of your book. Look at the map at the beginning of this chapter, and label Nigeria, Benin, Niger, and Cameroon. Use all capital letters.
2. Label Lake Chad and the Gulf of Guinea. Use all capitals to label the ocean south and west of the gulf.
3. Label Lagos, Abuja, and Ibadan.

7. Exploring the Savannas

Glossary Words

antelope

papaya

antelope (AN tuh lohp) A deerlike animal with pronged horns.

cassava (kuh SAH vuh) A tropical plant with a starchy root, often dried and ground into flour.

game reserve An area set aside to protect wild animals.

game warden An official responsible for the protection of wild animals.

harmattan (hahr muh TAN, hahr MAT uhn) A dry, dusty wind of northwestern Africa.

mango (MANG goh) A juicy oval fruit with a smooth yellowish red rind.

papaya (puh PAH yuh) A yellow melonlike fruit of the tropical region.

savanna (suh VAN uh) A large area of grassland in a warm region, sometimes partially covered with trees or shrubs.

sorghum (SAWR guhm) A stout canelike grass that is raised for grain or for its juice and fodder.

yam A kind of sweet potato that may grow as long as 2 feet.

A Trip to Zaria

The next morning Chuli made arrangements with the other workers of the cacao plantation so that he could be away a few days. Antonia and Clara took a walk outside the compound while they waited until everyone was ready for the trip. Palm trees swayed in the breeze, shading the compound from the morning sun. "How pleasant this place is!" said

LESSON AIM

To teach about the climates of Nigeria.

MAIN POINTS

- **Southern Nigeria has a warm, moist climate.** Fruits and vegetables can be grown. Tropical rain forests cover parts of the south.

- **Northern Nigeria has a warm, dry climate.** The harmattan blows from the Sahara, drying out the land, trees, and grass. [The name *Sahara* is preferred over *Sahara Desert* because *Sahara* means "desert."] Fulani herdsmen graze their cattle on the savanna. Few trees grow in northern Nigeria.

- **The amount of moisture in an area affects people's work, houses, and food.** This is true even when temperatures remain about the same.

RELATED POINTS

- **The Hausas.** These people are excellent at tinwork, pottery, and stone painting. They also weave, make sculptures, and work with brass. For a "souvenir" of Nigeria, the students can make a clay or stone paperweight as explained at the end of the chapter.

Clara. "Are those fruit trees yours? It looks as if oranges and lemons are growing on them."

"Yes, this is our orchard. We have grapefruits, bananas, *papayas*, and *mangoes* too. On the other side of the compound, we have a garden where we grow *cassava*, *yams*, tomatoes, and some other things."

"We raise tomatoes at home," said Clara. "And yams we call sweet potatoes."

"Let's pick some ripe oranges to take along on our trip," suggested Antonia.

Soon everyone was ready to leave, and the two families set out for Zaria. Trees and flourishing cropland provided interesting scenery. "Crops seem to be thriving," observed Brother Parker. "What is growing in the field to our right?"

"That is a patch of rice," answered Chuli. "We are also passing some yam, pepper, and *sorghum* fields," he explained.

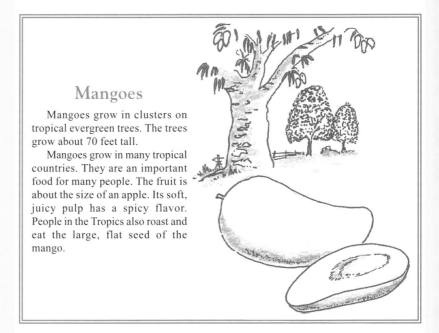

Mangoes

Mangoes grow in clusters on tropical evergreen trees. The trees grow about 70 feet tall.

Mangoes grow in many tropical countries. They are an important food for many people. The fruit is about the size of an apple. Its soft, juicy pulp has a spicy flavor. People in the Tropics also roast and eat the large, flat seed of the mango.

Clara looked at Antonia. "What is sorghum?" she asked.

Antonia pointed to a patch of tall grassy plants with heavy seed clusters at the top. "That is sorghum. The grains in the top part will be ground into flour. Some kinds of sorghum have sweet juice in the stalks. The juice is crushed out of the stalks, or canes. It can be boiled into a thick syrup. The crushed canes make good fodder for animals."

By and by the travelers came to a large river. "This is the Niger River," Chuli explained. "It is part of the big Y that divides Nigeria."

Sorghum is useful in many ways. The kind shown here is grain sorghum. Grain sorghum is good food for both livestock and people. In some countries, people grind the grain and make it into pancakes or mush.

Cassava roots are an important food in wet, tropical areas where potatoes do not grow well.

Drier Lands

"The landscape looks different here," commented Sister Parker. "There are trees here and there, but large stretches of grassland instead of forests and crops."

"This is the **savanna**," said Antonia's mother. "There used to be more forests here, but as trees were cut down, grasslands took their place. Many of the Fulani people herd their cattle in the savannas. As we go farther north, there will be fewer trees. The savannas are large areas with just grass and brush or scrubby little trees. The dry season is longer in the north and the *harmattan* is stronger."

Clara looked at Antonia again. "Whatever is a harmattan?" she asked.

Antonia smiled. "The harmattan is a wind," she answered. "As Mother said, the land gets drier as you go north. North of Nigeria is the Sahara (suh HAIR uh)—a great desert. The harmattan comes from the Sahara, and it is very dry and hot. The hot wind blows fairly regularly during the dry season, which is from November through March or April."

"That would dry your laundry in a hurry, if you hung it out," said Clara.

"It dries lots of other things too," agreed Antonia. "Many of the streams, wells, and rivers dry up when the harmattan blows. Trees can't grow well because the harmattan dries them so completely that the wood cracks. If you are out in the wind very long, your skin feels dry and your lips may crack from the dryness."

"Do I see some Fulani herdsmen?" asked Brother Parker, looking across the savanna at some figures in the distance. "It looks like a group of cattle and some men."

"I think you're right," agreed Chuli.

"How does the grass survive the harmattan?" asked Brother Parker. "Is pasture available for the cattle all year?"

"The grass turns to hay. Nomads simply travel on to new pastures when they need more food. And the grass springs up fresh and green when the rainy season comes again."

Wild Animals

"There are some more cattle," said Clara. "No, they are not as big as cattle, and there are no herdsmen. Are they deer?"

"That's a herd of *antelope*!" exclaimed Antonia. "Aren't they pretty? They are wild animals. See them run! They really seem nervous."

"Look over there!" exclaimed Chuli a short while later. "No wonder the antelope were excited. That lion has a fresh kill."

Everyone looked in the direction Chuli was pointing. They

saw a lion disappearing into the brush, dragging the body of an antelope with it. Clara's skin tingled. A wild lion! It looked big and dangerous.

"Is it common to find lions around here?" asked Brother Parker.

"No," answered Chuli. "Lions in this area mean danger to the Fulani cattle and goats. **Game wardens** often try to remove the lions safely to another area. They shoot the animals with darts, which have a drug that puts the lions to sleep. Then they load up the animals and haul them to a **game reserve**. Maybe on our trip back, we can visit the game reserve west of here."

Tropical Climates

Antonia passed out the oranges she had picked in the orchard that morning. "How sweet and juicy and refreshing!" exclaimed Sister Parker when she tasted hers. "Tree-ripened oranges are much better than the ones that ripen after they are picked."

"We don't see orange trees here," observed Brother Parker. "In just one day's trip, we have

This male lion lies lazily in the sunshine on the empty savanna. Lions help control the population of other animals, such as the antelope.

stepped from one kind of climate to another."

"That's right," agreed Chuli. "The southern part of our country has tropical rain forest. But in the north, some areas are nearly desert. It is all tropical, but the moisture makes a great difference. The difference affects the work we do, the things we eat, and the houses we build.

"For instance, I could not raise cacao trees in the dry savannas. We would not have oranges so plentifully here. The mud houses and roofs you see here would soften in the tropical rain forest. And if houses were built here with bamboo walls and leaf roofs as they are in the rain forest, the harmattan would dry them up and blow right through."

Lesson 7 Answers

Testing Your Understanding

A. 1. palm, papaya
   2. grain, canes
   3. north, rain
   4. dry, desert
   5. cattle, savanna
   6. bamboo, leaf

B. 1. They need to find new grazing land for their cattle.
   2. lions, antelope (There are others that are not mentioned in the text.)
   3. a. Northern Nigeria is dry; southern Nigeria is wet.
       b. All areas of Nigeria are tropical (*or* warm).

──────── **Testing Your Understanding** ────────

A. *Choose the correct words in parentheses.*

1. Clara saw (palm, cacao) trees and (papaya, coffee) trees near Antonia's house.

2. Sorghum is raised for flour from the (roots, grain) and sweet juice from the (leaves, canes).

3. There are fewer trees as one travels (north, south) because there is less (sunshine, rain).

4. The harmattan is a (dry, wet) wind that blows from the (desert, ocean).

5. The Fulani people herd their (antelope, cattle) in the (savanna, rain forest).

6. Many homes in the rain forest have (bamboo, stone) walls and (mud, leaf) roofs.

B. *Answer these questions.*

1. Why do the Fulani move about?

2. What are two kinds of wild animals that might be found in the savannas?

3. (*a*) How is the climate of northern Nigeria different from the climate of southern Nigeria? (*b*) How are they the same?

Further Study

1. Why is the harmattan stronger in northern Nigeria than in southern Nigeria?
2. How is the hay of the savannas different from the hay raised in a temperate zone? (Compare this lesson with Lesson 3.)

Map Exercises

1. On your map of Nigeria, label the city of Zaria.
2. Label the Niger River and the Benue River.
3. Use all capitals to label the areas where the main tribes of Nigeria live. Write HAUSA–FULANI across the northern section, IBO across the eastern section, and YORUBA across the western section.

Further Study
1. Northern Nigeria is closer to the Sahara.
2. The hay of the savanna is dried by the harmattan, and the cattle graze it while it is still standing. The hay raised in a temperate zone is cut and stored in barns until winter.

Map Exercises
(Individual work. Check maps for accuracy and neatness.)

8. A Drive Through a Game Reserve

Glossary Words

dam

custom (KUHS tuhm) The usual way of doing something.

dam A thick wall built across a river to control the flow of water.

generate (JEHN uh rayt) Bring into being; produce.

heron (HEHR uhn) A long-legged wading bird.

hyena (hy EE nuh) A wild, wolflike animal.

irrigation (ihr ih GAY shuhn) A system by which dry land is watered so that it can be used for farming.

Hot Days, Cold Nights

Antonia's and Clara's families rose early on the morning that they left Zaria. Clara shivered as she helped to put luggage into the car. "It's chilly this morning! It was so warm yesterday that I thought cool weather would be nice. But now I'm ready to see it warm up again."

"It will," Antonia assured her. "In the drier climate here, the days usually get hotter than they do in our area. But the nights get cooler. Farther north where it is drier yet, the daily temperature varies so much that it sometimes frosts at night, while the daytime temperature goes higher than 100 degrees."

Soon the Parkers were bidding farewell to the kind friends who had shared their home with them. The fellowship in Christ made them brethren and sisters, even though their skin was a different color and their homes and *customs* seemed strange to each other.

Clara and Antonia watched for antelope again as they traveled through the savannas. Several times they saw Fulani herdsmen with their cattle. "Look

LESSON AIM

To learn more about the savanna of Nigeria and some of the changes brought by man.

MAIN POINTS

- **Northern Nigeria has hot days and cold nights.** [This is typical in desert or semidesert lands because the dry air and barren ground do not hold heat well.]

- **Dams provide benefits.** Electricity can be generated, fishing is improved, a dependable supply of water is stored for irrigation, and the dam can be used as a bridge. But often lakes cover good farmland and villages.

- **God has provided a balance in nature.** Animals prosper best when they are in their natural settings. Game reserves are sections of land where animals are protected from hunting and trapping. This lesson mentions a number of animals that God has designed especially for tropical lands.

- **The sunrise, sunset, and daily temperatures stay about the same year round in lands close to the equator.** [This is because lands along the equator get the full rays of the sun every day of the year.]

RELATED POINTS

- **Tropical sun.** You may want to use a flashlight and a globe to show why the tropical sun climbs high, almost directly overhead, the year around. You can also show why the sun's rays do not come from directly overhead in areas outside the Tropical Zone.

ahead to the left," said Chuli. "That may be a herd of antelope, but there is something else with them."

"Ostriches!" exclaimed Antonia. A flock of about a dozen huge birds made the antelope look small. As the car drew near, all the animals sped away across the savanna.

"Such big steps!" cried Clara as she watched the ostriches stride swiftly across the grassland.

"Ostriches cannot fly, you know," explained Chuli. "But they can run very swiftly. Sometimes they reach a speed of 40 miles per hour. If they cannot get away from an enemy, they may kick with their powerful legs." Soon the animals were out of sight, and all that was left was a haze of dust on the savanna.

Kainji Dam and Lake

"It's warm enough now!" exclaimed Clara when they came in sight of the Niger River. She fanned her cheeks when Chuli stopped the car.

"I want to show you the Kainji Dam (kah EEN jih)," Chuli explained. "This *dam* holds back the water of the Niger to form Kainji Lake, which covers 500 square miles." Everyone got out of the car and looked at the great concrete wall. Below the dam, water poured out and flowed on downstream. "Waterpower is used here to *generate* electricity. Power lines carry electricity from the generators to our home area and to many other places."

An ostrich

A heron wades in shallow water, searching for food.

Above the dam, the lake spread out, vast and beautiful in the sunshine. A graceful pair of **herons** sailed overhead. "There go some beautiful fishermen," remarked Brother Parker.

"This lake is valuable in many ways," said Chuli. "It has more fish than there would be in the undammed river. There is also a more dependable supply of water for *irrigation*."

The two families went back to the car, and Chuli turned onto a roadway going across the top of the dam. "The dam gives us a bridge across the river too," Chuli said. "But there were some sacrifices as well as benefits in building the dam. Many villages were on the land that is now covered with water. We are coming to New Bussa. This town was built for the people who had to leave Bussa because the lake was going to cover it."

The Game Reserve

It was not far from Kainji Dam to the Borgu Game Reserve. "Keep your eyes open for the animals," said Chuli. "Some wild animals are in danger of dying off because people hunt them and take over their forests and grasslands. In the game reserve, the animals are protected from hunters. People are allowed to drive through the reserve to see the animals, but remember—they are wild animals, and they are not caged."

The girls soon spotted some monkeys scampering in the tree-tops. As the car drove slowly along, the monkeys followed curiously, jumping from branch to branch and hiding in the leaves.

The next animals to be seen were several giraffes in the distance, eating leaves from a tall tree. "I wish we could get closer and see how tall they really are," said Clara.

"If your father stood on the roof of the car and I stood on his shoulders, I would probably be high enough to reach a giraffe's

A giraffe's long neck enables him to reach high in the trees for food.

head," said Chuli. "That is, if the giraffe was standing by the car too."

"Is this where they take the lions they catch in the Fulani herdsmen's territory?" asked Sister Parker.

"Yes, lions are welcome here. But of course the giraffes do not welcome them. The lion is a natural enemy to the giraffe. In the heat of the day, we are not likely to see lions on the move. They rest and sleep as long as twenty hours a day when hunting is not difficult."

"I thought the animals are supposed to be safe from hunters here," said Clara.

"People are not allowed to hunt here," answered Chuli. "But lions and leopards are part of the natural setting for wild animals. They help to keep animals like deer from becoming too numerous. This is part of the pattern God created to balance nature."

"Do lions have any enemies in nature?" asked Antonia.

"Leopards and **hyenas** are a danger to the cubs. Older lions, especially those who are past their prime, may be hurt or killed in trying to kill their prey. For example, elephants defend themselves with their heavy feet and their tusks."

"I see some zebras grazing in the grassland to the right," said Brother Parker.

"There are some antelope out there too," said Chuli.

The travelers returned to Antonia's home in pleasant evening weather. "Does the sun always go down this early?" asked Clara. "We are used to having long days in the summer."

"Yes, sunset and sunrise are very regular all year round," answered Antonia. "We do not have summer and winter. Daylight is the same through rainy season and dry season. So is the temperature. That is because we live close to the equator."

Secretary Birds

Do you know of any birds that like snakes? Secretary birds do—at least they like to eat them! These large African birds also eat insects, mice, and other rodents. Secretary birds stand almost 4 feet tall. Their wings stretch out 6 to 7 feet when they soar.

Secretary birds were named for their crest feathers, which look like pens stuck behind the ears. Their gray and black feathers make them look somewhat like office workers dressed in business suits.

———— **Testing Your Understanding** ————

A. *Write the correct word(s) to complete each sentence. You will not use all the words.*

homes	game reserve	Niger	dry season
ice	temperature	bridge	electricity
fish	irrigation	Benue	equator
autumn	rainy season	spring	rainfall

1. The Kainji Dam was built across the ——— River.
2. It provides waterpower to generate ———.
3. It provides a ——— across the river.
4. It stores a large water supply for ———.
5. The dam forms a lake, which is a source of ———.
6. Because of the dam, many people had to find new ———.
7. Wild animals are protected in a ———.
8. In the Tropical Zone, the ——— changes more from day to night than it does from one season to another.
9. The seasons in the Tropical Zone are the ——— and the ———.
10. Near the ———, the amount of daylight does not change with different seasons.

B. *Answer these questions.*

1. List ten kinds of wild animals mentioned in this lesson.
2. Why was the game reserve needed?

Further Study

1. How would the balance of nature be disturbed if all animals such as lions and leopards were destroyed?
2. Discuss some reasons why tropical animals would find it difficult or impossible to live in areas that have cold winters.

Map Exercises

1. On your map of Nigeria, label the Kainji Lake.
2. Label the Borgu Game Reserve.

Lesson 8 Answers

Testing Your Understanding
A. 1. Niger
2. electricity
3. bridge
4. irrigation
5. fish
6. homes
7. game reserve
8. temperature
9. rainy season, dry season.
10. equator

B. 1. (Any ten) antelope, ostriches, herons, monkeys, giraffes, lions, leopards, hyenas, elephants, zebras, secretary birds (also fish)
2. The game reserve was needed to protect animals that were in danger of dying off.

Further Study
1. Other animals would become so plentiful that there would not be enough food for them all.
2. (Sample answers)
—Tropical animals do not prepare for cold weather by storing food or fat, growing thick coats of hair, migrating, or hibernating.
—Tropical animals need a regular supply of food all year. For example, the giraffe needs a steady diet of leaves, but many trees lose their leaves during cold winters.
—Tropical animals were created to endure heat rather than cold.
(*Note:* Zoos in the temperate zones are able to keep tropical animals by providing feed and shelter during the winter.)

Map Exercises
(Individual work. Check maps for accuracy and neatness.)

9. Resources of Nigeria

Glossary Words

mangrove trees

delta (DEHL tuh) Land that is built up when soil settles near the mouth of a river.

ferment (fur MEHNT) Go through a slow chemical change, thus becoming sour and giving off gas.

latex (LAY tehks) The milky sap of certain plants.

lubricant (LOO brih kuhnt) A substance such as oil that reduces friction between moving parts.

mangrove (MAN grohv) A tropical tree that spreads at the edge of water by growing new roots down from its branches.

natural resource (rih SAWRS, REE sawrs) Something useful provided by God in nature, such as water or coal.

petroleum (puh TROH lee uhm) A black oil that is used to make gasoline, kerosene, and other products.

plantation (plan TAY shuhn) A large farm with many workers.

A Cacao Farm

"Come along and see the cacao farm," invited Chuli the next morning as he was preparing for work. Many of the villagers had small farms in the surrounding forest, and they walked to them each day to care for their crops.

Under the shade of taller forest trees, Chuli had rows and rows of cacao trees. The fruit was not growing in the leafy treetops, but on little stems hanging from the trunks and branches.

"There are two times a year that the harvest is greater, but

LESSON AIM

To study some of Nigeria's resources and to teach how important natural resources are to any nation.

MAIN POINTS

- **Nigeria is a leading producer of cacao products.** The melonlike fruit grows on short stems, close to the trunk of the tropical cacao tree. The seeds are taken from the fruit and cleaned, roasted, shelled, and ground.

  [At some time in history, *cacao* was misspelled as *cocoa*. This accounts for the two similar words.]

- **Other tropical trees are important to Nigeria.** Oil palm trees produce two kinds of oil, one from the fruit and one from the kernels. Rubber trees produce latex, which is processed into rubber. Mahogany trees provide hard, beautiful wood. Banana and coffee trees are also grown.

- **Petroleum is the leading export of Nigeria.** Many oil wells have been drilled near the coast, especially in the delta area.

- **Deltas form at the mouth of some rivers.**

- **God has blessed Nigeria with many natural resources.** [The last few paragraphs of the text review some natural resources that are presented in this lesson, as well as a few others. Many more could have been added.]

RELATED POINTS

- **Importance of natural resources.** The students should be made aware of the resources they depend on. Mention some that are used to provide the necessities of everyday life—food, clothing, shelter, and things such as books and school supplies. To travel by car, resources of oil, iron, and rubber are needed.

some of the pods are ripening all year round," said Chuli. He reached for a cacao pod and cut it from the tree. It looked like a long cantaloupe. With a sharp knife, he split the pod, and then he showed the mass of beans inside in a soft pulp.

"Today we will be getting a batch of beans ready to *ferment*," said Chuli. He handed one half of the pod to Brother Parker and scooped a handful of beans from the other half. They looked like brown lima beans. "One pod may have from twenty to forty beans in it. We put a batch of them in a hole in the ground lined with leaves. For about a week they ferment, and we stir them frequently. The pulp drains away from the beans. Then we dry the beans, and they are ready for shipping."

"Do you have some dried beans on hand?" asked Brother Parker.

"Yes, come and see our drying shed." Chuli led the way to a long, thatched roof. Several tables were spread with chocolate-brown beans on mats that let the air circulate around the beans. Chuli opened a basket and scooped up a handful of dry beans.

A cacao tree

"They smell somewhat like chocolate," said Clara. "What must still be done to them to make chocolate?"

"They must be cleaned, roasted, and shelled," explained Chuli. "Then they are ground, and the fat in the beans makes a pasty mixture called chocolate liquor. This mixture may be pressed to separate it into cocoa butter and cocoa powder. Or the chocolate liquor may be made into chocolate by adding extra cocoa butter to it. The candy you like to eat has sugar and flavorings and probably milk solids added too."

Other Tropical Trees

"There are other trees important to Nigeria," Chuli remarked

• **Wise use of resources.** Discuss how resources are sometimes wasted or misused. Though we or any other people are blessed with many natural resources, we will lose them if we do not use them wisely.

as he pointed to some small palm trees near the drying shed. "These are oil palm trees. I have only a few wild ones, but some people grow them on farms or **plantations** the same as I grow cacao trees. Palm oil is made from the fleshy part of the fruit. Palm kernel oil is made from the nut inside the fleshy fruit. Making palm oil is an important business in this part of Nigeria."

"What is palm oil used for?" asked Clara.

This man is cutting a rubber tree to gather latex. Rubber trees grow 60 to 70 feet tall. They grow well in hot, moist climates. Rubber produced from the rubber tree is called natural rubber.

An oil palm

"It is used mostly in soap products, candles, and **lubricants**. The fat or oil taken from the palm kernel is used to make margarine."

"Another tree crop is rubber," stated Chuli. "Workers tap the trees by making a slanted cut in the bark halfway around the tree.

A mahogany tree

Oil Wells Near the Delta

"Are these tree crops the leading products of Nigeria?" asked Brother Parker.

"They are important products. Nigeria is one of the leading nations in producing cacao. But Nigeria's greatest export by far is *petroleum*. Many oil wells have been drilled near the coast, especially around the *delta* of the Niger River. Petroleum has had a big influence on the prosperity of the nation."

"We have a cousin who moved to Port Harcourt to get a job with

The thick white sap, called *latex*, runs down the cut to a spout and into a cup. It must be gathered quickly because it soon spoils. The latex is shipped to factories where it is processed to make rubber."

"I never imagined that trees gave chocolate, oil, and rubber," said Clara. "This is interesting."

"A tropical forest has many kinds of trees," answered Antonia. "Some of them, like mahogany, are used for their beautiful wood. Bananas and coffee are also raised in Nigeria."

This oil station in Nigeria controls the flow of oil from a number of wells.

The Niger River flows many miles through Nigeria. Water is a natural resource everyone depends on. God controls the water supply. "He sendeth the springs into the valleys, which run among the hills" (Psalm 104:10).

an oil company," said Antonia. "Once we went to visit him and his family. There the rain forest walks right out into the sea."

"What do you mean?" asked Clara.

"Have you ever seen ***mangrove*** trees?" wondered Antonia. "They grow right at the edge of the land, with seawater washing around their roots. New roots grow out of the branches and curve away from the tree, down to the water and mud. They make props for the branches, and in this way the trees spread over large areas. New trunks grow up where the roots anchor in the mud.

"All that maze of roots helps to slow down the water flowing from the mouth of the river. Soil carried by the water drops to the bottom and is held there by the roots. Slowly the delta grows as the land follows the trees into the water.

"The petroleum business walks right out into the sea too.

Cousin Ramat took us to see the oil wells. Some of them are out in the gulf, drilled down into the mud and rock under the water."

"Your land has surely been blessed with many *natural resources*," said Brother Parker.

"Yes, we are rich," agreed Chuli. "We have soil and water and a good climate for growing things. We just mentioned several kinds of trees, and there are many more. Many kinds of crops prosper in our land. In the drier northern part, peanuts and cotton are important crops. The

How a Delta Forms

The flow of water carries soil downstream.

The soil settles to the bottom when the water reaches a larger body of water at the river's mouth.

The soil gradually builds up to form new land.

Smaller streams cut through the new land and form a triangular-shaped delta.

plentiful rainfall in the southern part makes it possible to raise many of the crops that need more water.

"Our land is also rich in animal life. You have seen some of the animals of the grasslands. The rivers and lakes have an abundance of fish. And hidden under the ground are some other important resources. There is petroleum as well as coal and tin. The Lord has bestowed many riches on our land. We have much to thank Him for."

——————— Testing Your Understanding ———————

Lesson 9 Answers

Testing Your Understanding

A. 1. a. cacao
    b. oil palm
    c. mangrove
    d. rubber
    e. mahogany
 2. d. The beans are taken out of the fruit.
    a. The pulp around the beans ferments and drains away.
    e. The beans are dried and cleaned.
    c. The beans are roasted and then shelled and ground to make chocolate liquor.
    b. Chocolate liquor is pressed to make cocoa butter and cocoa powder.
 3. water, soil, lumber, animal life, tin, good climate, coal, petroleum

A. *Follow the directions.*

  1. Name each tree described here.
    a. It produces beans that are made into chocolate.
    b. It produces fruit and kernels that provide oil.
    c. It has long roots growing from the branches down into the mud.
    d. It produces a sap called latex.
    e. It provides beautiful wood.
  2. Write the letters of these steps in the correct order for processing cacao beans.
    a. The pulp around the beans ferments and drains away.
    b. Chocolate liquor is pressed to make cocoa butter and cocoa powder.
    c. The beans are roasted and then shelled and ground to make chocolate liquor.
    d. The beans are taken out of the fruit.
    e. The beans are dried and cleaned.
  3. From the list below, copy the names of eight natural resources in Nigeria that this lesson mentions.

lead	water	copper
soil	lumber	animal life
tin	silver	good climate
gold	coal	petroleum

Lesson 9   73

B. *Answer these questions.*

1. When do cacao pods ripen?
2. What kinds of oil come from trees?
3. What kind of oil comes from wells in the ground?
4. What is the leading export of Nigeria?

Further Study

1. Which of the natural resources of Nigeria are usually found only in the Tropical Zone?
2. How does a delta form?

Map Exercises

1. Before the Niger River flows into the Gulf of Guinea, it divides into several branches. This part of a river is called a delta. Print *DELTA* to label the Niger Delta on your map.
2. Label Port Harcourt on your map.
3. Draw a few oil well symbols (⚒ ⚒) in the gulf around the Niger Delta.
4. Color your map according to the Rules for Neat Maps that you copied in Lesson 4.

B. 1. Cacao pods ripen throughout the year, but the harvest is best two times a year.
2. palm oil and palm kernel oil
3. petroleum
4. petroleum

Further Study
1. Most of the tree products and animal life, and many of the crops of Nigeria are usually found only in the Tropical Zone.
2. A river carries soil particles with the water. At the mouth of the river, the water slows down and the soil drops to the bottom. Over a period of time, this builds up as extended land. The roots of mangrove trees help hold the soil of some deltas.

Map Exercises
(Individual work. Check maps for accuracy and neatness.)

10. Chapter 2 Review

——————— Testing Your Understanding ———————

A. *Write a glossary word for each definition.*

1. Sap of the rubber tree.
2. Oil from an oil well.
3. A useful material provided by God in nature.
4. Tree that is the source of chocolate.
5. Strong, dry wind that blows from the Sahara.
6. Person who moves about in search of pasture.
7. Habit or usual way of doing something.
8. The number of people in an area.
9. Place of protection for wild animals.
10. Vast, dry grassland.

B. *Write* true *or* false *for each sentence. Copy each false sentence, and change one word in it to make it true.*

1. Nigeria has the largest population of any country in Africa.
2. The rain forest of Nigeria is a band across the northern part of the country.
3. Ibadan is the capital city of Nigeria.
4. The dry season in Nigeria lasts from November through March or April.
5. Electricity is generated at the Kainji Dam.
6. There are over two hundred languages in Nigeria.
7. Cocoa is made from the seeds of the coconut tree.
8. Some natural resources of Nigeria are tree products, rainfall, and fish.
9. The Niger and Benue rivers form a great V across Nigeria.
10. English is the official language of Nigeria.

Lesson 10 Answers

Testing Your Understanding

A. 1. latex
2. petroleum
3. natural resource
4. cacao
5. harmattan
6. nomad
7. custom
8. population
9. game reserve
10. savanna

B. 1. true
2. false; The rain forest of Nigeria is a band across the ~~northern~~ southern part of the country.
3. false; ~~Ibadan~~ Abuja is the capital city of Nigeria.
4. true
5. true
6. true
7. false; Cocoa is made from the seeds of the ~~coconut~~ cacao tree.
8. true
9. false; The Niger and Benue rivers form a great ~~V~~ Y across Nigeria.
10. true

C. *Answer these questions.*

1. In what climate zone is Nigeria?
2. Why do the northern savannas have fewer trees than the southern savannas?
3. What are the two seasons in Nigeria?
4. In Nigeria, which causes a greater temperature change: the change from one season to another, or the change from day to night?
5. How does the amount of moisture in an area make a difference in what people eat?

Map Exercises

Use your completed map of Nigeria to do these exercises.

1. Name each of the following.
   a. The capital of Nigeria.
   b. The gulf that is south of Nigeria.
   c. The lake on the northeastern border of Nigeria.
   d. The two main rivers of Nigeria.
   e. The lake formed by the dam in western Nigeria.
2. Which tribe or tribes live in (*a*) northern Nigeria? (*b*) western Nigeria? (*c*) eastern Nigeria?
3. What is the name of a place where a river divides into several branches before flowing into the sea?

Review Study

1. Do you know the meaning of all the glossary words in Chapter 2?
2. Do you know how northern Nigeria is different from southern Nigeria?

C. 1. in the Tropical Zone
2. The northern savannas are drier than the southern savannas. (Also, the harmattan blows across the northern savannas.)
3. the wet season and the dry season
4. the change from day to night
5. People eat the crops or animals that they can raise with the amount of moisture in an area.

Map Exercises
1. a. Lagos
   b. Gulf of Guinea
   c. Lake Chad
   d. Niger and Benue
   e. Kainji Lake
2. a. Hausa and Fulani
   b. Yoruba
   c. Ibo
3. a delta

Review Study
(Individual work. Review the glossary words orally. Discuss ways that northern and southern Nigeria are different. Point out that the main differences are due to the amount of rainfall each area receives. Examples:
Southern Nigeria has much more rainfall than northern Nigeria.
The houses are built differently.
Different crops are grown.
More cattle are raised in the north.
The harmattan is stronger in the north.
The south has more oil wells.
Rain forests are in the south; savannas are in the north.)

Extra Activity

(This activity is designed to show the students that durable buildings can be made from clay. It should also help them to appreciate one of the Hausa crafts—stone painting that depicts Nigerian life.

Potter's clay may be used for the clay impressions; but if that is not available, you can probably get clay from the ground in your area. Most areas have a clay subsoil under several inches of topsoil, and this clay works almost as well as potter's clay.

A kind of clay can also be made by mixing 1 cup flour, 2 tablespoons salt, and 1 teaspoon vegetable oil, and adding enough water to make a pliable dough. Moisten your clay and keep it in a plastic bag until you are ready to use it.

Water colors may be used for the stone painting. You may need to explain what is meant by a silhouette.)

Extra Activity

Clay Impressions

Use clay to make a paperweight with an interesting impression—a fingerprint, a paw print of your pet, or a leaf impression like that in a fossil. You could also use a needle and thimble to make a picture or design. Or you could make a little house like the ones in Nigeria, as shown in the picture on page 50. When the Nigerians build these houses, they mix straw, hair, or grass with the clay to make it stronger.

Now you are ready for the drying. If it is a warm day, let your clay dry in the sun. This is the best way because the sun bakes it hard. If you need to use an oven, place your items on a cookie sheet and bake them slowly. When they are finished, you will understand better how the Nigerians' clay houses can last year after year, sometimes for centuries.

Stone Painting

The Nigerians do much painting of pictures showing animals or scenes from their daily life. They paint in caves, on stones, on pottery, and even on baskets. In weaving or basket making, they often use dyed threads or strips to work a figure into the finished product.

To make a painted stone paperweight, choose a smooth flat stone 3 to 6 inches in diameter. On your stone, paint a colored silhouette (a "shadow picture") of some animal that you have studied in this chapter. The Nigerian painters use colors like gray, brown, or forest green, but they seldom use bright colors. When you paint your stone, use dull and light colors, but not colors such as bright red or bright yellow.

So Far This Year

1. The (weather, climate) of an area is its usual temperature, rainfall, wind, and sunshine.

2. Match the climate zones to the descriptions.

   a. Region of four seasons, north of the equator.

   b. Cold region around the South Pole.

   c. Warm region along the equator.

   d. Cold region around the North Pole.

   e. Region of four seasons, south of the equator.

   Northern Frigid Zone
   Northern Temperate Zone
   Tropical Zone
   Southern Temperate Zone
   Southern Frigid Zone

3. Most of Brazil is in the (Temperate, Tropical, Frigid) Zone.

4. Seasons in the Tropical Zone are the (rainy season and dry season, hot season and cold season).

5. The (Nile, Amazon, Mississippi) River is a large river in Brazil.

6. Choose two: Some animals prepare for winter by (migrating, molting, hibernating, ruminating).

7. During summer in the (Tropical, Temperate, Frigid) Zone, the sun can be seen at midnight.

8. Nigeria is in the (Tropical, Temperate, Frigid) Zone.

9. Nigeria is on the continent of (Africa, Asia, Australia).

10. Dams help to provide all the following benefits except (fishing, irrigation, electricity, climate control, flood control).

11. Chocolate and cocoa come from (cacao, coconut, canola) seeds.

12. A deposit of soil at the mouth of a river is a (dam, delta, delegate).

So Far This Year

1. climate
2. a. Northern Temperate Zone
   b. Southern Frigid Zone
   c. Tropical Zone
   d. Northern Frigid Zone
   e. Southern Temperate Zone
3. Tropical
4. rainy season and dry season
5. Amazon
6. migrating, hibernating
7. Frigid
8. Tropical
9. Africa
10. climate control
11. cacao
12. delta

Manila is the largest city and capital of the Philippines. This commercial section of the city was once a swamp.

CHAPTER 3

THE PHILIPPINES, MORE THAN 7000 ISLANDS

"Sing unto the LORD a new song, and his praise from the end of the earth, ye that go down to the sea, and all that is therein; the isles, and the inhabitants thereof" (Isaiah 42:10).

11. At Home Near Manila

Glossary Words

frond

archipelago (ahr kuh PEHL uh goh) A large group of islands.

barrio (BAH ree oh) A village in the Philippines.

frond A long, wide leaf made up of smaller sections.

nipa (NEE puh) A large palm tree that grows in the Philippines.

peso (PAY soh) The main unit of money used in the Philippines, worth much less than an American dollar.

typhoon (ty FOON) A hurricane that occurs off the southeastern coast of Asia.

An Island Nation

Find the nation of Brazil on a globe or a world map. Move west and cross the Pacific Ocean just north of the equator. Halfway around the world from Brazil, you will find a cluster of islands called the Philippines.

There are more than 7,000 islands in the Philippine *archipelago*. Most of the people, called Filipinos, live on the eleven largest islands. Hundreds of the small islands have not even been named. Some are so small that they go underwater every time the tide rises.

Since the Philippine nation is in the Tropical Zone, it has a warm climate such as Brazil and Nigeria have. Filipinos do not need coats or furnaces. They enjoy eating many tropical fruits and vegetables.

The national languages of the Philippines are Pilipino (PIHL uh pee noh) and English. Many other native languages are spoken by small groups of people.

A Nipa Hut

Jose (hoh SAY) and Nena (NAY nuh) are ten-year-old twins who live on Luzon Island (loo

LESSON AIM

To introduce the students to the Philippines, an island nation in the Tropical Zone.

MAIN POINTS

- **The Philippines is an archipelago of over 7,000 islands.** Most of the Filipinos live on the eleven largest islands. Many of the islands are very small.

- **The Philippines is in the Tropical Zone.** The climate is warm year round.

- **Pilipino [also called Tagalog] and English are the national languages of the Philippines.** Many other local languages are also spoken.

- **Many Filipinos live in nipa huts.** These simple huts are well suited for the tropical climate, and they are often clustered in villages called barrios. Houses in the cities have windows and floors. Manila, the capital city, also has some skyscrapers.

- **Jeepneys provide a popular form of transportation.** The first jeepneys were converted army jeeps, but new ones are manufactured now. Many Filipinos do not travel much.

RELATED POINTS

- **The Philippine Islands are divided into three major groups.** The Luzon group in the north consists of the island of Luzon and the nearby smaller islands. The Mindanao group in the south includes Mindanao and the smaller islands around it. The Visayan Islands include the seven large islands and the thousands of smaller islands between Luzon and Mindanao.

The islands of Mindoro and Palawan are considered as separate smaller divisions or are included in the Luzon group.

ZAHN). Luzon is the largest Philippine island. Jose and Nena's home is near Manila, the capital city of the Philippines.

"Father!" Jose exclaimed, running through the doorway of their *nipa* hut and jumping to the ground.

Nena was right behind her brother and just as excited. But she took time to climb down the six steps to the ground.

"Father, I'm glad you're home!" Nena greeted him. She caught Father's hand and pressed it to her forehead.

"I am too," he replied, taking each of the children by the hand and leading the way to the hut. "The week seems long when I am away. Where is Mother?"

"Cooking rice," Nena answered. "Did you catch lots of fish?"

"Yes," Father replied. "I went out deep-sea fishing on one of the larger boats. The fish brought a good price at the market too."

"Good," Jose cried happily. "Now we will have more *pesos* to spend when we go to the city."

Father's fishing provided money for things his family needed, as well as fish to eat.

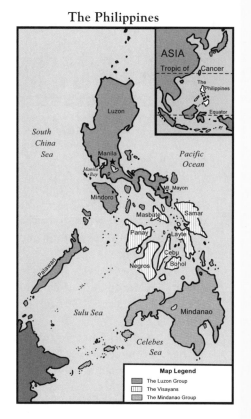

The Philippines

Their nipa hut was built on a small lot in a *barrio* near Manila. The lot was so small that there was no room to raise rice or keep animals. Thousands of huts like theirs were crowded together in their barrio. They had only a tiny garden where Mother raised vegetables.

This is a Filipino five-peso bill. The peso is the Filipino unit of money. The dollar is the unit of money used in the United States and Canada.

"Father," Jose began again, "school is out now. Will you take us to Manila next week to see the harbor, and the ships loading and unloading their cargoes?"

"And to see the skyscrapers in downtown Manila, and the beautiful Luneta Park?" Nena added wistfully.

The twins had not forgotten Father's promise to take them to Manila after school was out. They had never been farther away from home than they could walk. Families like theirs had no cars, and they usually traveled by walking—to school, to church, and to nearby marketplaces.

Father sat down on the top step of the nipa hut. "Do you know what I've been thinking? I think it would be nice if we would go and help Grandfather plant rice next week."

"Oh, yes!" cried Jose. "I could help him plow."

"But wouldn't we go to the city?" asked Nena.

"Yes, on our way home," answered Father. "We would spend several days with Grandfather, then we could go into Manila and see the harbor and Luneta Park."

"Yes, and I would like to see some of those big houses you told us about," said Nena. "I cannot imagine why people want glass windows in their houses. The sun shining through glass windows would make a house too warm. The air feels fresh coming in our open windows."

"I know," Jose agreed, "but rich people have fine furniture and beds. They would get all wet if they didn't have glass in their windows," he reminded his sister.

"I'm glad a little rain won't hurt the grass mats we sleep on," Nena replied. "Not much rain comes in anyway, except when the wind is strong during the rainy season. Sometimes a *typhoon* will drive in a lot of rain, but it runs right out again through the bamboo slats in the floor."

"Rich people have concrete or wooden floors in their houses," Father remarked. "Then the water can't get away if it rains in."

"I like the soft breeze that comes up between the bamboo slats on warm days," Nena commented. "That's why our huts are built up on stilts, isn't it?"

"That's partly right," answered Father. "Do you remember when the Pasig River (PAHS ihg) flooded? Weren't you glad our house was on stilts then?"

"I sure was!" exclaimed Nena. "And I'm glad we don't live closer to the river. Our stilts wouldn't have been high enough to keep us out of the water."

"Well, I suppose if we lived close to the river, we would build on higher stilts, as the other people do who live there," said Jose. "Here our stilts don't need to be so high. Just high enough to allow a good breeze to come in, and to keep the rats out. That's why Father nailed these pieces of tin around the posts."

"God made a useful tree when He made the nipa palm, didn't He?" observed Father. "There is nothing that makes such nice cool walls as mats woven of nipa palm leaves. And nipa *fronds* make a good roof too when they are laid tightly and overlapped. With our nipa walls and roof and bamboo floor, our little hut is shady and cool inside."

A Jeepney Ride

The warm tropical sun was just rising after a pleasantly cool night. "Jose! Nena!" Father called. "It's time to get up."

The twins jumped up, rolled up their sleeping mats, and stood them in a corner. Mother was already frying rice over a little fire outside the hut.

Thousands of Filipinos live in nipa huts on stilts.

84   Unit 2, Chapter 3 The Philippines, More Than 7000 Islands

Many jeepneys in the Philippines are lavishly decorated.

Jose and Nena were almost too excited to eat their breakfast. Today they were going to Grandfather's farm!

"I haven't ridden in a jeepney very often," Nena said, her eyes dancing.

"I haven't either," Jose said. "But I have seen them when I walked with Father out of the barrio to catch one. They are all brightly painted and decorated."

"The first jeepneys, many years ago, were made from old American army jeeps," explained Father. "Filipino mechanics rebuilt the jeeps and put truck beds on them. They put roofs over the beds and built seats inside. Then they went around picking up passengers. Today the jeepneys are made here in the Philippines. They are covered with so many decorations that they hardly look like army jeeps."

The breakfast bowls were washed and set on the shelf. The mosquito nets that had hung over their sleeping mats were folded and stacked by the mats.

"Are we ready?" Father called from outside. He had been making sure the fire was out.

"Yes," Mother replied, handing each child a sack. "Here are the things you will need while we travel."

Soon Jose and Nena were enjoying their jeepney ride on the highway alongside the Pasig River. They marveled at the speed they were traveling, as they passed small boats slowly making their way up the river.

———————— **Testing Your Understanding** ————————

A. *Write the correct word(s) to complete each sentence.*

1. The Philippines is in the ——— Zone.
2. The people of the Philippines are called ———.
3. The national languages of the Philippines are ——— and ———.
4. The capital of the Philippines is ———. It is on ———, the largest Philippine island.
5. Philippine villages are called ———.
6. Jose and Nena live in a ——— hut. It is built on ——— to keep out ——— and rats. The floor is made of ———.
7. In the Philippines, vehicles called ——— provide transportation for many people.

B. *Write* true *or* false *for each sentence.*

1. A large group of islands is called an archipelago.
2. There are over 7,000 islands in the Philippines.
3. All the Philippine islands are crowded with people.
4. Furnaces are not needed in the Philippines.
5. Many native languages are spoken in the Philippines.
6. Most Filipinos drive their own cars.
7. Some houses in Manila have glass windows and wooden floors.
8. Typhoons bring hot, dry weather.

Lesson 11 Answers

  Testing Your Understanding

A. 1. Tropical
   2. Filipinos
   3. Pilipino, English
   4. Manila, Luzon
   5. barrios
   6. nipa, stilts, water, bamboo
   7. jeepneys

B. 1. true
   2. true
   3. false
   4. true
   5. true
   6. false
   7. true
   8. false

9. false
10. false

Further Study

1. Many of the smallest islands are not named. Even if they all had names, it would be hard to learn the names of 7,000 islands.
2. (Individual work. Discuss the advantages and disadvantages of nipa huts. Help the students to see that for many Filipinos, a nipa hut is the best choice. Point out that people living in the Tropical Zone need less shelter than people living in the temperate or frigid zones.)

Map Exercises

(Individual work. Check maps for accuracy and neatness.)

9. Jose and Nena's mother cooks rice on a stove inside their hut.
10. The first jeepneys were made from old farm trucks.

Further Study

1. Give two reasons that teachers in the Philippines would not expect their students to learn the names of all the Philippine islands.
2. Would you enjoy living in a nipa hut? Give a reason for your answer.

Map Exercises

1. Trace Map B in the map section.
2. Label Manila.

12. A Visit to Grandfather's Farm

Glossary Words

terraces

carabao (kair uh BOW) The water buffalo of the Philippines.

paddy (PAD ee) A flooded field where rice is grown.

terrace (TAIR ihs) A level surface cut into the side of a hill, usually for raising crops.

volcano (vahl KAY noh) A mountain that is formed when pressure inside the earth throws out melted rock.

A Rice Farm

"*Kamusta!*" (kah MOO stuh) Grandfather called in Pilipino when he saw the twins running toward him. His greeting meant "How are you?"

"*Mabuti, ho!*" (mah BOO tee hoh) the children called back, meaning "Fine." (*Ho* is a Filipino term showing respect for older people.)

"We are glad to see you, Grandfather!" Jose cried. He ran to help hold a large wooden plow while Grandfather hitched it to his *carabao*.

"Oh, a water buffalo!" Nena exclaimed.

"No," Jose corrected her, "this is Grandfather's carabao."

"You are both right," Grand-

father said with a smile. "You need to come to the farm more often."

"We will plow this small rice

These Filipino farmers are preparing their fields for rice. This photograph was taken near Manila, the capital city of the Philippines.

LESSON AIM

To learn about raising rice, the influence of foreigners in the Philippines, and the Ring of Fire.

MAIN POINTS

- **Rice is the most important crop in the Philippines.** [Most Filipinos eat rice every day.] More rice is raised on the central plain of Luzon than anywhere else in the Philippines. Rice is raised to some extent on all the major islands.

- **The Philippine Islands have a rainy season and a dry season.** Rice grows well during the rainy season, since the paddies need to be flooded part of the time. Some farmers grow rice during the dry season by irrigating it.

- **Carabaos are used for plowing.** Tractors are used on some of the larger farms. [Some Filipino farmers use a machine that resembles a large rear-tine tiller.]

- **The Filipinos have been influenced by many foreigners.** The first Filipinos came from neighboring islands or the mainland of Asia. The Ifugao tribe built rice terraces in the mountains of northern Luzon. Later, Arab traders brought the Muslim religion, and the Spanish started Catholic churches. Eventually the Americans drove out the Spanish and introduced the English language. Some Filipinos have joined Bible-believing churches that were started by missionaries.

- **The Philippine Islands are located on the Ring of Fire.** This is a circle around the Pacific Ocean that has many volcanoes and earthquakes. [California and Mexico are on the opposite side of the circle.] Typhoons also cause damage along the coasts of the Philippine Islands.

bed this morning," Grandfather went on to explain. "This afternoon you can help me sow the rice seed. We start the rice in small beds, but the plants become crowded as they grow. In about three weeks, we will set the plants out in rice **paddies**, like those over there."

Nena looked where Grandfather pointed. "I thought those were ponds," she said in a surprised voice.

"No, the water is only a few inches deep."

Later the twins helped to drop rice seeds on the freshly plowed soil. Grandfather explained, "The rice plants are about a foot tall when we plant them in the rice paddies. About that time the rainy season will start. Until the rains come, I will need to keep this bed watered.

"Some people grow rice during the dry season, when there is almost no rain at all. Those farmers irrigate their crops with water from a river. We grow rice only during the rainy season so that the rain floods our paddies.

"We will harvest our rice after the rainy season. Some farmers

In the Philippines, millions of young rice plants are set out by hand each year.

RELATED POINTS

- **The rice terraces in northern Luzon rise to about 5,000 feet above sea level—the highest existing structures made by early civilizations.** How the Ifugao did all that digging, and why they raised rice in the mountains instead of in level and more fertile areas remain mysteries to this day.

  The terraces are irrigated by stone canals, which bring water to the rice from mountain streams and springs. Dams of stone and earth are built along the edges of the terraces to prevent erosion.

- **The typhoons of the Philippines are hurricanes that strike in the western Pacific Ocean.** Filipinos call them *baguios* (bahg YOHS).

These paddies are filled with lush, green rice plants. Notice that the plants are standing in water. Most of the buildings in the background are used to raise ducks.

spread their rice out on the road to dry. They rake it often with large wooden rakes to make sure it dries properly. They don't want it to spoil."

"Don't people drive over it?" Nena asked.

"Oh, no. Rice is our country's food," Grandfather explained. "The rice is always kept on one side of the road, and the drivers carefully stay off that side until the rice is dry. Then the rice is sent to cities and sold in stores or put on ships to be taken to other countries."

"Is rice raised on all the Philippine islands?" asked Nena.

"Rice is raised on the eleven main islands and on many of the smaller islands," Grandfather explained. "But more rice is raised here on the central plain of Luzon than anywhere else in the Philippines. Thousands of tons of rice are raised here every year."

"Why don't you have a tractor, Grandfather?" Jose asked as they finished plowing. "I noticed many of the big farms out here have tractors. Wouldn't that be easier?"

Preparing Rice in the Philippines

The rice is washed and then boiled in water over a small outside fire in a large, black kettle. The water is boiled away until the rice is white, dry, and fluffy. It is eaten with dried fish for breakfast.

For lunch and supper the rice is served with an *ulam* (OO lahm). The *ulam* (topping) is made by lightly cooking small cubes of carrots and *sayote* (sy OH tee), a pear-shaped vegetable, with bits of beef or pork in a watery sauce.

"Yes," Grandfather replied thoughtfully. "Some are getting tractors, but I see many advantages in carabaos. Their broad feet do much better in mud than tractor tires do. Carabaos give milk, and they have new calves. When a carabao is too old to work, it can be killed and eaten, and the hide is also useful. Carabaos are hard workers, yet they are gentle and patient.

"Tractors do make some work easier and faster, but they are expensive. I would have to buy gasoline and oil, and repair the tractor if it broke down. The carabao costs me very little. I have plenty of grass for it to eat."

Learning About the Past

After supper that evening, Nena asked, "Have people always lived on these islands?"

Grandfather chuckled. "We can't be sure when men first found these islands. We do know that many Filipinos are descendants of tribes that came from Asia or nearby islands before the birth of Christ. One ancient tribe, the Ifugao (EE foo GOW), built rice **terraces** high into the mountains of northern Luzon. Their descendants still grow rice there today.

"Traders from Asia have visited the islands for hundreds of years. About the year 1400, Arab traders introduced the Muslim religion. There are still many Muslims on Mindanao (mihn duh NAH oh), the second largest island in the Philippines."

"I remember studying about them in school," Jose told his grandfather. "Many people on the other islands accepted Catholic beliefs after the Spanish took over the Philippines in the 1500s."

"You are right," Grandfather agreed. "Our way of life has been influenced by many foreigners. When the Americans ruled several hundred years later, we learned some American ways too, including their English language. That is why some children have Spanish names and others have English names.

"Some of us have also been influenced by foreign missionaries. I first heard the truth about

Do you see the white dust rising around the carabao's legs? The ground is covered with white ash from a volcano named Mount Pinatubo. Mount Pinatubo erupted in 1991, covering hundreds of acres of good cropland with ash.

Jesus and the Bible from one of them. But most Filipinos are still Catholic."

The Ring of Fire

"Grandfather, have you ever seen a *volcano*?" Jose asked suddenly.

"Yes," Grandfather replied. "There are ten active ones in the Philippines. I have seen most of them. I saw Mount Mayon (mah YAWN) in action."

"You have traveled a lot," Jose said, "and you have seen many things."

"Mount Mayon is one of the most perfectly shaped volcanoes in the world," Grandfather continued. "That is why it is so famous.

"Many of our mountains, and even many islands, were formed by volcanoes. The ashes that fall from their eruptions make the soil rich. That is one reason why plants grow so well here.

"Did you know we are living

The
Ring of
Fire

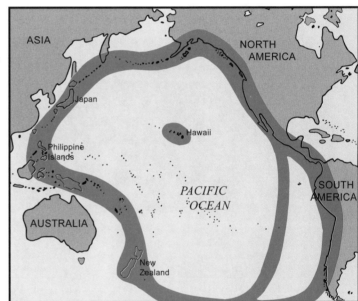

The Ring of Fire is an area around the Pacific Ocean where many earthquakes and volcanoes occur. The Philippines lie along the Ring of Fire.

along the Ring of Fire"? Grand-father asked.

"Yes," Jose replied. "I learned that in school. But why is it called the Ring of Fire? Is it because we have lots of volcanoes?"

"Yes, you are right," Grand-father said. "Over the years, scientists have noticed that there is a ring of volcanoes around the Pacific Ocean. There have also been many earthquakes along that ring."

"We must live in a dangerous place," said Nena.

"There are some dangers in the Philippines, from volcanoes and earthquakes as well as from storms. But no place on earth is perfectly safe from danger. God has blessed us with good soil and cool, refreshing ocean breezes. Typhoons and tropical storms do not hit as hard here near shel-tered Manila Bay as they do in many areas along the coast. And we can trust God to care for us during earthquakes or volcanic eruptions."

Testing Your Understanding

A. *Choose the correct words.*

1. *"Kamusta"* means ("How are you?" "Fine") in Pilipino.
2. (Rice, Wheat) is raised on all the main Philippine islands.
3. Rice is raised in (paddies, ponds).
4. Rice grows best during the (rainy, dry) season.
5. Rice is (irrigated, dried) after it is harvested.
6. Many Filipinos use carabaos instead of tractors because trac-tors are (expensive, hard to use).
7. The (Ifugao, Muslims) built rice terraces in the mountains of northern Luzon.
8. Catholic churches were started by the (Spanish, Americans).
9. The Ring of Fire is an area with many volcanoes and (typhoons, earthquakes).
10. The Ring of Fire lies around the (Atlantic, Pacific) Ocean.

Lesson 12 Answers

Testing Your Understanding
A. 1. "How are you?"
2. Rice
3. paddies
4. rainy
5. dried
6. expensive
7. Ifugao
8. Spanish
9. earthquakes
10. Pacific

B. 1. in the central plain of Luzon
2. by irrigating the fields
3. Mindanao
4. The Filipinos were ruled by Spanish-speaking people for a time. Later they were ruled by Americans, who spoke English.
5. Mount Mayon

Further Study

1. Tractors make the work simpler and faster on the largest farms.
2. The ashes that fall from volcanic eruptions make the soil rich, and better crops can be grown.

Map Exercises

(Individual work. Check maps for accuracy and neatness.)

B. *Answer the following questions.*

1. In what area of the Philippines is the most rice grown?
2. How is rice raised during the dry season?
3. On which Philippine island do many Muslims live?
4. Why do some Filipinos have Spanish names and others have English names?
5. Which volcano in the Philippines is known for its almost perfect shape?

Further Study

1. Why do some Filipinos buy tractors even though farming with carabaos has many advantages?
2. How have volcanoes helped the Filipinos?

Map Exercises

1. Use all capital letters to label the eleven largest Philippine islands. They are Luzon, Mindoro, Palawan, Panay, Masbate, Samar, Leyte, Cebu, Negros, Bohol, and Mindanao.
2. Mark Mount Mayon with a ▲ symbol, and label it.

13. Fishing With Father

Glossary Words

cannery (KAN uh ree) A place where foods are canned.

mainland A landmass such as a continent; not an island or a peninsula.

pearl A smooth, round stone that forms in an oyster and is valued for its beauty.

sponge A sea animal whose body is full of holes.

The jeepney was coming back into Manila when Father spoke. "Jose and Nena," he said, "we will soon be getting off. We are almost at Luneta Park, where Mother plans to spend a few days while I do some fishing. She will be weaving baskets and small mats. You may stay and help with the weaving, or you may go fishing with me."

Both children cried excitedly,

Most Filipino fishermen use small boats and do not go far out into the ocean. They sometimes fish at night, using lights on their boats to attract the fish. In the foreground, a fresh catch of squid is drying.

LESSON AIM

To learn about the resources from the waters of the Philippine Islands and to consider the beauty of natural wonders that God has made.

MAIN POINTS

- **Fishing is an important occupation in the Philippines.** Some fish are raised in flooded rice paddies after the rice is harvested. Fish are also caught in rivers and lakes, in channels around the islands, and in the deep waters of nearby seas and oceans. Fish are sold in markets or processed at canneries.

- **Other important resources from the sea include pearls, sponges, and shells.**

- **Oceans and seas separate the Philippine Islands from neighboring countries.** The Pacific Ocean lies east of the islands. The South China Sea lies to the west and separates the Philippines from the mainland of Asia. The Sulu and Celebes seas separate the Philippines from the islands of Indonesia and Malaysia.

- **Forests cover about half the land in the Philippines.** Trees provide beauty and useful wood products. Mangrove trees help keep the soil along the coast from washing away.

RELATED POINTS

- **Many other small seas, gulfs, bays, straits, and channels lie around and between the islands of the Philippines.** Fish are abundant in these waters. The total coastline of the islands is over 10,000 miles.

96   Unit 2, Chapter 3 The Philippines, More Than 7000 Islands

"We will go fishing! We will go fishing!"

"Fishing is hard work," Father warned.

"But we can do weaving at home." Nena's eyes sparkled. "I'm so eager to go out on the boat and help pull the fish in."

"If you catch any," Jose said, laughing. "Father, are we going in a boat today?"

"How else would we fish?" Nena asked.

"In a rice paddy," Jose replied.

Nena stared at her brother in disbelief.

"Jose is right, Nena," Father explained. "Not all fishing is done from boats. Many farmers stock their rice paddies with fish after the rice is harvested. They get double benefits by doing that. The fish fertilize the paddies for the next crop, and of course the fish grow and the farmers can sell them at the market. When they are ready to catch the fish, they simply drain the water out of the paddy."

There are many villages along the rivers and coasts of the Philippines. These huts are built on high stilts to keep high tides and floods from coming into them. Many of the people in this village make their living by fishing.

Large fishing boats help to provide a living for the Filipinos that go deep-sea fishing.

"But you don't catch fish that way, do you, Father?" asked Nena.

"No, I usually fish in the Pasig River, where we will go today. Next week I may go along on a bigger boat to do some more deep-sea fishing. But here is where we get off, so you will need to come along quickly."

Luneta Park was a lovely place. It had so many large, shady mango trees, beautiful flowers, and colorful birds that Nena almost changed her mind and decided to stay here with Mother.

"Let's go," said Jose, eager to be off with Father.

"You will still have some time to spend in the park when you return from fishing," Mother reminded Nena as she waved good-bye.

Fishing on the Pasig River

"Fishing is good today," Father observed. "God has blessed us with a large catch. Often when I'm out fishing, I think of Jesus' disciples who were fishermen."

"We have anchovies (AN choh veez), herring, mackerel, and sardines," Jose remarked. "But these probably won't bring as many pesos as the big sea bass and the shrimp you catch when you go deep-sea fishing. Will they, Father?"

"No, but they will provide us good food for the rest of the week," Father replied. "And we will have some to sell."

"I didn't know there were so many kinds of fish," Nena remarked as she removed a herring from a hook. "Father is right; fishing is hard work." She yawned and curled up for a nap in a corner of the gently rocking boat.

Jose helped Father with his net. Whenever they found a

Pearls and Sponges

An oyster begins making a pearl when a sharp object such as a grain of sand gets inside its shell. The object hurts the soft oyster, so the oyster covers it with a smooth, hard material. A pearl is formed as layer after layer is added.

Pearls are valued because of their beauty. Jesus told a parable about a man who sold all that he had so that he could buy a special pearl (Matthew 13:45, 46).

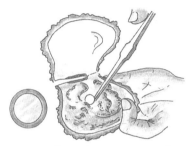

A pearl inside an oyster and an enlarged cross section of a pearl

A sponge

Sponges look like strange plants growing on rocks in the sea. But they are considered animals because they get their food by straining tiny plants and animals out of the water.

After divers gather sponges, the sponges are cleaned and dried until only their skeletons remain. Then they are sold in stores and used for many purposes.

Sponges have been gathered for thousands of years. When Jesus was dying on the cross, the Roman soldiers used a sponge to offer Him a drink (Matthew 27:48).

A few natural sponges are still used in America today. But most sponges sold in stores are made of rubber or some other material.

school of sardines or anchovies, the net was soon filled. "Father, what will we do with all these little fish?" Jose asked.

"Oh, we will sell them to the *cannery*. They pack them in cans to sell in stores. Some will be sent to other countries.

"There are other resources from the sea that bring in good wages too," Father told Jose. "Some people make their living by diving for *pearls* or *sponges*. Sometimes they drag nets on the sea floor and bring in tons of shells."

"What are shells good for?" Jose asked.

"They are used to make buttons and ornaments. Some people make wind chimes out of them."

"Father, will you be on the Pacific Ocean next week?" Jose wondered. "Could you find us some pearls?"

"No, I don't dive. Pearls are hard to get. I only go after fish. A person has to be a good diver to go down and find pearls. Besides, I won't be on the Pacific Ocean. The Pacific is east of the Philippines. I go out west of Manila on the South China Sea."

"That's the sea that separates the islands from the *mainland* of Asia," Jose remembered. "And the Sulu and Celebes seas separate our islands from the islands of Indonesia and Malaysia. There is lots of water around our islands, and lots of wealth in those waters, isn't there?"

"Yes," Father replied, "God has given us many good things and plenty of food, but we must work to get it."

The Luneta Park

Two tired children came back to stay with Mother at Luneta Park. Father left some of the fish for them to enjoy, and then he hurried to the market to sell the rest.

The park hummed with activity as many other people, like Mother, were making and selling their crafts. Strangers from all over the islands were spending a few days in Luneta Park as they passed through Manila on business trips or vacations.

"Let's take a walk through the park," suggested Jose. "Let's see how many different kinds of flowers there are."

Luneta Park is a busy park in Manila. Beautiful flowers and trees grow there.

"And trees," said Nena. "Look at those beautiful narra trees. Their bright yellow blossoms must be in full bloom!"

"Yes," replied Jose, "our trees are a real blessing from God. I remember reading that forests cover about half of the land in the Philippines. Besides their beauty, trees are useful for lumber and plywood.

"And that's not all," Jose added as they strolled through the park together. Pointing out a mangrove tree, he said, "Those trees are especially good for holding the soil and keeping the coast from washing away."

Testing Your Understanding

A. *Write the correct word(s) to complete each sentence.*

1. Some Filipinos raise —— in rice paddies after the rice is harvested.

2. Small boats are used by fishermen on the —— River and other rivers and lakes of the Philippines.

Lesson 13 Answers

Testing Your Understanding

A. 1. fish
   2. Pasig

3. Larger boats are used for ——— fishing in the waters around the islands.

4. Sardines and anchovies are packed in cans at ———.

5. Divers gather ——— and ——— from the seas.

6. Tons of ——— are brought up from the sea floor with nets.

7. The ——— Ocean is east of the Philippines.

8. The ——— Sea is west of the Philippines.

9. Fresh fish and many other goods are sold at ———.

10. About half the land in the Philippines is covered with ———.

B. *Answer these questions.*

1. What two benefits do farmers get from raising fish in rice paddies?

2. What two seas separate the Philippine Islands from the islands of Indonesia and Malaysia?

3. Besides being beautiful, how are the trees of the Philippines useful?

Further Study

1. Why did Jose and Nena want to go fishing rather than help Mother weave baskets and mats?

2. Why is fishing more important in the Philippines than in Nigeria?

3. So far this year you have visited Brazil, Ohio, Baffin Island, Nigeria, and the Philippines. Which of these are on the mainland of a continent?

Map Exercises

1. Label Manila Bay on your map of the Philippines. (You may need to label it outside the land area and draw an arrow pointing to its location.)

2. Use all capital letters to label the Pacific Ocean. Also label the South China Sea, the Sulu Sea, and the Celebes Sea.

3. deep-sea
4. canneries
5. pearls, sponges
6. shells
7. Pacific
8. South China
9. markets
10. forests (*or* trees)

B. 1. The fish fertilize the paddies, and the farmers can sell the fish.
2. the Sulu Sea and the Celebes Sea
3. The trees are used for lumber and plywood, and the roots of the mangrove tree help to keep the soil along the coasts from washing away.

Further Study
1. They could help Mother weave when they were at home, but they did not often get to go fishing.
2. The Filipinos have more places to fish than the people of Nigeria do.
3. Brazil, Ohio, and Nigeria

Map Exercises
(Individual work. Check maps for accuracy and neatness.)

14. At the Docks and the Market

Glossary Words

abaca

abaca (ab uh KAH) 1. A plant similar to a banana plant that is grown for its strong fiber. 2. The fiber itself, which is used to make ropes.

copra (KOH pruh, KAHP ruh) Dried coconut meat.

export (EHK spohrt) 1. *noun* A product that one country sends to another country to be sold. 2. *verb* To send (a product) out of a country.

import (IHM pohrt) 1. *noun* A product brought in from another country to be sold. 2. *verb* To bring (a product) into a country.

At the Harbor

When the jeepney stopped at Manila Bay, the children ran down to the docks with Father.

Someone called, "*Kamusta!*"

"*Mabuti*," they replied, running toward a tall, brown-skinned young man.

"Uncle Marcos!" Jose exclaimed. "I hoped you would be at the docks today."

Some people around them spoke in Pilipino or in English. Others spoke in dialects the twins could not understand. "I'm glad we know Pilipino and English at least," Nena said as she listened to the many strange voices.

After discussing some business with Father, Uncle Marcos turned to the children. "So school is out, and you have come to Manila at last," he said.

"Yes," Jose replied, watching a dozen men hurrying on and off a large boat. "What are they unloading?"

"Bananas," Uncle Marcos replied.

"Aren't there plenty of bananas grown here?" Nena asked.

"Yes, plenty for us. These will be shipped to other countries on

LESSON AIM

To learn the importance of Philippine imports, exports, and markets.

MAIN POINTS

- **Manila Bay provides a good, safe harbor for ships.** Large ocean-going ships dock at Manila and at a few other large ports in the Philippines. Smaller ships and boats carry supplies between the islands.
- **The Philippine Islands import and export many products.** Some are traded between islands, and others are shipped to and from other countries. Philippine products that are mentioned in this lesson include bananas, pineapples, coconut, sugar, rice, gold, corn, cattle, abaca, coal, and lumber.

- **Local products are bought and sold at markets.**
- **Coconut trees provide many useful products.**

  the coconut (coconut oil, copra, shredded coconut)

  oil (soap, cooking oil, margarine)

  copra (feed, fertilizer)

  shells (charcoal)

  husks (mats, ropes)

  trees (lumber for building houses and bridges)

  leaves (thatch roofs, strips for weaving)

  leaf ribs (brooms)

  sap (sugar, vinegar)

  unripe coconuts (sweet drink)

big ocean-going freighters. The bananas come from a small island where big ships can't go because the water is too shallow. They are brought here on smaller boats, and later they are loaded onto bigger ships. The bananas will be *exported* along with other products."

"What other products?" wondered Jose.

"Do you see that big red ship over there, where men are carrying cargo on?" Uncle Marcos asked.

"Yes," Nena and Jose answered. "What are they loading?"

"Canned pineapple, and also coconut and sugar. All three of those products are processed here before we export them.

"See the blue ship? It is loaded with farm equipment, steel, and computers. They are being *imported*, or brought into the Philippines. We also import flour, butter, canned milk, and cloth. Some of the imports will be used here, and the rest will be loaded onto smaller boats and taken to the small Philippine ports."

Nena nodded. "We import what we need but cannot produce here, and we export what we have too much of."

"Right," Uncle Marcos agreed.

"Is there always so much activity here?" Nena asked. She was trying to see everything at once.

"Yes," Uncle Marcos replied. "Manila Bay provides one of the best natural harbors in the world. It is deep enough for large ocean

Every day, much exporting and importing is done at busy harbors in the Philippines.

RELATED POINTS

- **There are many similarities and differences between the natural resources of Nigeria and the Philippines.** Some of the differences may be discussed in class.

- **Abaca is a useful native plant of the Philippines.** Abaca fibers are removed from the sheath that grows around the stalk of the plant. After the fibers are dried, they are twisted into many kinds of strong, durable cords and ropes.

The streets of Manila are busy with automobile and pedestrian traffic.

ships, yet it is protected from severe storms and high waves. You see, Filipinos do a lot of buying and selling between our own islands and with many other lands."

"Does each island export just one main product?" asked Jose.

"Most islands export a number of products. Luzon is known for its rice, but it also has gold mines, corn, and cattle. Mindanao is called the Land of Promise because it still has many undeveloped resources. It is a world leader in the production of *abaca*. The main export of Cebu (see BOO) is corn, but it also ships coal, rice, and sugar cane. Lumber is an important export from a number of islands. Each of the main islands has much to offer."

The Market

Mother served buns the next morning for breakfast. She had bought them from a lady who was carrying them in a large basket on her head. After breakfast, Mother quickly prepared her baskets and other woven crafts.

"Today we will see some of the big markets in Manila at last!" Nena exclaimed.

"We will take a jeepney up to Market Street," Father decided.

When they arrived at the market, Nena clung to Father's hand to keep from getting lost in the jostling crowd. There were hundreds of people—Filipinos as well as tourists.

"Look!" Jose cried. "It's like a hundred of our barrio markets all put together."

"I never saw so many fish!" Nena exclaimed as they watched several young men cleaning and selling fish.

"Some of them may be the ones we caught yesterday," Father explained. "I sold them here."

"I see fruit stands up ahead," said Nena. "Look at them—all the bananas, mangoes, kalamansi,

Kalamansi and Sayote

Kalamansi (kah lah MAHN see) are citrus fruits with a very tart flavor. Their juice can be used to make a delicious drink much like lemon juice. Kalamansi grow on small trees with glossy leaves. They have green rinds and are about the size of large marbles.

Sayote (sy OH tee) are pear-shaped vegetables with green skins and crisp, crunchy white meat. Sayote is often cut into small cubes and cooked with carrots and meat to make an ulam for rice.

and papayas, and all the vegetables too."

"The children will soon think they are hungry if we stay here," Mother said, laughing.

"Look; some stands even have American fruits," Jose cried. "Apples and pears!"

"What are those little fruits?" Nena asked.

"Grapes," Father told her. "But American foods are too expensive for us to buy, especially since the Lord provides us with so many delicious fruits of our own."

Coconut Products

"That must be a whole boatload of coconuts!" Jose exclaimed, staring at an enormous mound.

"Maybe a small boat," Mother commented.

The man behind the stand grinned at the children. "I am Regino from the island of Samar (SAH mahr). Do you like coconut?" he asked, offering Jose and Nena each a fresh piece of sweet white coconut meat.

"Yes, *salamat*," Nena replied, taking the coconut and biting into it.

The Filipinos often use horses to bring coconuts from the plantations to the roadside, where the coconuts are loaded on trucks.

Filipinos eat much fish. These fresh fish are stacked on a market stand, waiting for buyers.

"A lot of people must like coconut, to eat all that you have here," remarked Jose.

Regino laughed heartily. "Don't you know how many other uses there are for coconut? We don't raise coconuts just to eat. The shells are made into charcoal for use in cooking fires. The husks are made into mats, ropes, and other things. Coconut oil is used for soap, cooking oil, or margarine. After the oil is taken out, the *copra* is used in feed and many other things.

Even young, unripe coconuts are useful. They are filled with a sweet, milky liquid that makes a delicious drink.

"Coconut trees are also valuable. You can build houses and bridges with the lumber. Coconut leaves are used to thatch roofs, or they are cut into strips to weave many useful things. You can make sugar and vinegar from the sap of the tree. Brooms are made from the ribs in the leaves."

"That is a very useful tree,"

Like cities in every country, Manila is a city of contrast. The shacks of poor people contrast sharply with an expensive skyscraper.

Jose agreed. "How often do you harvest the coconuts?"

"Every three months," Regino replied. "Some trees bear over a hundred coconuts a year."

The twins and their parents moved on to a stand where Mother traded her baskets and mats for several pieces of cloth. There they also saw pretty embroidered pillows, rag dolls, and many other handmade things.

Late that afternoon Nena and Jose boarded a jeepney with their parents and headed back toward their own little barrio. They were tired, but it had been a rewarding day.

Testing Your Understanding

Lesson 14 Answers

Testing Your Understanding

A. 1. Large ocean-going ships dock at **[c]** deep harbors like the one at Manila.

A. *Choose the best ending for each sentence. Write the complete sentences.*

1. Large ocean-going ships dock at
    a. many of the small Philippine islands.
    b. all the Philippine islands.
    c. deep harbors like the one at Manila.

2. Smaller ships and boats carry
   a. only exports.
   b. products between the Philippine islands.
   c. products to the mainland of Asia.
3. The island of Mindanao is known for its
   a. production of abaca.
   b. gold mines.
   c. coal and sugar cane.
4. The market at Manila
   a. was much larger than the barrio markets.
   b. was a place where only Philippine products were sold.
   c. had only a small amount of business.
5. Coconuts are
   a. raised only for their sweet white meat.
   b. imported into the Philippines from other countries.
   c. used to make many products.

B. *Answer these questions.*
   1. What two things make the Manila Bay an excellent harbor?
   2. How is an import different from an export?
   3. List four Philippine fruits besides coconuts that the twins saw at the market.
   4. Which island did the owner of the coconuts come from?
   5. How often are coconuts harvested?

Further Study

1. Some of the products mentioned in the lesson are named below. Write the headings **Exports** and **Imports**, and write the names under the correct headings.
   bananas, pineapples, computers, coconuts, flour, sugar, butter, gold, abaca, cloth, grapes, lumber

2. Smaller ships and boats carry **[b]** products between the Philippine islands.
3. The island of Mindanao is known for its **[a]** production of abaca.
4. The market at Manila **[a]** was much larger than the barrio markets.
5. Coconuts are **[c]** used to make many products.

B. 1. It is deep enough for large ships, and it is protected from severe storms and high waves.
   2. An import is a product brought into a country, and an export is a product shipped out of a country.
   3. bananas, mangoes, kalamansi, papayas
   4. Samar
   5. every three months

Further Study

1. Exports	Imports
bananas	computers
pineapples	flour
coconuts	butter
sugar	cloth
gold	grapes
abaca	
lumber	

2. a. 4
   b. 5
   c. 8
   d. 3
   e. 1
   f. 9
   g. 2
   h. 7
   i. 6

2. Match these coconut products with the ways they are used.

a. shells	1. lumber
b. husks	2. sugar, vinegar
c. oil	3. feed
d. copra	4. charcoal
e. trees	5. mats, ropes
f. leaves	6. brooms
g. sap	7. sweet drink
h. unripe coconuts	8. soap, margarine
i. leaf ribs	9. thatch roofs

Map Exercises

(Individual work. Check maps for accuracy and neatness.)

Map Exercises

1. The map in Lesson 11 shows how the islands are often divided into three groups: the Luzon group, the Visayans, and the Mindanao group. On your map of the Philippines, lightly shade each group a different color.

2. Make a map legend in a corner of your map to show the color of each island group.

3. Color the bodies of water according to the Rules for Neat Maps that you copied in Lesson 4.

15. Chapter 3 Review

═══════ Testing Your Understanding ═══════

A. *Write a glossary word for each definition.*

1. A plant grown for its strong fiber.
2. A Philippine village.
3. The Philippine unit of money.
4. A product that is shipped out of a country.
5. A large group of islands.
6. A large landmass.
7. A palm tree that grows in the Philippines.
8. A flooded rice field.
9. A product that is shipped into a country.
10. A violent tropical storm.

B. *Write* true *or* false *for each sentence. Copy each false sentence, and change one or two words to make it true.*

1. There are more than 10,000 Philippine islands.
2. The Philippines are in the Tropical Zone.
3. The national languages of the Philippines are English and Spanish.
4. More rice is grown on the central plain of Mindanao than anywhere else in the Philippines.
5. The Philippines have a rainy season and a dry season.
6. Many Filipinos use family cars to travel.
7. Tractors are more expensive than carabaos.
8. Many Muslims live on Mindanao.
9. Fish are sold to canneries and in markets.
10. Forests cover about two-thirds of the land in the Philippines.
11. Ships in the Manila Bay are usually safe from typhoons.
12. The Filipinos import coconut products.

Lesson 15 Answers

Testing Your Understanding

A. 1. abaca
   2. barrio
   3. peso
   4. export
   5. archipelago
   6. mainland
   7. nipa
   8. paddy
   9. import
  10. typhoon

B. 1. false; There are more than ~~10,000~~ 7,000 Philippine islands.
   2. true
   3. false; The national languages of the Philippines are English and ~~Spanish~~ Pilipino.
   4. false; More rice is grown on the central plain of ~~Mindanao~~ Luzon than anywhere else in the Philippines.
   5. true
   6. false; Many Filipinos use ~~family cars~~ jeepneys to travel. [*or*] ~~Many~~ Few Filipinos use family cars to travel.
   7. true
   8. true
   9. true
  10. false; Forests cover about ~~two-thirds~~ half of the land in the Philippines.
  11. true
  12. false; The Filipinos ~~import~~ export coconut products.

C. *Answer these questions.*

1. Why are nipa huts better suited for the climate in the Philippines than for the climate in Ohio?
2. Why is much of the rice grown during the rainy season?
3. What is the Ring of Fire?
4. What three resources other than fish are found in the seas around the Philippines?
5. Why do the Filipinos import some products?

Map Exercises

Use your completed map of the Philippines to do these exercises.

1. Name the ocean east of the Philippines.
2. Name the sea that separates the Philippines from the mainland of Asia.
3. Name two other seas that are south or west of the Philippines.
4. Name the largest Philippine island.
5. Name a large island in the southern part of the Philippine archipelago.
6. Name the three main groups of Philippine islands.

Review Study

1. Do you know the meanings of all the glossary words in Chapter 3?
2. Can you find the Philippines on a world map?
3. Can you name
   a. the most important Philippine crop?
   b. the capital city?
   c. the tribe that built rice terraces in northern Luzon?
   d. a famous Philippine volcano?
   e. two ways the Filipinos use small boats?

C. 1. (Sample answer) Nipa huts provide the shade and the shelter from rain that is needed in countries with a warm climate, but they would not be warm enough for Ohio's cold winters.
2. The heavy rains of the rainy season provide the water to flood the rice paddies. Rice raised during the dry season must be irrigated.
3. It is a circle around the Pacific Ocean where there are many earthquakes and volcanoes.
4. pearls, sponges, and shells
5. The Filipinos import products that they need but cannot produce in their country.

Map Exercises
1. Pacific Ocean
2. South China Sea
3. Sulu Sea, Celebes Sea
4. Luzon
5. Mindanao
6. Luzon group, Visayans, Mindanao group

Review Study
1. (Individual work.)
2. (Individual work.)
3. a. rice
   b. Manila
   c. Ifugao
   d. Mount Mayon
   e. for fishing, to carry products between islands
   (Review the glossary words orally. Have a student find the Philippines on a globe or a world map. Call on students for the answers to number 3.)

So Far This Year

1. Match the climate zones to the places. Answers may be used more than once.
   - a. Most of Brazil
   - b. Baffin Island
   - c. Nigeria
   - d. Ohio
   - e. Philippines

   Northern Frigid Zone
   Northern Temperate Zone
   Tropical Zone
   Southern Temperate Zone
   Southern Frigid Zone

2. Seasons in the Tropical Zone are the (rainy season and dry season, hot season and cold season).

3. The (Nile, Amazon, Mississippi) River is a large river in Brazil.

4. When animals sleep through the winter, they (hibernate, migrate).

5. During winter darkness in the Frigid Zone, some light is provided by the (sun, northern lights).

6. A great desert in northern Africa is the (Niger, Sahara, Fulani).

7. The sunrise, sunset, and daily temperatures stay about the same the year round in lands near the (equator, North Pole).

8. Chocolate and cocoa come from (cacao, coconut, canola) seeds.

9. (Corn, Wheat, Rice) is the most important grain in the Philippines.

10. (Carabaos, Horses, Oxen) are important farm animals in the Philippines.

11. The Ring of Fire lies around the (Atlantic, Pacific) Ocean.

12. An (import, export) is brought into a country, and an (import, export) is shipped out of a country.

So Far This Year
1. a. Tropical Zone
   b. Northern Frigid Zone
   c. Tropical Zone
   d. Northern Temperate Zone
   e. Tropical Zone
2. rainy season and dry season
3. Amazon
4. hibernate
5. northern lights
6. Sahara
7. equator
8. cacao
9. Rice
10. Carabaos
11. Pacific
12. import, export

UNIT THREE
Temperate Lands

God created much barren land in the Australian outback.

CHAPTER 4

AUSTRALIA, THE LONELY CONTINENT

"I give waters in the wilderness, and rivers in the desert, to give drink to my people, my chosen" (Isaiah 43:20).

116   Unit 3, Chapter 4 Australia, the Lonely Continent

16. A Trip to Grandfather's Station

Glossary Words

verandah

outback The thinly settled inland part of Australia.

station A sheep or cattle ranch in Australia.

verandah (vuh RAN duh) A porch running along the outside of a house.

An Island Continent

Find the Philippines on a globe or map. Move south across the equator to the continent of Australia. The Tropic of Capricorn runs through the center of Australia. Northern Australia is in the Tropical Zone, and southern Australia is in the Southern Temperate Zone. Our visit to Australia will be mainly to the part in the Temperate Zone.

Australia is called a continent because it is too big to be called an island. Greenland is the world's largest island, and Australia is about three and one-half times as large as Greenland. But Australia is still the smallest continent.

Australia is the sixth largest country in the world. It is about the same size as the United States not counting Alaska and Hawaii. But Australia does not have very many people—only about 18 million live in all its vast territory. By comparison, the same area in the United States has a population of over 200 million people!

Australia is called the "lonely" continent because it is separated from the other continents by great stretches of water. The continent of Australia lies south of the equator, in the Southern Hemisphere. For this reason it is said to be "down under." The only other continent entirely south of the equator is Antarctica.

Do you remember the other continents you have visited? They are North America, South America, and Africa. Two other continents are Europe and Asia.

LESSON AIM

To introduce Australia as a continent in size, an island in isolation, and a country in climate.

MAIN POINTS

- **Location and size of Australia.** Australia is in the Southern Hemisphere. It is called the "lonely" continent because it is separated from the other continents. Northern Australia is in the Tropical Zone, and southern Australia is in the Southern Temperate Zone.

  Australia is the smallest continent. It is about the size of the United States without Alaska and Hawaii, but its population is much smaller.

- **Most Australians live in a few large cities.** Sydney is Australia's largest city. [About one-fifth of the population of Australia lives in Sydney.]

- **Australia is flatter than the other continents.** The Great Dividing Range is the largest range of mountains. Mount Kosciusko is the highest peak. It is much lower [at 7,300 feet] than the highest mountains on the other continents.

- **Most of Australia is dry.** The Murray River and its tributaries provide some water for irrigation. The amount of water available has been increased by a system of dams and lakes [called the Snowy Mountain Hydroelectric Scheme].

- **The outback of Australia has many large stations.** Cattle and sheep need large areas of the dry land to find enough to eat. Airplanes and two-way radios have improved transportation and communication between the widely scattered stations. Many outback children do their school lessons at home.

All these, together with Australia and Antarctica, make up the seven continents of the world.

Australia's Largest City

Let us go with Mark and Susan, who are from Canada, as they visit their grandparents in Australia. They have just taken off from the Sydney (SIHD nee) airport with Grandfather in his small airplane. Their cousins Andrew and Margaret, who live

on Grandfather's cattle **station**, are with them.

Mark and Susan looked out over Sydney as they circled the city and headed west. "Sydney is larger than I expected it to be," Susan remarked. "I thought Australia was thinly settled."

"Most of Australia is thinly settled," replied Grandfather. "You will see plenty of open space when we get to our cattle station in the **outback**. But Australia

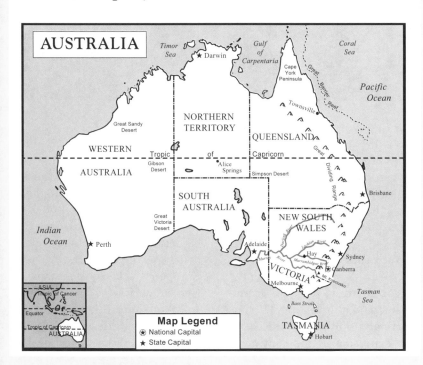

- **The seasons of the Southern Hemisphere are opposite from the seasons of the Northern Hemisphere.** [Review the "Reason for the Seasons" interest block in Lesson 3, page 26. Point out that when the Northern Hemisphere is getting more heat and light from the sun, the Southern Hemisphere is getting less.]

RELATED POINTS

- **Isolation of Australia.** Use a world map to show the students how far Australia is from North America (7,400 miles), South America (6,500 miles), Europe (9,000 miles), and Africa (5,600 miles).

- **Australia's population.** The population of Australia is very unevenly distributed. Only about one-tenth of the people live in the country. Most of the cities are clustered in the southeastern corner. Large areas in the central and western parts of the continent are nearly uninhabited.

Sydney is Australia's largest city.

has a few large cities too. In fact, most of the people of Australia live in cities. More people live here in Sydney, Australia's largest city, than on all of Australia's farms and stations together."

Mountains and Rivers

"We will soon be crossing the Great Dividing Range," Grandfather said a little later. "It runs north and south along the entire eastern coast of the continent. This part of the Great Dividing Range is called the Australian Alps. It includes Mount Kosciusko (kahs ee UHS koh), the highest mountain in Australia. But even though these mountains are the highest in Australia, they are not nearly as high as the Alps of Europe or the Rocky Mountains of North America."

"Are there other mountain ranges in Australia?" Mark asked as they passed the highest peaks.

"There are some smaller ranges of mountains and hills, but God made Australia with land that is generally flatter than on the other continents. Much of the land is level enough for crop farming, but most of it is too dry for crops to grow. Over half of the land is used for grazing sheep and cattle. Large sections of the continent are too dry even for grazing."

"Could the land be irrigated so that crops can grow?" Susan asked.

"Yes, some irrigation is used where water is available," answered Grandfather. "The Murray River and its tributaries flow west from these mountains and provide water for raising a variety of fresh fruits and vegetables. Do you see that lake below us? That is one of the lakes that was formed when the government built dams along the rivers. The lakes provide a steady supply of water all year long. But even this large irrigation project has water for only a small part of Australia's dry lands."

"Is that the Murray River flowing from the lake?" asked Susan.

"No, we are flying over the Murrumbidgee (mur uhm BIHJ ee),

a tributary of the Murray River. We will follow it most of the way to my station. The Murray with all its tributaries makes up Australia's largest river system."

"Can you tell which fields are irrigated?" questioned Andrew.

The mountain in the background is part of the Great Dividing Range. Sugar cane is produced on much of the flat, irrigated land in the foreground.

The Murrumbidgee River supplies water for these irrigated fields in New South Wales.

"That's easy," replied Mark. "The irrigated fields are much greener than the surrounding land."

Large Stations

"I can see plenty of open space now," commented Susan about an hour later. "I haven't seen many towns since we crossed the mountains. Even the houses are far apart here."

"Farms and stations that do not have water for irrigation must be large," Grandfather explained. "Cattle and sheep need to graze large areas to find enough to eat. Some of the stations farther west are larger than the state of Rhode Island in the United States. I often use this plane to travel because of the long distances between places."

"Do you fly to school in airplanes?" Mark asked Andrew.

"No, we walk to school," answered Andrew with a smile. "But we do not need to walk far. Many children in the country are too far from towns, so we are allowed to do our lessons at home by correspondence courses or the

School of the Air. The School of the Air has teachers who talk to their students with two-way radios. We use Bible-based correspondence courses from Christian publishers in America.

"Two-way radios are also used to warn neighbors of floods or bush fires in the outback. The two-way radios serve as telephones in places where there are no telephone lines."

"Our station is just ahead!" exclaimed Margaret a few minutes later.

Seasons of Australia

After receiving a warm welcome from Grandmother, Uncle David, and Aunt Elizabeth, the children visited with Grandfather on his screened-in *verandah*. The verandah was built on all four sides of the long, spacious one-story house. "This

verandah helps keep us cool in the hot months of December, January, and February," Grandfather remarked.

Susan looked puzzled. "That's when we have our coldest time in Canada. Our warmest months are June, July, and August."

"Those are the coldest months here," Margaret told her. "July is the coldest, often with temperatures of 5 to 10 degrees Celsius [40 to 50 degrees Fahrenheit]. We have some frosts, but usually the temperature is above freezing."

"You are north of the equator, and we are south of it," Grandfather explained. "That makes the seasons exactly opposite. Our area here is about as far from the equator as the southern part of the United States. So even though our winters are much milder than yours, we still need a fire to keep warm."

--------- Testing Your Understanding ---------

A. *For each number, copy the phrase that best describes Australia.*

1. (a) large continent   (b) small continent
2. (a) Southern Hemisphere   (b) Northern Hemisphere
3. (a) many large cities   (b) a few large cities
4. (a) many high mountains   (b) low mountains and level land
5. (a) dry climate   (b) wet climate
6. (a) small farms   (b) large ranches
7. (a) cold July   (b) hot July

Lesson 16 Answers

Testing Your Understanding

A. 1. (b) small continent
   2. (a) Southern Hemisphere
   3. (b) a few large cities
   4. (b) low mountains and level land
   5. (a) dry climate
   6. (b) large ranches
   7. (a) cold July

B. 1. true
2. false; Australia is called the ~~"friendly" island~~ "lonely" continent.
3. true
4. true
5. false; Most Australians live in ~~the outback~~ cities. [or] ~~Most~~ Few Australians live in the outback.
6. false; ~~Murray~~ Sydney is the largest city in Australia. [or] The Murray is the largest ~~city~~ river in Australia.
7. false; Over half of the land in Australia is used for ~~crop farming~~ grazing.
8. true

Further Study

1. a. The Murray River and its tributaries
   b. The Murray River system provides water for irrigating the dry land.
2. The children on different stations live so far apart that they cannot go to school together.

Map Exercises

(Individual work. Check maps for accuracy and neatness.)

B. *Write* true *or* false *for each sentence. If a sentence is false, rewrite it to make it true.*

1. Australia's size is about the same as the United States without Alaska and Hawaii.
2. Australia is called the "friendly" island.
3. Australia is said to be "down under" because it is entirely south of the equator.
4. Mount Kosciusko is the highest mountain in Australia.
5. Most Australians live in the outback.
6. Murray is the largest city in Australia.
7. Over half of the land in Australia is used for crop farming.
8. Airplanes are useful in the outback because most stations are far apart.

Further Study

1. (*a*) What is the largest river system in Australia? (*b*) Why is this river system important?
2. Why do children on a cattle or sheep station receive their schooling at home?

Map Exercises

1. Trace Map C in the map section.
2. Mark the Great Dividing Range with ⋀⋀ symbols and Mount Kosciusko with a ▲. Then label them.
3. Label the Murray River and the Murrumbidgee River.

17. Sights and Sounds on Grandfather's Station

Glossary Words

eucalyptus

koala

kookaburra

artesian well (ahr TEE zhuhn) A well from which water flows without being pumped.

brumby A wild horse (an Australian word).

dingo (DIHNG goh) The wild dog of Australia, having reddish brown fur, a face like that of a fox, and a bushy tail.

eucalyptus (yoo kuh LIHP tuhs) A kind of evergreen tree that originally grew only in Australia.

kelpie (KEHL pee) A kind of herding dog used in Australia.

koala (koh AH luh) A marsupial with large ears, gray woolly fur, and no tail. It lives in trees and eats eucalyptus leaves.

kookaburra (KOO kuh bur uh) A large Australian bird in the kingfisher family, known for its harsh laughing cry.

mammal A class of warm-blooded creatures that produce milk for their young.

marsupial (mahr SOO pee uhl) A mammal that carries its newborn young in a pouch.

porous (PAWR uhs) Having many pores (small holes) that allow liquids to soak in.

wallaby (WAHL uh bee) A small kangaroo of Australia and New Guinea.

LESSON AIM

To learn about the artesian wells, unusual animals, and eucalyptus trees of Australia.

MAIN POINTS

- **Australia has many unusual animals and trees.** Animals that are introduced in this lesson include kookaburras, kangaroos, koalas, kelpies, brumbies, dingoes, and wallabies. Animals that carry their young in a pouch, such as kangaroos, koalas, and wallabies, are called marsupials.

  Many kinds of eucalyptus trees grow in Australia. Some of them grow as tall as 300 feet and live as long as 1,500 years or more. Eucalyptus trees are unusual in that they shed their bark instead of their leaves. Koalas eat nothing but the buds and leaves of the eucalyptus tree.

- **Men have learned to use the available resources of the outback.** Artesian wells are a special blessing to the dry, isolated stations of Australia. The water from the wells is usually somewhat salty, but many of the wells produce water good enough for cattle to drink. [Water from Australia's artesian wells is usually too salty to use for irrigation.]

  Horses and kelpies are used to herd cattle.

- **Australia's climate is warmer than Canada's climate because Australia is closer to the equator.**

RELATED POINTS

- **Cattle in Australia.** Australia is one of the world's largest producers of beef. Much of the beef comes from large stations in the tropical north, but cattle stations are also found in other areas where there is sufficient moisture.

Unusual Animals

Mark awoke the next morning to shrill screams of laughter coming from outside the bedroom window. "What is that noise?" he asked.

"That is the **_kookaburras_**," replied Andrew. "They are large birds in the same family as kingfishers."

This wallaby has two joeys in her pouch. The wallaby is a small kangaroo of Australia and New Guinea.

At the breakfast table, Uncle David announced, "Today I need to look for some stray cattle. You children may ride along and get a good look at this station if you would like."

As Uncle David went to get the horses, a large animal, almost as tall as Susan, hopped over a shrub near the children and went bounding past. "What's that?" Susan shrieked.

Andrew laughed as he replied, "That is Joey, our pet kangaroo." He called, "Come, Joey, and sit." The animal bounded back and sat beside Andrew, using its large tail to balance itself. Andrew and the others petted the kangaroo, and Andrew explained more about him. "Kangaroos can be wild and ill-tempered, but Joey is very safe and friendly."

Artesian Wells

Soon Uncle David had five horses saddled. The children eagerly mounted and followed Uncle David as he started out on a winding dirt trail. Not far from the station buildings, they saw a large group of cattle around a watering trough. "Where do you get enough water for the cattle?" Mark asked.

• **Artesian wells.** The water in artesian wells comes from a porous layer of rock that traps water when it rains. The trapped water builds up pressure; and when the rock layer is penetrated, the water comes to the surface by its own pressure.

To explain how an artesian well works, you could use the illustration of a balloon filled with water. If it is put under pressure, a pinhole near the neck will allow the water to spout upward.

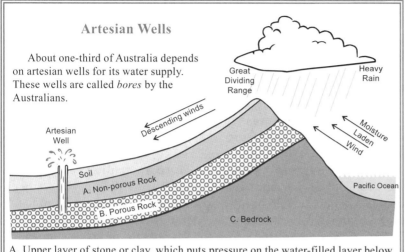

Artesian Wells

About one-third of Australia depends on artesian wells for its water supply. These wells are called *bores* by the Australians.

A. Upper layer of stone or clay, which puts pressure on the water-filled layer below.
B. Porous layer where water becomes trapped and put under pressure.
C. Lower layer of rocks, which does not let water escape.

"Rain is scarce here, but God has provided water for us in another way," Uncle David replied. "The water for our cattle comes from **artesian wells**. We live at the southern end of the Great Artesian Basin, which has many such wells. Some artesian wells are too salty, but several on our station produce water that is good enough for the cattle."

"What is an artesian well?" asked Mark.

"Deep underground there is a layer of water," Uncle David explained. "In an artesian well, the water comes to the surface by its own pressure. You don't need a pump. But in some areas of our country, there is just no water. Deserts cover about one-third of Australia."

Eucalyptus Trees and Koalas

"What kind of trees are these?" asked Susan. "They are really tall."

"Those are **eucalyptus** trees. There are hundreds of kinds of eucalyptus trees in Australia.

These that you see are red gum eucalyptus. Under good growing conditions, some of them grow 300 feet tall. Some live 1,500 years or more. Just think—some of these trees could have been growing already in the time of Christ!"

"Aren't eucalyptus trees the kind that *koalas* like to eat?" asked Mark.

"Yes," Margaret stated. "Australia is the only land where koalas live in the wild because they eat nothing but the buds and leaves of eucalyptus trees. The kangaroo and the koala are just two of the *marsupials* that live in our country."

"What are marsupials?" Susan wondered.

"They are *mammals* with a pouch, where they carry their newborn young," answered Uncle David. "The common opossum of North America is also a marsupial."

As Uncle David led the way down the trail, Susan asked, "Do eucalyptus leaves change color and drop off in the fall?"

"No," answered Uncle David. "Eucalyptus trees shed their bark instead of their leaves. Our trees do not shed their leaves because our winters are milder than the ones you have in Canada. Do you know why?"

"Is it because you are closer to the equator?" Susan wondered.

"Yes. Actually, almost half of Australia lies north of the Tropic of Capricorn, in the Tropical Zone."

More Australian Animals
Uncle David had been watching a brushy area off to the left of the trail. Suddenly he spoke to the dogs. "Button, Shep, bring!" The dogs ran into the brush and began barking. The children heard snorts and the crackle of breaking brush. Suddenly two steers charged out of the brush, each with a dog at his heels.

Uncle David smiled and said, "Good *kelpies* are a big help. They'll run the steers a little until they tire out. Then they will bring them back to us." Seeing the puzzled looks of Mark and Susan, he added, "A kelpie is a kind of herding dog."

"How did you know where those cattle were hiding?" asked Mark.

"Usually I can tell from past

These men are herding their cattle along a road in New South Wales.

experience or just by careful listening. Of course we all make mistakes sometimes. Once in a while it is a mob of ***brumbies*** instead of stray cattle. Brumbies are wild horses," Uncle David explained.

Suddenly there was an eerie howling that made chills go up Susan's back. "Was that a wolf?" she asked.

"It sounded like a ***dingo*** to me," said Margaret.

"What is a dingo?" asked Mark.

"Dingoes are the wild dogs of Australia," Uncle David explained. "Their main food for many years was the ***wallaby***, which is a small kind of kangaroo. After men began to raise sheep in Australia, the dingoes became pests and killed many sheep. A dingo looks like a medium-sized dog with straight ears and a bushy tail. Dingoes howl, but they hardly ever bark."

That morning Uncle David and his helpers rounded up about fifty head of cattle. The children and the dogs helped to keep the livestock together and herd them toward home. They were all tired by lunchtime, and the ranch buildings were a welcome sight.

Grandfather came out to help drive the cattle into a corral, and then all the workers went into the house for a delicious meal of roast beef. "I certainly was glad for all the good help I had today," said Uncle David as they sat down. "Let's bow our heads and thank God for the blessings He has given us in this land."

Testing Your Understanding

A. *Write the correct word(s) or number to complete each sentence. For the first blank of each exercise, choose one of these: kelpie, koala, eucalyptus, wallaby, dingo, kangaroo, kookaburra.*

1. The ⸺ tree sheds its ⸺ instead of its leaves. It may grow ⸺ feet high and live ⸺ years or more.
2. The ⸺ eats only the buds and leaves of the ⸺ tree. Like all marsupials, it carries its young in a ⸺.
3. Uncle David had a kind of dog called a ⸺. These dogs are used for ⸺ cattle and sheep in Australia.
4. The ⸺ is in the same family as the kingfisher. Its calls sound like shrill screams of ⸺.
5. The ⸺ is a large marsupial that hops on its hind legs. It uses its ⸺ to balance itself.
6. The ⸺ is the wild dog of Australia. It ⸺ like a wolf or coyote, but rarely barks. It has become a pest because it kills ⸺.
7. The ⸺ is a small type of kangaroo. This animal was once the main food of the ⸺.

B. *Answer these questions.*

1. Why is no pump needed to get water out of an artesian well?

Lesson 17 Answers

Testing Your Understanding

A. 1. eucalyptus, bark, 300, 1,500
2. koala, eucalyptus, pouch
3. kelpie, herding
4. kookaburra, laughter
5. kangaroo, tail
6. dingo, howls, sheep
7. wallaby, dingo

B. 1. The water flows out of the well by its own pressure.

2. Why are artesian wells a special blessing to the outback of Australia, even though they are somewhat salty?

3. Why is the eucalyptus tree very important to the koala?

4. Why are the winters in Australia milder than the winters in Canada?

Further Study

1. (*a*) How did the habits of the dingo change after sheep were brought to Australia? (*b*) Why did its habits change?

2. Name a marsupial of Australia and describe it in detail. (Use an encyclopedia if necessary.)

3. Name and describe a marsupial that lives in your country.

Map Exercises

1. On your map of Australia, use all capital letters to label the Northern Territory and the five states on the continent of Australia. Also label the island state.

2. Use all capital letters to label the Tropic of Capricorn.

2. Rain and water are scarce, and many of the wells produce water good enough for cattle to drink.

3. The koala eats nothing but the buds and leaves of the eucalyptus tree.

4. Australia is closer to the equator than Canada is. (The Tropic of Capricorn passes through Australia.)

Further Study

1. a. Instead of feeding mainly on the wallaby, the dingo began to kill and eat sheep.

 b. Sheep are easier to catch.

2. (Individual work)

3. (The following answer is correct for North American pupils.) The only marsupial living in North America is the opossum. (Description is individual work.)

Map Exercises

(Individual work. Check maps for accuracy and neatness.)

18. A Flight Over the Outback

Glossary Words

aborigine (ab uh RIHJ uh nee) One of the people who originally lived in a certain area.

fleece A sheep's coat of wool.

merino (muh REE noh) A kind of sheep that has fine silky wool.

mutton (MUHT uhn) The meat from fully grown sheep.

Wheat Farms

The next morning the children boarded Grandfather's plane, and he took them for a flight toward the northwest. They first passed over Hay, the closest town. Then they flew over rich, irrigated farmland near the Lachlan River (LAHK luhn). As they traveled on, the lush green slowly thinned to spotty green and gray. Large fields of wheat could be seen here and there.

Thousands of acres of wheat are planted and harvested each year in Australia. Wheat can grow better in dry conditions than crops such as corn and soybeans.

LESSON AIM

To acquaint the students with Australia's wheat farms and sheep stations, major deserts, and early inhabitants and explorers.

MAIN POINTS

- **Wheat is the most important farm crop in Australia.** Wheat does not need as much rainfall as many other crops. But most of Australia is too dry even to raise wheat.

- **Deserts cover much of Australia.** The Simpson Desert is in the eastern half of Australia. The Great Sandy Desert, the Gibson Desert, and the Great Victoria Desert are in the western part.

  Dry salt lakes are usually dry, but they fill with water when the land receives an unusual amount of rain. [They are salty because of the minerals left behind when the water evaporates.]

- **Aborigines lived in Australia before the Europeans discovered it.** Some of the aborigines still live like their ancestors.

  The English started the first white settlement when they brought prisoners to what is now Sydney.

- **Australia has many large sheep stations.** Most sheep are raised for their wool, which is sheared once each year. Merino sheep have the best wool. Some sheep are raised for their meat.

Australia has been called the driest continent in the world. Dry areas and deserts cover much of the continent.

"How does the wheat grow in this dry land?" asked Susan.

"Wheat can be grown in areas like this that receive some rainfall," answered Grandfather. "Because it can grow with less moisture than many crops, wheat has become the most important farm crop in Australia. But cattle and sheep are even more important because they can graze on land that is too dry to raise wheat. Australia is a world leader in producing sheep, wool, beef, and wheat."

Deserts and Dry Salt Lakes

"What is that?" Mark asked, after they had been flying for more than an hour. He was pointing toward a large bare spot in the landscape, cracked and dry in the heat. "It looks like a crater on the moon."

"That is a dry salt lake," answered Grandfather. "There are many of those in Australia, but very few freshwater lakes. Dry salt lakes fill with water during rainy seasons, but the rest

RELATED POINTS

- **Largest dry salt lake.** Lake Eyre (AIR) is the largest of the dry salt lakes; it covers 3,700 square miles, but it is only a few feet deep and is often dry. At 52 feet below sea level, this dry lake is also the lowest spot in Australia.
- **The boomerang.** This was the main weapon of the aborigines. Two types of boomerangs were used: the returning type and the nonreturning type.

of the time they are usually dry. Some of them have not been full for years."

"Is this a desert?" asked Susan.

"This area is dry, but not actually a desert," answered Grandfather. "We would need to fly another hour or two to reach the edge of the Simpson Desert. The Simpson Desert is the main desert in the eastern half of Australia. In the western part of the country, there are three other deserts. The Great Sandy Desert is in the northwest, the Gibson Desert in the west central area, and the Great Victoria Desert in the southwest.

"The names show which deserts are the largest—the Great Sandy and the Great Victoria. In the Great Victoria Desert, there are sand dunes 200 miles long. Before you go back home, I think you will see why Australia is called the driest continent in the world."

Inhabitants of Australia

"Who are those people?" Susan asked. "Their huts look like a village."

"Those are the Australian *aborigines*," answered Margaret.

"Their ancestors were the first inhabitants of our country in the same way that the Indians were of America. Some aborigines still live like their ancestors. They use stone and wooden tools and kill game with a spear or boomerang. Others are sheep or cattle herders, and still others have become workers in the city. Words such as *koala* and *kangaroo* come from the aboriginal languages."

"Who were the first white people in Australia?" asked Mark.

"The Portuguese have records of a visit to our country in 1542," answered Margaret. "Several explorers also saw Australia in the 1600s. One explorer, Abel Tasman, discovered the island that is named for him—Tasmania (taz MAY nee uh).

"In 1788 an Englishman named Captain Arthur Phillip came to establish a colony with people who had been prisoners in England. Of the one thousand people aboard his ships, over seven hundred were prisoners. Their settlement grew into what is now Sydney. The first white settlers were from England, so English became Australia's official language."

"Did they ever bring more prisoners?" asked Mark.

"Thousands of them," replied Andrew.

"Were there women too?" Susan wondered.

"Yes," said Grandfather. "Those men and women were really the ones who settled this country. But many of them were in prison only because they were too poor to pay their debts."

A Visit to a Sheep Station

Grandfather banked the plane and flew over a large ranch house and several other buildings. "We'll land here, and you can meet the owner of a sheep station. His name is Pat O'Meer, and he

These sheep are grazing near Canberra, the national capital of Australia. Can you find Canberra on the map on page 117? The hills in this photograph are the foothills of the Australian Alps.

is a friend of mine. His Irish and your English ancestors were some of the first white settlers in Australia."

By the time the plane had landed and taxied to a small hangar, Pat was walking out to meet them. "William, how are you today?" Pat greeted Grandfather warmly. "These must be your grandchildren from Canada."

"Yes, they are," replied Grandfather. "I thought they might enjoy seeing an Australian sheep station in action."

"There's some action over in that long building—the shearers are at work today." As they walked

---

Egg-laying Mammals

The echidna (ih KIHD nuh) and the platypus (PLAT ih puhs) are the only mammals in the world that lay eggs. Both are found in Australia.

The echidna, also called the spiny anteater, is a marsupial like the kangaroo and the koala. It is a little more than a foot long, has a long, tapered nose, and is covered with stiff hair and sharp spines.

Echidna

Platypus

The platypus is a strange-looking mammal. It has a bill like a duck, a tail like a beaver, and a body covered with fur. But its bill is leathery, not hard like a duck's bill.

toward the building, Pat continued, "We used to raise *merino* sheep because they have the best wool. But today scientists have developed good wool-producing sheep whose meat has a good flavor too. Much lamb and *mutton* is eaten here in Australia, where sheep outnumber people by about ten to one."

"How is all that wool used?" asked Susan as they entered the building.

"It is used in blankets, *jumpers* [the Australian word for sweaters], coats, rugs, and other things," Pat told her. "Wool is very strong and warm."

The children watched with great interest as the shearers, using clippers, quickly but carefully clipped the *fleece* from each sheep. This left the sheep with only a short white coat to cover its bare skin. As one man put the finished sheep into a holding pen, another brought the next sheep to a shearer, and a third man took the fleece away. The short wool was removed from the fleeces, and then they were sorted and put into bins.

"The men work so fast," Susan observed.

"Will the sheep go back out to the pasture now?" asked Mark.

"Yes," Pat replied. "We will drive them to the outback, and they will stay on the range until shearing time next year."

―――――― Testing Your Understanding ――――――

A. *Write the correct word(s) to complete each sentence.*

1. The most important farm crop in Australia is ―――. It can grow with less ――― than many crops.

2. A desert in eastern Australia is the ―――. The two largest deserts in Australia are the ――― and the ―――.

3. A dry salt lake is ――― most of the year.

4. The words *koala* and *kangaroo* come from the ――― languages.

5. In 1542 the ――― became the first white men to see Australia. The English brought ――― in 1788 and started a colony.

Lesson 18 Answers

Testing Your Understanding

A. 1. wheat, moisture (*or* rainfall)
   2. Simpson Desert, Great Sandy Desert, Great Victoria Desert.
   3. dry
   4. aboriginal
   5. Portuguese, prisoners

6. wool, ten
7. shearers

B. 1. Most of the land in Australia is too dry for wheat to grow.
   2. Both were the first people to live in their particular land.
   3. Sydney
   4. (Possible answers) blankets, sweaters (jumpers), coats, rugs

Further Discussion

1. There are large deserts in western Australia.
2. No. Many of the first white settlers were prisoners only because they were poor. (In those days the really dangerous criminals were usually put to death.)

Map Exercises

(Individual work. Check maps for accuracy and neatness.)

6. Merino sheep are known for their fine ———. Sheep outnumber the people of Australia by about ——— to one.
7. The ——— are the men who skillfully clip the fleeces from the sheep.

B. *Answer these questions.*

1. Why is more land in Australia used for grazing than for growing wheat?
2. How are the aborigines of Australia like the Indians of America?
3. What city has developed from the first white settlement in Australia?
4. What are three products made from wool?

Further Study

1. Why do some large areas of western Australia have very few people?
2. Would it be right to say that most of the first white settlers in Australia were dangerous criminals? Explain.

Map Exercises

1. On your map of Australia, label the town of Hay and the city of Sydney.
2. Label the Lachlan River.
3. Label the Simpson Desert, the Great Sandy Desert, and the Great Victoria Desert.

Lesson 19   137

19. The Pacific Coast

Glossary Words

atoll

coral

atoll (AT ahl, AY tahl) A ring-shaped island of coral, partly or completely surrounding a lagoon.

coral (KAWR uhl) A hard substance made of limestone and calcium, produced by tiny sea animals and appearing in many shapes and colors.

lagoon (luh GOON) A shallow body of water, often connected to a larger body.

polyp (PAHL ihp) A tiny water animal, often living with many others in a colony.

reef A ridge of rocks, sand, or coral at or near the surface of water.

Capital Cities and an Island State

On another early morning, the children were again in the air with Grandfather. "Where are we heading this time?" asked Mark as the plane flew southward.

"I'm going to give you a tour of the east coast. Today we will fly around the southeastern corner of Australia and up to Brisbane (BRIHZ buhn). Tomorrow I plan to fly to Townsville. There we can take a boat ride and see the Great Barrier Reef.

"Over there you can see the city of Melbourne (MEHL burn).

It is almost as large as Sydney and has a very busy harbor on Port Phillip Bay."

"What is out there across the water?" asked Susan, pointing south. "Antarctica?"

Grandfather laughed. "Yes," he said as he turned the plane east along the coast. "But there is also a large island out there much closer than the continent of Antarctica. It is the island state of Tasmania. The water between the mainland and the island is called Bass Strait."

The plane swung around to the northeast, and Grandfather

LESSON AIM

To acquaint the students with the Pacific coast of Australia and with the Great Barrier Reef.

MAIN POINTS

- **Most of Australia's major cities are along its southeastern coast.** [The three state capitals mentioned in the first part of this lesson are the largest cities.] Canberra is the national capital.

- **The island of Tasmania is a state of Australia.** The Bass Strait separates the island from the mainland. [Tasmania is the smallest and perhaps the most beautiful state of Australia. A photograph of Tasmania's scenery is on the front cover of *Homelands Around the World*.]

- **Oceans and seas surround Australia.** Use a globe to point out the Pacific and Indian oceans. Smaller bodies of water that are mentioned in this lesson include the Port Phillip Bay, Bass Strait, Tasman Sea, Coral

Sea, Gulf of Carpentaria, and the Timor Sea.

- **The Great Barrier Reef is a beautiful natural wonder along the eastern coast.** The Great Barrier Reef is the world's largest coral reef. It stretches along the eastern coast for about 1,200 miles. [If possible, obtain a few pieces of coral to show the class.]

- **God has blessed Australia with many important resources.** Many rich mines are in western Australia. [Other important minerals, such as coal and oil, are found in eastern Australia.]

RELATED POINTS

- **Coral reefs.** There are three kinds of coral reefs: fringing reefs, barrier reefs, and atolls. A fringing reef is a submerged layer of living coral that extends from the shore out into the sea. A barrier reef follows the shore but is separated by a channel of water. An atoll is a ring-shaped coral island in the open sea.

Melbourne is a modern Australian city. Notice that two of the skyscrapers have cranes mounted on top of them. The cranes are used to build the skyscrapers.

pointed out Mount Kosciusko. He also showed them Canberra (KAN bur uh), the capital of Australia, and he pointed out the Tasman Sea off the coast of Sydney. Late that afternoon they arrived at Brisbane, the capital of Queensland.

"You have seen three of our state capitals now," said Grandfather. "Sydney is the capital of New South Wales; Melbourne is the capital of Victoria; and Brisbane is the capital of Queensland."

"This is the Pacific Coast of Australia, isn't it?" asked Mark.

"Yes," replied Grandfather. "That is the South Pacific Ocean out there. Tomorrow we will see the Great Barrier Reef, where the waters between Australia and New Guinea (GIHN ee) are called the Coral Sea."

"But it's really all one body of water, isn't it?" asked Margaret.

"Yes, it is," said Grandfather. "But when a section of the ocean is between two bodies of land, it usually has a name of its own.

The Coral Sea was named for the ***coral*** that thrives in it. Other seas may be named for the men who discovered or first explored them."

A Boat Ride Over the Great Barrier Reef

The next day as the travelers continued their flight north, Grandfather pointed to his right. "If you look out to sea, you will notice the beginning of the largest coral ***reef*** in the world. The Great Barrier Reef starts here and runs nearly 1200 miles north along the coast. Coral reefs are a beautiful part of God's creation, but they have also sunken many ships."

"There are other coral reefs in the world, too, aren't there?" asked Mark.

"Yes," answered Grandfather. "There are many, mostly in the Pacific, but no other reef is as large as the Barrier."

Later in the day, the plane landed at Townsville, and the children were soon boarding a

Fish swim past coral in the Great Barrier Reef. This photograph was taken through the glass on a glass-bottomed boat.

The Emu

The emu (EE myoo) is a large, graceful Australian bird similar to an ostrich. Emus may be as much as 7 feet tall. Emus never fly, but they can run 30 miles per hour.

glass-bottomed boat with Grandfather. They peered down into the water with keen interest as the boat moved slowly out over the reef.

"Look how clear it is!" Susan gasped.

Their guide smiled and said, "Yes, usually the water is so clear that we can see over 30 meters down [100 feet]."

"I just can't believe how many colors there are!" exclaimed Margaret.

"There are over 350 colors," replied the guide. "We will be coming to an **atoll** soon, so keep your eyes open."

"What is an atoll?" Mark asked, looking around curiously.

"It is a ring-shaped island made completely of coral, surrounding or nearly surrounding a **lagoon**."

"Is a coral reef made of the skeletons of dead animals?" asked Susan.

"It is more like a protective house of limestone for the coral **polyps**," the guide explained. "When they die, the old houses gradually build up on top of each other. This goes on year after year until finally there is a reef."

On the atoll, the children continued their eager exploration. Soon they were traveling back to the mainland.

The travelers spent the night at Townsville. After an early breakfast, they were in the plane and flying again. "We are flying southwest over the Great Dividing Range," Grandfather

Ayers Rock is a large red rock in central Australia. This rock is 1½ miles long and 1,000 feet high.

informed them. "To the north is the Cape York Peninsula reaching out toward New Guinea. The Cape York Peninsula separates the Gulf of Carpentaria (kahr pihn TAIR ee uh) from the Pacific Ocean."

"What large bodies of water are to the west?" asked Susan.

"West of the city of Darwin, the water is called the Timor Sea (TEE mawr). Beyond the Timor Sea is the Indian Ocean."

Grandfather pointed ahead. "Look; we have crossed the mountains. Now we will turn south and head toward home."

"What would we cross if we flew directly west from here?" asked Mark.

"The land would become drier and drier until we reached the Simpson Desert," replied Grand-father. "Beyond the Simpson Desert, we could land at the town of Alice Springs, the only real town or city in all of central Australia.

"The large western deserts cover much of the continent west of Alice Springs. But many of Australia's rich mines are also located in the west. God has blessed Australia with iron ore,

A huge shovel loads iron ore into a dump truck at an Australian mine.

Australia is rich in mineral resources. Iron ore is dug from this open-pit mine. This mine in western Australia is the largest open-pit iron ore mine in the world.

copper, uranium, gold, coal, and other important resources. We would need to travel all the way to the west coast to see Perth, the capital of Western Australia and the only major city in the west."

That evening as they neared Grandfather's station, Mark commented, "I understand better now why Australia is called a continent instead of an island. Australia is large, even though it is the smallest continent."

Grandfather smiled as he prepared to land his airplane. "Yes, it is, and we saw only a small part of it on this trip. But most of the people live in this southeastern corner of the continent."

──────── **Testing Your Understanding** ────────

A. *Write the correct word(s) for each description.*

atoll	Coral Sea	Indian Ocean
polyp	Timor Sea	Great Barrier Reef
coral reef	Bass Strait	Gulf of Carpentaria

1. Narrow stretch of water between Australia and an island state.
2. Sea west of Darwin.
3. Tiny sea animal.
4. Sea northeast of Australia.
5. A large body of water reaching into northern Australia.
6. Hidden danger to ships.
7. Ring-shaped coral island surrounding a lagoon.
8. Stretches about 1,200 miles along the east coast of Australia.
9. Huge body of water west of Australia.

B. *Write the answers.*

1. Which city of Australia
   a. is the capital of New South Wales?
   b. is the capital of Australia?
   c. has a busy harbor on Port Phillip Bay?
   d. is the capital of Queensland?
   e. is the largest city in western Australia?
2. In Australia, the ──── Ocean lies to the east and the ──── Ocean to the west. In North America, the ──── Ocean lies to the east and the ──── Ocean to the west.
3. Why is western Australia important, even though most of the people live in the east?

Lesson 19 Answers

Testing Your Understanding
A. 1. Bass Strait
   2. Timor Sea
   3. polyp
   4. Coral Sea
   5. Gulf of Carpentaria
   6. coral reef
   7. atoll
   8. Great Barrier Reef
   9. Indian Ocean

B. 1. a. Sydney
      b. Canberra
      c. Melbourne
      d. Brisbane
      e. Perth
   2. Pacific, Indian, Atlantic, Pacific
   3. Many of Australia's rich mines are located in the west.

Further Study

1. The many coral reefs in the area make it too dangerous for large ships.
2. The Tasman Sea was named for Abel Tasman.

Map Exercises

(Individual work. Check maps for accuracy and neatness.)

Further Study

1. Why is it unlikely that many large ships pass through the area of the Great Barrier Reef?
2. The Tasman Sea lies southeast of Australia. Who was it named for? (Hint: Read in Lesson 18 about the explorers of the 1600s.)

Map Exercises

1. On your map of Australia, label Melbourne, Canberra, Brisbane, Darwin, Alice Springs, and Perth. Also label Adelaide, the capital of South Australia; and Hobart, the capital of Tasmania.
2. Label the Indian Ocean and the Pacific Ocean, using all capital letters. Then label the Bass Strait, the Tasman Sea, the Coral Sea, the Gulf of Carpentaria, and the Timor Sea.
3. Label the Great Barrier Reef and the Cape York Peninsula.
4. Color your map according to the Rules for Neat Maps.

20. Chapter 4 Review

=========== Testing Your Understanding ===========

A. *Write* true *or* false *for each statement.*

1. Australia is the smallest continent in the world.
2. In general, Australia is colder than Canada.
3. Both Africa and Australia are entirely south of the equator.
4. Seasons in Australia are opposite from seasons in the Northern Temperate Zone.
5. The climate of southern Australia is much like the climate of the Philippines.
6. A station in Australia is usually larger than a farm in North America.
7. The continent of Australia is heavily populated.
8. The continent of Australia has many high mountain ranges.

B. *Write a word for each definition.*

1. Thinly settled inland part of Australia.
2. The largest city of Australia.
3. A well that does not need a pump.
4. An animal that lives on eucalyptus buds and leaves.
5. A man who clips wool from sheep.
6. The most important farm crop in Australia.
7. First people in Australia.
8. A kind of sheep grown for their fine wool.
9. The national capital of Australia.
10. The meat from fully grown sheep.

C. *Answer these questions.*

1. Where do the Australians get water for irrigation?
2. What are the two largest deserts in Australia?

Lesson 20 Answers

Testing Your Understanding

A. 1. true
2. false
3. false
4. true
5. false
6. true
7. false
8. false

B. 1. outback
2. Sydney
3. artesian
4. koala
5. shearer
6. wheat
7. aborigines
8. merino
9. Canberra
10. mutton

C. 1. from the Murray River and its tributaries (and from dams)
2. the Great Sandy Desert and the Great Victoria Desert

3. They all carry their newborn young in a pouch.
4. The platypus and the echidna are the only two mammals that lay eggs.
5. a. the Tropical Zone
   b. the (Southern) Temperate Zone
6. Large ships are in danger of being sunk by the many coral reefs around the Great Barrier Reef.

Map Exercises
1. a. Canberra
   b. Sydney
   c. Melbourne
   d. Brisbane
2. a. Great Dividing Range
   b. Mount Kosciusko
3. a. Gulf of Carpentaria
   b. Cape York Peninsula
   c. Great Victoria Desert
4. Tasmania
5. a. Pacific Ocean
   b. Indian Ocean

Review Study
(Individual work. Review the glossary words orally. Then have the students tell you the names of the states and cities as you point to them on the blank map in the back of the book.
Discuss some ways that Australia is different from North America.
Examples:
Australia is drier than most of North America.
Australia is smaller than North America.
Australian seasons are opposite from those in North America.
Most of Australia is warmer than much of North America.
Australia is more thinly settled than most of North America. (But the Arctic lands and the deserts of North America are also thinly settled.)

3. The kangaroo, the koala, and the opossum are all known as marsupials. Why?
4. How are the platypus and the echidna different from all other mammals?
5. The Tropic of Capricorn passes through Australia. (a) In which climate zone is the northern part of the country? (b) In which climate zone is the southern part?
6. Why is the Great Barrier Reef dangerous to large ships?

Map Exercises
Use your completed map of Australia to answer these questions.
1. What is the capital of (a) Australia? (b) New South Wales? (c) Victoria? (d) Queensland?
2. (a) Name the mountain range in eastern Australia. (b) What is the highest mountain in it?
3. Name (a) the gulf in northern Australia. (b) the peninsula in northeastern Australia. (c) the great desert in southwestern Australia.
4. Name the island state of Australia.
5. What ocean is (a) east of Australia? (b) west of Australia?

Review Study
1. Do you know the meaning of all the glossary words in Chapter 4?
2. Can you label the states and major cities of Australia on a blank outline map?
3. Can you name some ways that Australia is different from North America?

So Far This Year

1. Much coffee comes from large (ranches, rain forests, fazendas) in Brazil.

2. When animals go to a warmer place for the winter, they (hibernate, migrate).

3. During (summer, winter) in the Frigid Zone, the sun can be seen at midnight.

4. Nigeria is on the continent of (Asia, Africa, Australia).

5. Dams help to provide all the following benefits except (fishing, irrigation, electricity, climate control, flood control).

6. A deposit of soil at the mouth of a river is a (delta, dam, delegate).

7. A large group of islands is an (arena, archipelago, architect).

8. Choose two: Along the Ring of Fire, there are many (earthquakes, forest fires, tornadoes, volcanoes).

9. (Corn, Wheat, Rice) is the most important grain in the Philippines.

10. Australia is the (smallest, largest) continent in the world.

11. When the Northern Hemisphere has summer, the Southern Hemisphere has (spring, summer, autumn, winter).

12. The first European settlers in Australia were (criminals, debtors, heretics).

So Far This Year
1. fazendas
2. migrate
3. summer
4. Africa
5. climate control
6. delta
7. archipelago
8. earthquakes, volcanoes
9. Rice
10. smallest
11. winter
12. debtors

A heavily loaded barge pushes past modern towns and medieval castles on the Rhine River.

CHAPTER 5

LANDS ALONG THE RHINE RIVER

"The LORD is my rock, and my fortress, and my deliverer; my God, my strength, in whom I will trust" (Psalm 18:2).

21. Europe, a Land of Many Countries

Glossary Words

Anabaptist (an uh BAP tihst) A member of a Christian group that started in the 1500s, teaching that people should not be baptized as infants but on their confession of faith in Jesus.

ancestor (AN sehs tur) One from whom a person is descended, such as a grandmother or great-grandfather.

Catholic Church (KATH uh lihk) A large church that performs infant baptism and many special ceremonies; the state church in Europe for hundreds of years.

Protestant Church (PRAH tihs tuhnt) A large church that separated from the Catholic Church but continued to work closely with the civil government and to perform many special ceremonies; the state church of some countries in Europe.

state church The church that is officially recognized by the government of a nation; sometimes the only church allowed in that nation.

Swiss Brethren Anabaptists in Switzerland who formed a church in 1525.

A Small Continent With Many Nations

Find the continent of Europe on a map or globe. Europe is across the Atlantic Ocean from the United States and Canada. This continent is not surrounded by water as Australia is. It is connected to Asia along its wide eastern edge. Europe and Asia are really one huge landmass, but they are considered as two separate continents.

Europe is the next to smallest continent in the world. Only Australia is smaller. Yet Europe has more people than any other continent except Asia. Europe does not have a few large nations such as the United States and Canada. Instead, it is divided into many small nations.

LESSON AIM

To introduce the European countries that border the Rhine River and also to introduce the United Kingdom (Great Britain and Ireland).

MAIN POINTS

- **Europe is a small continent across the Atlantic Ocean from North America.** The continents of Europe and Asia are actually one huge landmass, [which is sometimes called Eurasia. The boundary between Europe and Asia is the Ural Mountains, but a stronger reason for considering these as separate continents is the great difference between European (western) culture and Asian (eastern) culture.]

- **The United Kingdom (Great Britain and Ireland) depend heavily on shipping and trading because they are island countries.**

- **The warm waters of the Gulf Stream provide good fishing grounds.** This warm ocean current causes a mild climate along the coasts of Europe, [even though they should be colder according to their latitude. Fogs and wet weather are common.]

- **The English Channel separates Great Britain from the rest of the continent.** [It is about 20 to 100 miles wide, the shortest distance being from Dover, England, to Calais, France. The many boats traversing the Channel often battle rough waters. Frequent dense fogs also hinder travel.]

- **The Alps are some of the highest mountains in Europe.** [The mountain range extends from near the Mediterranean Sea in France, through Switzerland and Austria, and into northern Yugoslavia. The entire system is about 750 miles long. But the Caucasus Mountains, between Europe and Asia, are higher.]

Most of Europe is in the Northern Temperate Zone and has four seasons. Only a small part is in the Northern Frigid Zone, and none is in the Tropical Zone. Summers in Europe are generally warm, although they are cooler in the north and in the mountains. Spring and autumn are usually pleasant seasons. Winters are often cold, with heavy snow in some places.

Western Europe has many islands and peninsulas. The ocean water is warmer than the cold winter air, and it helps to keep the winters from getting extremely cold. The western coasts are warmed by an ocean current called the Gulf Stream.

Eastern Europe is wider than western Europe. Much of this land is far from the warm seas, and winters are often bitterly cold.

Many rivers of Europe begin in high mountain ranges. They

Western Europe

- **The Swiss Brethren (or Anabaptists) began a new church near Zurich, Switzerland.** They were persecuted, and many fled into the hills and forests to hide.

RELATED POINTS

- **Europe consists of many countries.** Some neighboring countries that contain the Alps are Italy, Austria, and the tiny countries of Luxembourg and Liechtenstein.

- **The British Isles include Ireland and Great Britain.** Ireland is mainly an agricultural land, with most of its population belonging to the Catholic Church. A small part in the north has strong ties with Great Britain and is predominately Protestant. There has been civil unrest between the "two Irelands" in the past. Dublin is the capital of Eire (the southern part). Belfast is the capital of Northern Ireland.

Great Britain consists of three countries on one island: Scotland to the north, England to the south, and Wales to the west. These three and Northern Ireland are unified under one government, centered in London. The term *United Kingdom* refers to these unified lands.

- **Many immigrants came to America from these European nations for religious freedom and economic improvement.**

The beautiful rolling hills of Ireland are ideal for pasturing cattle and sheep.

start out as rushing streams and grow larger as they flow toward the seas. One of the most important rivers in Europe is the Rhine River. It begins in Switzerland and flows north to the Netherlands. In this chapter, we will join David and Ruth as they and their parents visit some countries along the Rhine.

Land of Long-ago Ancestors

David and Ruth Martin gazed out the plane windows. Below they could see nothing but water, for they were flying over the Atlantic Ocean. Other people in the plane were dozing, but David and Ruth were too excited to rest.

The Martin children had been looking forward to this trip for several months. Their father was a minister, and he had told them, "Children, I want you to learn more about Europe. We are planning to go there and meet some Christians to whom I have been writing. One family lives in Switzerland, the land that your great-great-great-grandfather left many years ago. He took a boat down the Rhine River through Germany to the port at Rotterdam, the Netherlands. We'll travel much the same path that he did." Now they were on their way!

Suddenly Ruth pointed. "Look," she said. "Land! What is that land down there, Father?"

"That is the island country of Ireland," he replied. "Some people call it the Emerald Isle because the misty, mild climate causes the grass and fields to have a bright green color. The people who live there are called the Irish. Do you remember Mrs. Killarney at the nursing home? Her *ancestors* came from this island long ago."

Ruth thought awhile. "Wasn't Mrs. Killarney a member of the *Catholic Church*?"

"Yes, Ruth. In fact, most Irish people are Catholic. There is a small area in the northern part of the island that is mostly *Protestant*. That small part of the island has strong ties with the country of Great Britain, which we will soon see."

David had been listening to the conversation, but his attention was still out the window of the plane. Many ships were in the waters below.

Father said, "David, we are flying over one of the busiest

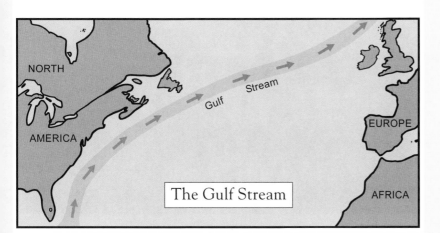

The Gulf Stream

shipping areas in the world. Over there you can see the shores of Great Britain. Great Britain is an island nation, so it depends on ships to carry products to and from other countries."

"Are all of those trading ships?" asked David.

"I doubt it," answered Father. "Probably some of them are fishing ships. The warm waters of the Gulf Stream provide good fishing grounds for Great Britain and the west coast of Europe."

The Mainland of Europe

Sometime later, Father spoke again. "Children, we will soon be flying over the English Channel, which separates Great Britain from the rest of the continent of Europe. Do you see the white chalk cliffs of Dover along the shore of England?"

"The channel isn't very wide, is it?" observed David. "I can see land on the other side."

"No, it isn't," said Father. "Here it is only about 20 miles

The white chalk cliffs of Dover.

God has blessed France with some flat, fertile farmland.

wide. "That is France you see on the other side of the channel."

Soon the plane was flying over France. The Martin family admired the neat farms below, with streams winding through them. Father pointed out a river that he said was the Seine (SAYN). He told the children that the Seine River flows through Paris, the capital of France.

"The French are good farmers," said Father. "They raise more crops and animals than any other nation in Europe. They have been blessed with good, fertile land to farm. See how nice and level it is?"

"Is all of France like this?" asked Ruth.

"Oh, no," answered Father. "France has many hilly parts. Here in the north it is level. What you see is in the Northern Plain of Europe. Farther south it is hilly. In the southeastern part next to Switzerland, France has high mountains. They are part of the Alps."

"I remember reading about the Alps," said David. "They are

156   Unit 3, Chapter 5 Lands Along the Rhine River

some of the highest mountains in Europe. And many of them are in Switzerland, aren't they?"

"Yes, they are. It was in Switzerland that a new church was started long ago. The members of the new church called themselves Brethren and were later known as the *Swiss Brethren*. But the leaders of the *state church* called them *Anabaptists* and persecuted them. Many Anabaptists fled to the hills and forests for safety."

The sun was setting, and darkness settled over the land. Off in the distance, Ruth noticed something white, with a rosy tint, standing above the clouds. "What is that?" she asked Father.

Father studied it a moment. "I wonder if that isn't one of the higher peaks of the Alps," he said. "They are snow-covered, you know. The sunset is making it look pink. Isn't that beautiful?"

"It certainly is!" exclaimed Ruth. "I think Europe is a lovely place."

Lesson 21 Answers

Testing Your Understanding

A. 1. Atlantic
2. Asia
3. Most, a small part
4. Ireland, Great Britain
5. a. English Channel
   b. 20
6. land (or soil)
7. Alps
8. Anabaptists

———————— **Testing Your Understanding** ————————

A. *Write the correct word(s) to complete each sentence.*

1. Europe lies across the ——— Ocean from the United States and Canada.

2. Europe is connected to the continent of ———.

3. (Most, A small part) of Europe is in the Northern Temperate Zone, but (most, a small part) is in the Northern Frigid Zone.

4. ——— and ——— are two island countries northwest of France.

5. a. The ——— separates Great Britain from the rest of Europe.
   b. It is about (20, 50, 100) miles wide near Dover.

6. The French have good farms because God gave them fertile ———.

7. The ——— of Switzerland are some of the highest mountains in Europe.

8. The ——— were a group of persecuted Christians who fled to the hills and forests to hide.

B. *Write the answers.*

1. Why do some people call Ireland the Emerald Isle?

2. Why is shipping very important to the country of Great Britain?

3. Write *Europe* or *Australia* for each description.
   a. A continent of one nation.
   b. A continent of many nations.
   c. A continent completely surrounded by water.
   d. A continent joined to another continent.
   e. A heavily settled continent.
   f. A thinly settled continent.

4. Why are winters colder in eastern Europe than in western Europe?

5. Name an important river of Europe that begins in Switzerland and flows north to the Netherlands.

6. (*a*) What city is the capital of France? (*b*) What river flows through the capital?

Further Study

1. What are some problems of having many nations on one continent, as Europe has?

2. One of the most important rivers in Europe is the Rhine River. Give a good reason why it is so important.

3. Find out if your ancestors came from Europe. What country did they come from?

Map Exercises

1. Trace Map D in the map section. Use blue to color the oceans, seas, and lakes.

2. Label these countries on your map: Great Britain, Ireland, France, Switzerland, Germany, and the Netherlands.

3. Label the capitals of Great Britain, Ireland, France, Switzerland, Germany, and the Netherlands.

B. 1. The misty, mild climate causes the grass and fields to have a bright green color.
2. Great Britain is an island nation.
3. a. Australia
   b. Europe
   c. Australia
   d. Europe
   e. Europe
   f. Australia
4. Eastern Europe is far away from the seas that warm western Europe.
5. the Rhine River
6. a. Paris
   b. the Seine River

Further Study

1. Travelers must get special permission to go from one nation to another. The people may speak different languages. Wars may start when the nations have disagreements.
2. Inland countries of Europe use the Rhine River as a waterway to the sea.
3. (Pupils may obtain information from their parents or grandparents. Most people with an English background have ancestors from Great Britain. Most people with an Anabaptist background have ancestors from Switzerland, Germany, or the Netherlands.)

Map Exercises

(Individual work. Check maps for accuracy and neatness.)

22. Switzerland, Land of the Alps

Glossary Words

bannwald

avalanche (AV uh lanch) A large mass, usually of snow and ice, that slides swiftly down a slope.

bannwald (BAHN vahlt) A triangle-shaped grove of trees on Swiss mountainsides that help to stop avalanches.

cargo (KAHR goh) A load of goods carried by a ship or plane.

lock A "step" in a "water stairway" by which a ship can go from one water level to another.

pass A lower place in a mountain range, where people pass through the range.

quality (KWAHL ih tee) Having a high degree of excellence.

tourist (TOOR ihst) A person who travels for pleasure to places of interest.

The Martins spent the night in Zurich, Switzerland, and the next day they spent some time in the city. One part had old buildings and very narrow streets—some only about 6 feet wide. They paused by the Limmat River. Father told the family about Felix Manz, who had been drowned in this river because he was faithful to God.

In 1525, Felix Manz and some other men had started a new church in Zurich, based on full obedience to the Bible. Leaders of the state church did not like this new group, which they called Anabaptists. The Anabaptists were persecuted, and many, such as Felix Manz, died for their faith.

The Martins rented a car and headed for the Alps. "We will see only a very small part of the Alps," Father told the children.

LESSON AIM

To acquaint students with the country of Switzerland and to introduce the persecuted Swiss Brethren.

MAIN POINTS

- **The Swiss Brethren (called Anabaptists by their enemies) started a church in 1525 based on full obedience to the Bible.** They were severely persecuted, and many were killed for their faith. [The church-state alliance of that time viewed the new church as a threat—one that must be exterminated.]

- **Avalanches are dangerous in mountain areas of high snowfall.** A warm wind [called a foehn, like the chinook of the western United States and Canada] can cause avalanches. The Swiss try to reduce the danger by preserving forests to stop the massive slides.

- **Switzerland is a country of few natural resources.** It depends on tourism and its skilled craftsmen for an income. The country specializes in precision goods produced by trained engineers. [Swiss banks are also famous worldwide, and the country enjoys one of the world's highest standards of living.]

- **Mountain passes have long been important routes through the Alps.** Tunnels have been bored in recent years to make travel easier.

- **Since Switzerland is landlocked, the city of Basel and the Rhine River are its link to the sea.** Basel is a busy port city, vital to Switzerland's economy. [For ships going upstream, this city is usually the last stop on the Rhine because of a large waterfall and other hindrances beyond Basel.]

"But it is said that some of the most beautiful peaks are in this area near Zurich."

"Oh, how lovely!" cried Ruth as the first towering, snowcapped peak came into view. As they came closer to the Alps, they saw many cattle blocking the road ahead.

"Look, Father! Dozens of cattle, and some little dogs barking at them! What is happening?"

"I'm not sure, but maybe we can find out if we ask."

"Don't the people speak Swiss here?" Ruth asked.

"No," Father replied. "Most of them speak German, and some use French or Italian. But Europeans commonly study English in their schools, so we should be able to talk with some of them."

Mother and the children stood nearby as Father talked to a

The Limmat River flows through the city of Zurich. Here Felix Manz, one of the first Anabaptists, was drowned for his faith in God.

- **Some people make their living by hauling cargo on boats.** These boats must be narrow enough to pass through the many locks on the Rhine. The family travels along, having their living quarters on the boat. [School children learn from different teachers along the river as the children make regular trips upstream and downstream.]

- **Locks allow ships to be raised or lowered from one water level to another.** Many European rivers are linked to the Rhine River by canals. Since the water level in those canals and rivers is not the same, locks are needed so that ships can pass from one water level to another.

RELATED POINTS

- **Grazing in Alpine pastures.** During summer, herders have traditionally lived in mountain huts in the high pastures. Much cheese is made in the huts, and it brings part of the herder's income. *Heidi,* the classic children's story by Johanna Spyri, gives an interesting picture of Swiss life in the Alps.

- **Mountain passes in Switzerland.** These are treacherous during winter. Centuries ago at St. Bernard Pass, monks built hospices (inns) for weary travelers. They also trained the famous St. Bernard dogs to rescue lost travelers and victims of avalanches.

- **Source of the Rhine River.** The Rhine begins from glaciers in the Alps. It has two sources, the Hinter Rhein and the Vorder Rhein, the former being considered the more scenic.

During the summer, Swiss farmers graze their herds on hilly pastures nestled high in the Alps.

herder. The air was filled with the constant musical tinkling of many cowbells.

"It is time to move the cattle to lower pastures," said the herder. "For centuries, our grazing lands have changed with the seasons. As the snow melts in the springtime, fresh grass grows farther up the mountains, and we take our herds where the pasture is. Now the autumn season is here. We are taking the cattle down the slopes, as the upper pastures get too cold."

The family talked with the herder for a while longer. Then Father thanked their new friend and handed him a Gospel tract. Soon the Martins were on their way again.

"We will go higher into the Alps," said Father. "I want you to see how people have learned to live in these high, cold mountains that God has made."

The family drove on twisting roads higher and higher into the mountains. David noticed a patch of trees and some fencelike structures clinging to the mountain that towered above a village.

He pointed these out to his father.

"Such a patch of trees is called a *bannwald*, which means 'forbidden forest.' No people or animals are to be in it, for the bannwald and the fences above it are a protection from *avalanches*. Avalanches have killed many people.

"Sometimes a warm, dry wind causes a huge mass of snow and ice to melt and suddenly come sliding down a mountain. The snow may weigh a million tons and travel 200 miles per hour. Forests are one of the best ways to stop avalanches from burying the villages below."

Father drove into the village and parked the car. Many shops were there, and people seemed happy to see the Martins. "They would like us to buy something while we are here," Father explained. "Many Swiss people depend on *tourists* to earn their living. Switzerland is a country with few natural resources. So there are many factories that

Switzerland

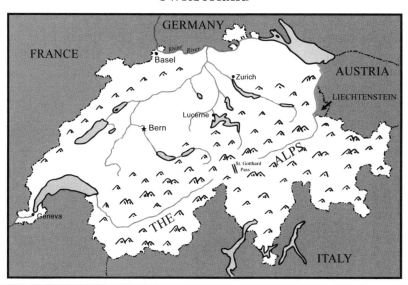

An avalanche

make **quality** goods to sell, such as fine watches, cloth dyes, and medicines."

Soon the family was driving on through the Alps. Near sundown Father said, "We have come up a mountain **pass**. This one is called the St. Gotthard Pass (GAHT urd). For centuries, mountain passes were the only way to get through the Alps. To make travel easier, men have now cut numerous tunnels through solid rock. We could have ridden on a train through the St. Gotthard Tunnel, which is about ten miles long. If we continued down the south side of the Alps, we would come to Italy."

Father pointed toward the west. "Look at that beautiful sight! That's the sunset reflecting off the snow and ice of the Alps. It is called the alpenglow."

The family watched quietly as God painted a beautiful picture in the sky. Soon they found a place to spend the night in the land of their great-great-great-grandfather.

A few days later, Father took the family to Basel, a city along the Rhine River. This port and the river are Switzerland's link to the ocean. The Martins went to the busy docks along the Rhine, where ships were being loaded and unloaded by huge machines.

"Come and meet Captain Hans!" said Father. "He will take us for a ride down the Rhine River on his riverboat."

"Hello!" boomed a deep voice in English. "My name is Hans Becker. I'm glad to meet Christians from America! We are planning to ride down the Rhine to Rotterdam, in the Netherlands. Come aboard and meet my family. This boat is our home!"

David and Ruth looked at each other. It would be fun to live on a boat, they thought! Eagerly they followed Hans and their parents to a long, narrow boat lying low in the water. They were soon introduced to Mrs. Becker, Emil, Hermann, and Johanna.

Mrs. Becker showed the family their sleeping quarters. Then Johanna and her brothers gave the Martin children a tour of the boat, including a look at its *cargo*. "Couldn't you carry a bigger load if you had a bigger boat?" asked David.

"You will soon see why our boat isn't bigger!" Emil said, smiling. "Did you hear the three rings of the bell? That means our boat is leaving the dock!"

Emil led the way to the pilot-house. There they found Father and Hans Becker, who was steering the boat. Soon a *lock* came into view. "Has your family ever gone through a set of locks?" Hans asked.

"No, we haven't," Father replied. "Please tell us why they are needed."

The Martin family listened closely as Hans told about the "watery steps" in the Rhine River. "Many canals join the Rhine with other rivers of Europe. But the water in those canals and rivers is not all at the same level. Locks are needed to raise or lower ships from one water level to another."

The boat glided slowly into the first lock. Big doors closed behind the boat. The water level dropped lower and lower as water drained out of the lock. When it was at the right level, a door opened in front of the boat and they glided into the next lock to

Basel is an important port city in northern Switzerland. The Rhine River flows downstream from Basel to the North Sea.

be lowered again. After going down through seven locks in a row, the boat came out into open water again. The children saw another ship about to enter the locks from the opposite direction.

Emil said, "That boat will be going uphill through the locks. We came downhill. By the way, David, do you see why we don't have a bigger boat?"

"Yes! Your boat wouldn't fit into those locks if it were any bigger!"

Testing Your Understanding

A. *Write the correct word(s) to complete each sentence.*

1. The Anabaptists were persecuted by the ——— church.
2. Cattle in Switzerland are moved to lower pastures in the (spring, fall).
3. Sometimes a huge mass of snow and ice goes sliding down a mountain. Such a sliding mass is called an ———.
4. A patch of trees called a ——— gives some protection against sliding snow and ice.
5. Switzerland has (many, few) natural resources. Many people depend on ——— from other countries for their income.
6. Sunlight reflecting off the snow and ice of the Alps is called the ———.
7. The ——— River and the city of ——— are Switzerland's link to the ocean.
8. The goods that a boat carries are called its ———.

B. *Write the answers.*

1. (*a*) In what year was the Anabaptist church started? (*b*) Why was Felix Manz drowned?
2. (*a*) What language do most Swiss people speak? (*b*) Name three other languages that are used in Switzerland.
3. Why are Swiss cattle brought down from the mountains at certain times of the year?
4. Name two things that are made in Swiss factories.

Lesson 22 Answers

Testing Your Understanding

A. 1. state
2. fall
3. avalanche
4. bannwald
5. few, tourists
6. alpenglow
7. Rhine, Basel
8. cargo

B. 1. a. in 1525
b. Felix Manz was drowned because he was faithful to God.
2. a. German
b. English, French, Italian
3. The upper pastures get too cold for grazing.
4. (Sample answers) watches, dyes, medicines

5. What are two ways of getting through the Alps from Switzerland to Italy?
6. Why are locks needed on some rivers?

Further Study

1. Many Swiss people can speak two or three languages. How is this especially helpful to them? (Think about what you have learned in this lesson.)
2. Would it be correct to say that a pass is a low place through a mountain range? Explain.

Map Exercises

1. On your map of Europe, label the cities of Basel and Zurich.
2. Make ∧∧ symbols on your map to show the Alps. Label the Alps and the Rhine River.

5. by using a mountain pass, by going through a tunnel
6. so that boats can go from one water level to another.

Further Study
1. Many foreign tourists come to Switzerland. For the Swiss people who have things to sell, it is very helpful if they can speak the tourists' languages.
2. No. Although a pass is lower than the surrounding mountains, it may still be hundreds or thousands of feet high. A pass is usually the best place to cross a mountain range, but it still requires a long climb.

Map Exercises
(Individual work. Check maps for accuracy and neatness.)

23. Visiting Germany and France

Glossary Words

aqueduct

mouth

aqueduct (AK wuh duhkt) A manmade channel that brings water from a distance.

autobahn (OW toh bahn) A large superhighway in Germany.

baron (BAIR uhn) A European nobleman.

castle A large thick-walled stone building used for refuge from attack, usually the home of a nobleman or ruler.

cathedral (kuh THEE druhl) A large, elaborate church building.

engineer (ehn juh NEER) A person who plans and builds roads, bridges, canals, and so forth.

mouth The end of a river where it empties into another body of water.

ore (AWR) Rock containing a valuable metal.

scenic (SEE nihk) Having beautiful scenery.

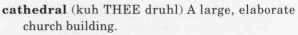

"The Rhine is certainly a busy and *scenic* river," Mother said as she watched a boat floating by. "I notice an area in the distance where some trees look darker than the ones around them. Are those evergreen trees?"

"Yes," Mrs. Becker replied. "That is part of the Black Forest. It has that name because most of the trees are dark fir and spruce trees."

Later the boat stopped at a dock near Freiburg, Germany. Soon the Martin and Becker families were riding in a van with the Gottlieb Otto family to their home in the Black Forest. Johanna Becker and Greta Otto were good friends, and they made the Martin children feel welcome. The Ottos could also speak English.

LESSON AIM

To acquaint students with the geography and lifestyles of the Rhineland and the Black Forest area of Germany and to present a few more details about the Anabaptists.

MAIN POINTS

- **The Rhine is a scenic river.** The nearby Black Forest is a hilly area, mostly covered with dark evergreen trees.

- **Most farms are small in southern Germany.** Cold-weather crops like hay, potatoes, cabbages, and wheat are grown on narrow valley slopes. Germany has to import many foods because the output of the small farms is not enough to meet the need.

- **Anabaptists were also persecuted in Germany.** Many of the persecuted Swiss Brethren fled to the Palatinate region, and many from that area later migrated to America. [Pennsylvania Dutch—actually a dialect of

German (Deutsch)—has its roots in the Palatinate.]

- **The first Bible produced by a printing press was printed by Johann Gutenberg in Mainz, Germany.** Gutenberg is credited with inventing the first printing press that used movable type. Before that invention, Bibles were extremely expensive because each one had to be copied by hand.

- **The Alsace-Lorraine region has large deposits of iron ore, coal, and oil.** The Rhine River is a valuable route for transporting these heavy materials to the factories that use them.

- **The Ruhr is the industrial heart of Germany.** This region seems like one continuous city. [It is about 30 miles wide. Over eight million people live in the Ruhr.] Water pollution is a major problem for this area, and Germany and the other Rhineland countries are working together to solve it.

Ruth watched the cars zooming past them. "Why are people driving so fast?" she asked Johanna and Greta.

"We are on an *autobahn*," Johanna explained. "In Germany, there are no speed limits on these superhighways. Cars travel up to 120 miles per hour."

"Are there many accidents?" questioned Ruth.

Mr. Otto answered from the driver's seat. "Yes, there are," he said soberly. "Too many people do not drive carefully, and sometimes

An autobahn speeds travel through a hilly area in Germany. Notice the tall concrete pillars supporting the highway.

The Black Forest is a wooded mountain region in southern Germany. Its name comes from the dark fir forests on the high slopes. The region also has some farmland.

RELATED POINTS

- **Germany has mountainous regions to the south, near the Alps.** Northern Germany, part of the Northern Plain, has flat, low land like the Netherlands.

- **On many German farms (especially older ones), the house and barn are under the same roof.** This arrangement conserves heat and makes animal care easier in cold weather.

- **Alsace and Lorraine are regions of France.** Alsace was predominately German at one time, but the younger generation is becoming more and more French. These provinces have seen much fighting in history because of their rich deposits of iron ore and coal, two necessary ingredients for making steel.

- **The French are noted for their fine foods and wines.** The drinking of wine is common in Europe because much of the water is contaminated. This is one reason that grapes are an important crop in the Rhineland. Christians, of course, should abstain from alcoholic drinks.

the roads are icy. On the autobahn, many souls meet their Maker unprepared."

Soon they arrived at the Otto farm. It was small, as most farms are in Germany. The steep-roofed farmhouse with several balconies looked inviting.

"I smell sauerkraut!" Ruth cried. "You must have made something for dinner that we are used to."

Greta laughed. "We are having frankfurters and sauerkraut, a

**Germany and
Northeastern France**

German meal that traveled to America. We also eat lots of pork, potatoes, and cabbage.

"Father raises wheat, hay, and potatoes on the slopes and in that narrow valley down there," Greta continued. "But even though Germany has many small farms, it must still import many farm products."

After dinner Johanna suggested that the girls walk out to a potato field, where their parents and the boys had gone. They walked up in time to hear David ask if the Anabaptists had also been persecuted in Germany.

Mr. Otto replied, "Yes. Many German Christians gave their lives rather than deny their faith. Later the persecution was less severe, and many Anabaptists from Switzerland moved in. They were allowed to live in the Palatinate, a part of Germany along the Rhine River."

"My ancestors lived in that area," said Mother. "They moved to America because they were suffering hard times even in the Palatinate. The Christians were persecuted because they did not help in the many wars Germany was fighting at that time."

"How did they get to America?" David asked.

"They rode in boats down the Rhine to Rotterdam, where they boarded larger ships. These larger ships took them to America, but many people died on the way. The ships were crowded and unhealthful. I'm sure the ones who made it to America were very thankful to God. At last they were allowed to serve God in freedom."

"Did you know that the first Bible ever printed was printed in Germany?" asked Mr. Otto. "Johann Gutenberg, who lived in Mainz, invented the printing press in the mid-1400s. Before then, people had to copy everything by hand. Bibles were very expensive and hard to get. The first thing Gutenberg printed on his new press was the Bible. After that, more people could buy Bibles."

The families spent several worthwhile days together, visiting, singing hymns, and making new friends. All too soon, it was time to leave. The Beckers and the Martins boarded the riverboat once more, and soon they were traveling on down the Rhine.

This statue of Johann Gutenberg stands in Strasbourg, France.

As the boat neared Strasbourg, France, Hans Becker told the Martins about the city. "Strasbourg is the capital of Alsace, France," he said. "Canals link this city with some of the great rivers in France. In fact, the Alsace area has been very important to both France and Germany for many years. Do you know why?"

Father knew. "God has blessed the Alsace-Lorraine area of France with large amounts of iron *ore*, coal, and oil. These natural resources are needed to make and run machinery. The Rhine River makes it easy to ship these heavy materials to the factories that use them."

Hans smiled. "Correct." Then he told about Pilgram Marpeck, an Anabaptist who labored in this area in the early 1500s. "Pilgram Marpeck had a God-given ability that was a great benefit to Strasbourg. He was an excellent *engineer*, and he organized the building of *aqueducts* for the city's water supply. But the city had one problem with Pilgram Marpeck."

"What was that?" Ruth asked.

Hans chuckled. "Marpeck was a zealous Anabaptist minister! The leaders wanted him as an engineer, but they did not want his preaching. Finally he was arrested and ordered to leave the city. He took the Gospel to other German cities and used his gift to

Canals help provide transportation in Strasbourg, France, where Pilgram Marpeck once labored. Strasbourg is in the Alsace-Lorraine area of France.

One of the greatest resources of France is rich soil. Grape production is the leading form of agriculture in France.

help them. Pilgram Marpeck did not die as a martyr, mostly because the leaders needed his engineering skills too much."

As the boat traveled downstream from Strasbourg, the river became more and more crowded. The Martins saw stone **castles** along the river, and they learned about the robber **barons** that had once lived in those castles. Emil said that riverboats were forced to stop and pay money for the right to sail by. "Sailors who refused usually lost their cargo

and sometimes their lives," Emil said. "I'm glad that doesn't happen here today!"

Father pointed out the many vineyards growing on both riverbanks. "This area is well known for its grapes and wine," he said. "Grape-harvesting season is so busy that schools are closed during that time. The harvest may be going on right now."

One day, another large city came into sight. "This city is Cologne, the largest city on the Rhine," Hans explained. "Notice the beautiful *cathedral* with its two towers. Some consider that to be the most beautiful church building in the world. It is lovely, but I'm glad we don't need such a place to worship the Lord."

Later Hans said, "We are now entering the Ruhr (ROOR), an area of many factories. This area makes much of the iron and steel for Germany and other nations. See how much smoke is coming out of the factories, and how dirty the river is! Not long ago, the countries along the river got together to clean up the air and water."

"This area looks like one big factory!" exclaimed Mother. "Many of the riverboats are loaded with coal, aren't they?"

"Yes," said Hans. "The Ruhr produces most of Germany's coal. From this part of the Rhine to its *mouth*, the boat traffic is very heavy. We will soon be entering the Netherlands."

Lesson 23 Answers

Testing Your Understanding

A. 1. autobahn
   2. small
   3. Palatinate
   4. Johann Gutenberg, Mainz
   5. Strasbourg
   6. iron ore, coal, oil, machinery
   7. castles, vineyards
   8. Cologne, cathedral

Testing Your Understanding

A. *Write the correct word(s) to complete each sentence.*

1. An —— is a big highway in Germany.
2. Most farms in Germany are (small, large).
3. Many Anabaptists from Switzerland lived in the —— region of Germany for a time.
4. —— produced the first printed Bible on his printing press in ——, Germany.
5. The capital of Alsace, France, is ——.
6. The Alsace region is important to both France and Germany because it has large amounts of ——, ——, and ——. These resources are used to make and run ——.
7. Down the Rhine from Strasbourg, —— and —— can be seen along the river.
8. The largest city on the Rhine River is ——. This city has a large, beautiful church building called a ——.

Lesson 23   173

9. The ——— area has many factories, which make much of Germany's ——— and ———. But the factories also make the river ———.

10. An Anabaptist named ——— had such useful skills that he was not persecuted as much as other Anabaptists. He was an excellent ———.

B. *Write the answers.*

1. Why does the Black Forest have its name?
2. What is the speed limit on an autobahn?
3. Name two crops grown on German farms. Also name a food that came to America from Germany.
4. Why did many Anabaptists of the Palatinate move to America?
5. How were Bibles made before the printing press was invented?
6. Long ago, why was it unsafe for boats to travel down the Rhine River from Strasbourg?

Further Study

1. Traffic laws are made for the good of people who use the highways. How is that truth shown in this lesson?
2. How did Pilgram Marpeck show that he did not hate the people who persecuted him?
3. What do you think the countries along the Rhine River did to clean up the air and water?

Map Exercises

1. Label these cities on your map of Europe: Strasbourg, Cologne, Mainz, Freiburg, and Bonn.
2. Label the Black Forest and the Palatinate regions.

---

9. Ruhr, iron, steel, dirty
10. Pilgram Marpeck, engineer

B. 1. Most of the trees are dark fir and spruce trees.
2. An autobahn has no speed limit.
3. (Sample crops) wheat, hay, potatoes; (Sample foods) frankfurters, sauerkraut
4. They were persecuted in the Palatinate. (They refused to help in the many wars Germany was fighting.)
5. All Bibles had to be copied by hand.
6. Robbers lived in castles along that part of the Rhine.

Further Study
1. When people drive at high speeds, they are likely to be killed or seriously injured in accidents. Speed limits help to prevent such accidents.
2. Marpeck used his skills to help people even in cities where he was persecuted.
3. They asked factories to clean up their waste water before returning it to the river and to reduce their output of smoke (by burning cleaner fuels, using scrubbers to remove smoke particles, and by other methods).

Map Exercises
(Individual work. Check maps for accuracy and neatness.)

24. The Netherlands, Land From the Sea

Glossary Words

herring

barge A large, flat-bottomed boat that carries freight and is pushed or pulled by a towboat.

dike A wall of earth built to hold back water.

herring (HEHR ihng) A small food fish of the northern Atlantic. Young herring are canned as sardines.

klompen (KLAHMP uhn) Shoes made entirely of wood.

klompen

polder (POHL dur) A piece of land reclaimed from a body of water and protected by dikes.

stevedore (STEE vuh dawr) A worker who loads or unloads the cargo of a ship.

tide The rise and fall of the ocean about every twelve hours.

barge

As the riverboat traveled through the Netherlands, Ruth suddenly exclaimed, "The land is flat! What happened to the Alps?"

Father laughed. "We left them soon after entering Germany. The land is so flat because we have entered the Northern Plain region. We are nearing the place where the river empties into the sea. The mouth of the Rhine River is a large triangle-shaped delta that covers much of the Netherlands. Have

LESSON AIM

To introduce the unique geography and economy of the Netherlands.

MAIN POINTS

- **The low, flat delta land of the Rhine and Maas Rivers covers much of the Netherlands.** This land is costly and valuable because the Dutch need to protect it from flooding. [About 40 percent of the land is below sea level.]

- **The Netherlands is traditionally known for tulips, windmills, and wooden shoes.** Many people call the country Holland, but that is the name of only two provinces—North Holland and South Holland. (*Holland* means "hollow land.") [This would be like referring to the United States as Carolina or to Canada as Ontario.]

- **The Dutch use dikes to reclaim land from the sea.** Five years are needed to remove enough water and salt from the polder soil to raise decent crops. [Small polders were made as early as the 1200s in Friesland. Polder land is very fertile, and is often used as pastureland for cattle.]

- **Amsterdam is the capital and largest city of the Netherlands.** Land in Amsterdam is so marshy that posts (piles) must be driven into the deeper, solid ground to support the weight of the buildings. [A city called The Hague is also an important city of the Netherlands. It contains the main government offices.]

- **Flower bulbs are a major export of the Netherlands.** Fields of beautiful flowers are raised southwest of Amsterdam [near Haarlem]. Flower heads are cut off during the peak blooming period to produce bulbs of higher quality.

you ever heard about this little country, Ruth?"

Ruth thought a little and then replied, "I thought it was called Holland. Isn't this the country that is known for tulips, windmills, and wooden shoes?"

Father smiled. "You are right. However, only a part of the Netherlands is actually called Holland. That name means 'hollow land.' Much of the land in this area would be underwater at high *tide* if it were not for the *dikes* that the Dutch people have built. When we get to Rotterdam, we will meet another English-speaking family that will tell us more about this land."

Hans expertly guided the riverboat through the crowded waterways. Tugboats helped to push the boat into an empty place at the busy dock. Then *stevedores* took over, and the cargo was soon emptied into waiting trucks.

Finally it was time for the Martins and the Beckers to part, and the families exchanged fond farewells. The Martin family stood waving as the Beckers' boat pulled away from the dock.

A man had been standing nearby, watching quietly. Now he introduced himself as Claus Willems. "Welcome to the Netherlands!" he said. "Come, and we can visit as we drive to my home. My mother is expecting us for dinner soon."

The Martin family was soon in Claus's small car, and they started off. David noticed how many canals they passed over. Claus said that cars sometimes went into the canals if the drivers were not careful!

Netherlands

- **Menno Simons, a former Catholic priest, helped to organize and unify the Anabaptists in the Netherlands.** For this reason they became known as Mennonites. Menno Simons was a hunted man, but he did not die a martyr's death.

RELATED POINTS

- **Why land is reclaimed from the sea.** A main reason is the high population density in the Netherlands. This averages about 900 persons per square mile, whereas the average in the United States is only 65 persons per square mile.

- **Anabaptists in the Netherlands.** In the 1500s, the Netherlands included the present country of Belgium. The Catholic Church was strong in the part of Belgium known as Flanders, and Dutch Anabaptists were severely persecuted. Later, the Calvinists also persecuted Anabaptists. Some estimate that the number of martyrs in Flanders was between 500 to 1,000.

- **Religious toleration.** William I, Prince of Orange, ruled the Netherlands in the 1580s. He was the first European ruler to let people worship as they chose, as long as they did not harm others. It was because of this religious toleration that the Pilgrims were in the Rotterdam area before they left for America.

These Dutch fishermen use nets to catch fish.

"Thank you for your encouraging letters, Brother Martin," Claus said. "My widowed mother and I live in the province of Zeeland. We have been alone ever since the flood of 1953. In February of that year, the North Sea broke through the dikes because of high tides and fierce winds. About 1,800 souls went to meet God that day, including my father and my sister."

The little car traveled on. Sometimes the road followed the tops of dikes, and sometimes it passed between fertile fields. Pastures did not need fences because drainage ditches kept the cattle from roaming. It seemed that more people rode on bicycles than in cars.

Finally the car came to a stop before a neat little house. Claus's mother, Tetje, came to greet them, smiling.

"Welcome, friends! Come inside. Dinner is waiting!"

The visitors entered the Willems' spotless home. A tasty meal of **herring**, potatoes, and cheese was served.

"Herring are very important fish to our country," Tetje Willems explained. "Fishermen, like my son Claus, have earned their living for years by selling these little fish from the warm waters off the coast. Herring are usually salted and dried for export."

Father asked David and Ruth if they remembered what made the coastal waters warm. David said, "Is it because of the Gulf Stream? But I thought that was near England."

"You're right, David. But we

aren't far from England now—only about 100 miles! It is the same Gulf Stream that warms these coasts."

The next morning, the Martin family went with Claus and his mother to see more of the country. The car crossed a number of dams and several islands. "I wonder if you would explain how the Dutch

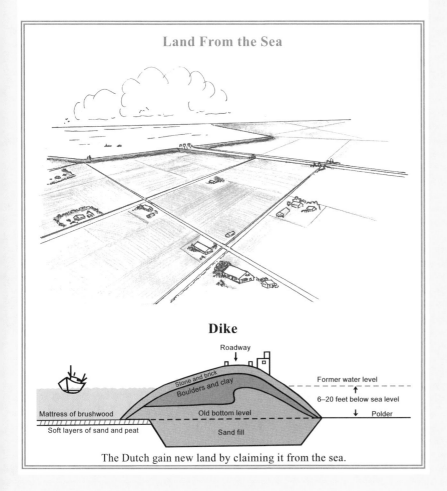

Land From the Sea

Dike

Roadway

Stone and brick
Boulders and clay

Former water level

6–20 feet below sea level

Mattress of brushwood

Old bottom level

Polder

Soft layers of sand and peat

Sand fill

The Dutch gain new land by claiming it from the sea.

get their land from the sea," said Father.

"Surely! First we decide what land we want. Then we surround that area with a dike and begin pumping the water out into the sea. Next we scrape off the saltiest soil. Rain helps to wash the rest of the salt out of the soil. After about five years, the *polder* is ready to be farmed.

"We need many canals to keep the polder land drained. The canal water is pumped over the dike and into higher canals that empty into the sea. Electric pumps now do most of the work, but there are still a few windmills

Years ago, large windmills like this were used to pump water over the dikes. Now electric pumps do most of the work.

around to show how the pumping was done in the old days.

"Farmland in this country is expensive because of all that must be done to gain and keep it," Claus explained. "Some people have started raising crops in greenhouses. Vegetables can be grown year round and sold to European countries where the winters are severe."

Next they drove to Amsterdam, the country's largest city. "Amsterdam is the nation's capital," said Tetje Willems. "The wet, marshy ground here and in other cities won't support the weight of a building, so most of these buildings are built on posts driven into the ground. The wet ground is also the reason for our wooden shoes, or *klompen*. They keep our feet drier than leather shoes, and they don't cost as much.

"In the springtime," Tetje continued, "the area southwest of Amsterdam is full of colorful tulips, daffodils, and other kinds of flowers. Tourists are surprised to see *barges* full of pretty flower heads taken out to be dumped into the sea or used in compost. The reason is that bulbs are the

Menno Simons

Menno Simons became a Catholic priest in 1524. Five years later he left the Catholic Church and became an Anabaptist. He had begun to doubt some of the Catholic teachings. By reading the Bible, he had found that those teachings were not true.

Menno Simons was soon a persecuted and hunted man. He traveled about constantly, and at least one man was put to death for giving him food and shelter. Rulers promised large sums of money to anyone who could capture him. But God always allowed Menno Simons to escape. He died a natural death in 1561, when he was more than sixty years old.

Menno Simons was the most outstanding leader that the Anabaptists had. He preached the Gospel, organized many churches, and did much writing. The Anabaptists came to be called Mennonites because of the great influence of Menno Simons.

Menno Simons was a Catholic priest in this church before he joined the Anabaptists.

export. When the blooms are cut off, the bulbs become stronger."

Father asked Claus if he had read the writings of Menno Simons. "Yes, I have," Claus replied. "Menno Simons lived in the northern part of the Netherlands in the 1530s. At that time the Anabaptists were about the only church in the Netherlands other than the Catholic Church, and the Anabaptists were severely persecuted. Later they were called Mennonites because Menno was one of their main leaders."

"It is getting late," said Tetje. "Let's return home and rest for the night. You have had a busy day!"

The Martin family stayed with the Willems for two days. They learned to appreciate the clean, orderly ways and the friendly hospitality of the Dutch people. Then it was time to return to Rotterdam and leave for America, as their ancestors had done long ago. But the Martins would be traveling by plane rather than by ship.

Tetje Willems put a round cheese into Mother's hands. "It is a gift for you made in our country," she said. "Please take it! Your family has encouraged us so much. Pray for us!"

After the Martins boarded the plane, Father put his feelings into words. "I enjoyed the interesting places and customs we saw," he said. "But it was the time we spent with Christian friends that I treasure most. Let us tell our friends and family back home what the Lord has done for us!" Soon the jet left the runway and headed toward home.

The cities of the Netherlands use many canals for transportation. Although the Netherlands is a small country without many natural resources, the Dutch have learned to use their water and land wisely.

—————— **Testing Your Understanding** ——————

A. *Write the correct word(s) to complete each sentence.*

1. The Northern Plain of Europe is a region of (level, hilly) land.

2. Much of the Netherlands is part of the triangle-shaped ——— of the Rhine and other rivers. This land is (high and dry, low and wet).

3. When many people think of the Netherlands, they think of ———, ———, and ———.

4. ——— is a busy shipping city at the mouth of the Rhine River. The men who load and unload the ships are called ———.

5. Many Dutch people drive cars, but more people ride on ———. Many pastures do not need fences, because ——— keep the cattle from roaming.

6. Long ago the Dutch used ——— to keep the water pumped out of their polders. Today most of the work is done by ——— pumps. The water is carried away by ——— that empty into the sea.

7. ——— is the capital and largest city in the Netherlands. Buildings in this city rest on ——— driven into the ground. Many people who work outdoors wear wooden shoes called ———.

8. Flower ——— are grown for export. The flower heads are cut off, loaded on ———, and taken away.

9. Long ago, about the only church in the Netherlands other than the Catholic Church was the ———. Later these people were called Mennonites because ——— was one of their main leaders.

B. *Write the answers.*

1. Why is *Holland* not a correct name for all of the Netherlands?

2. Explain why the coastal waters of the Netherlands are warm.

3. Copy the paragraph that tells how the Dutch get their land from the sea. (You do not need to copy the first word.)

Lesson 24 Answers

Testing Your Understanding

A. 1. level
   2. delta, low and wet
   3. tulips, windmills, wooden shoes
   4. Rotterdam, stevedores
   5. bicycles, ditches (canals)
   6. windmills, electric, canals
   7. Amsterdam, posts, klompen
   8. bulbs, barges
   9. Anabaptists, Menno Simons

B. 1. Only a part of the Netherlands is actually "hollow land."
   2. because of the Gulf Stream
   3. First we decide what land we want. Then we surround that area with a dike and begin pumping the water out into the sea. Next we scrape off the saltiest soil. Rain helps to wash the rest of the salt out of the soil. After about five years, the polder is ready to be farmed.

4. because of all that must be done to gain and keep it

5. so that the flower bulbs become stronger

Further Study

1. a. the Niger River

   b. As a river flows into the sea, its water slows down and drops the soil it is carrying. This soil builds up and forms a delta.

2. The Netherlands is the home of these people, and they take pride in their hard-won land. They face the danger of floods, but other lands also have dangers, such as earthquakes, volcanoes, avalanches, tornadoes, and hurricanes.

3. A large part of the water and nutrients in a plant is used to produce the flower (and the seed that develops later). When the flower is cut off, the rest of the plant (including the root or bulb) receives more benefit from the water and nutrients.

Map Exercises

(Individual work. Check maps for accuracy and neatness.)

4. Why is farmland expensive in the Netherlands?

5. Why do growers cut off the heads of the flowers they raise?

Further Study

1. (*a*) What river in Nigeria has a delta at its mouth? (*b*) Can you explain how a delta is formed?

2. The Dutch have struggled for many years to gain land from the sea and keep it from being flooded. Why do they keep doing this instead of moving somewhere else?

3. Why does the bulb of a flower become stronger when the flower head is cut off?

Map Exercises

1. On your map of Europe, label the city of Rotterdam and the area of Zeeland.

2. Color your map according to the Rules for Neat Maps.

25. Chapter 5 Review

===== Testing Your Understanding =====

A. *Write a glossary word for each definition.*

1. Churches that persecuted sincere Christians long ago (two answers).
2. A barrier for protection from avalanches.
3. A German superhighway.
4. Land reclaimed from the sea.
5. A large, elaborate church building.
6. A group of persecuted Christians (two answers).
7. A large, flat-bottomed boat for carrying freight.
8. One from whom a person is descended.
9. A fish that is used for food.
10. A place to get through a mountain range.

B. *Choose words from this list to fill in the blanks. Do not use any word more than once. You will not use all the words.*

tides	dikes	ancestors
aqueduct	quality	castles
mouth	stevedores	klompen
scenic	avalanches	tourists
ore	lock	engineer
barges	cargoes	natural resources

Many (1) ——— come to Switzerland to visit. In the winter, warm winds may melt the heavy snow and cause dangerous (2) ———. Many Swiss people are skilled workers who make (3) ——— goods such as fine watches. One reason is that Switzerland does not have many (4) ———.

A boat on the Rhine River must be narrow so that it will fit into a (5) ———. The boats carry iron (6) ——— and many other (7) ———. At Rotterdam, the boats are unloaded by (8) ———.

Lesson 25 Answers

Testing Your Understanding

A. 1. Catholic Church, Protestant Church (*Also accept* state church.)
2. bannwald
3. autobahn
4. polder
5. cathedral
6. Anabaptists, Swiss Brethren
7. barge
8. ancestor
9. herring
10. pass

B. 1. tourists
2. avalanches
3. quality
4. natural resources
5. lock
6. ore
7. cargoes
8. stevedores

9. engineer
10. aqueduct
11. castles
12. mouth
13. dikes
14. tides
15. klompen

C. 1. a. Gulf Stream
    b. English Channel
    c. Basel, Rhine River
    d. Johann Gutenberg
    e. Cologne
  2. so that boats can go from one water level to another
  3. The upper pastures get too cold for grazing.
  4. The small farms do not produce all the food that the people need.
  5. a. to find freedom of worship (or to escape persecution)
    b. Rotterdam

Map Exercises

1. a. London
   b. Bern
   c. Berlin
   d. Amsterdam
2. a. the Alps
   b. the Rhine River

Pilgram Marpeck was a gifted (9) ——— who built an (10) ——— for the city of Strasbourg. Many old (11) ——— can be seen along the Rhine River. Long ago, robber barons lived in them.

Most of the Netherlands is located on the delta at the (12) ——— of the Rhine River. The Dutch have built (13) ——— to make polders. In 1953, fierce winds and high (14) ——— caused a serious flood. Many people wear (15) ——— to keep their feet dry on the soggy soil of the polders.

C. *Answer these questions.*

1. What is the name of
   a. the warm ocean current that keeps England and the Netherlands from getting very cold?
   b. the waterway that separates Great Britain from the continent of Europe?
   c. the port and the river that link Switzerland to the sea?
   d. the man who first used a printing press to produce a Bible?
   e. the largest city along the Rhine?
2. Why are locks needed in some rivers?
3. In the Alps, why are cattle brought down from the mountains in the fall?
4. Why must Germany import many foods for its people?
5. (*a*) Why did many Anabaptists move to America? (*b*) From what port in Europe did they leave?

Map Exercises

Use your completed map of northwestern Europe to do these exercises.

1. What is the capital of each country named below?
   a. England   c. Germany
   b. Switzerland   d. Netherlands
2. (*a*) What high mountains are in Switzerland? (*b*) What

important river begins in these mountains and flows through the Netherlands?

3. What large forest is in Germany?
4. In what region of Germany did many Anabaptists live for a time?

Review Study

1. Do you know the meaning of all the glossary words in Chapter 5?
2. Can you find Europe on a world map or a globe? Can you find Ireland, Great Britain, Switzerland, France, Germany, and the Netherlands?
3. Do you know where the Alps are, and how people get through this mountain range?
4. Do you know where the Gulf Stream is and how it affects the climate?

3. the Black Forest
4. the Palatinate region

Review Study
1. (Review glossary words in class.)
2. (Have students point out these items on a globe and a world map.)
3. in Switzerland (and nearby countries); through mountain passes and through tunnels
4. The Gulf Stream flows along the northern coast of Europe. It causes a mild, damp climate.

So Far This Year

So Far This Year

1. a. Tropical Zone
   b. Northern Temperate Zone
   c. Tropical Zone
   d. Tropical Zone, Southern Temperate Zone
   e. Northern Frigid Zone
   f. Tropical Zone
   g. Northern Temperate Zone
2. Amazon
3. northern lights
4. a place of safety for wild animals
5. cacao
6. Jeepneys
7. import, export
8. Australia
9. marsupials
10. Great Dividing Range
11. Asia
12. watches

1. Match the climate zones to the places. Answers may be used more than once.

   a. Most of Brazil
   b. Ohio
   c. Nigeria
   d. Australia (two zones)
   e. Baffin Island
   f. Philippines
   g. Most of Europe

   Northern Frigid Zone
   Northern Temperate Zone
   Tropical Zone
   Southern Temperate Zone
   Southern Frigid Zone

2. The largest river in the world is the (Amazon, Nile, Rhine) River in Brazil.

3. During winter darkness in the Frigid Zone, some light is provided by the (sun, northern lights).

4. A game reserve is (a safe place for playing games, a place of safety for wild animals).

5. Chocolate and cocoa come from (cacao, coconut, canola) seeds.

6. (Trains, Taxicabs, Jeepneys) provide a popular form of transportation in the Philippines.

7. An (import, export) is brought into a country, and an (import, export) is shipped out of a country.

8. The smallest continent is (Africa, Australia, Asia).

9. All (mammals, marsupials, marmots) carry their young in a pouch.

10. The largest range of mountains in Australia is the (Great Dividing Range, Great Barrier Reef).

11. Europe is connected to the continent of (Asia, Africa, Australia).

12. The Netherlands is known for all the following except (tulips, windmills, watches, wooden shoes).

A traditional Japanese castle stands in stark contrast to the skyscrapers in the background.

CHAPTER 6

JAPAN, LAND OF THE RISING SUN

"They that go down to the sea in ships, that do business in great waters; these see the works of the LORD, and his wonders in the deep" (Psalm 107:23, 24).

26. The Japanese Archipelago

Glossary Words

archipelago (ahr kuh PEHL uh goh) A large group of islands.

hibachi (hih BAH chee) A small charcoal burner used by the Japanese for heating or cooking.

kimono (kuh MOH nuh) A long, loose robe fastened with a wide band of material.

kotatsu (koh TAH tsoo) A small charcoal or electric heater kept in a square hole under the table of a Japanese house.

miso soup (MEE soh) Soup made by mixing soybean paste with seaweed, vegetables, or other foods.

tatami (tah TAH mee) A straw mat used as a floor covering.

Islands of Japan

The islands of Japan lie in the western part of the Pacific Ocean near the coast of Asia. They stretch about 1,200 miles from northeast to southwest. Cool, snowy islands are in the north, and warm, sunny islands are in the south.

Like the Philippines, Japan is an *archipelago*. In fact, the Philippines are only about 1,000 miles south of the main Japanese islands. Japan is also a neighbor to China, Korea, and Russia. Can you find Japan on a globe?

Japan's islands are all in the Northern Temperate Zone. Like the United States, the Japanese islands have spring, summer, autumn, and winter. The southern islands are nearly in the Tropical Zone.

Japan has four main islands. The largest is Honshu (HAHN shoo), where most of the people live. North of Honshu is Hokkaido (hah KY doh), the second largest island. Shikoku (SHEE kaw koo), the smallest of the four main islands, is directly south of Honshu. Farther southwest lies Kyushu (kee OO shoo). There are more than 3,500 other islands in Japan, but they are all very small.

LESSON AIM

To introduce Japanese islands and some traditional Japanese customs.

MAIN POINTS

• **Japan is a nation of islands off the coast of Asia.** The archipelago includes four large islands and more than 3,500 small islands. [The Japanese call their country *Nippon*, which means "source of the sun." It is called the Land of the Rising Sun because it is the easternmost Asian land in the middle latitudes.]

• **All the Japanese islands are in the Northern Temperate Zone, but some of the southern islands are nearly in the Tropical Zone.**

• **Japanese farmers often live in villages.** Their wooden houses are built close together.

• **Japanese customs are different from American customs.** [The Japanese are becoming more and more like North Americans and Europeans, especially in the cities. But the customs listed below are still widely practiced.]

—Bowing and other gestures that show politeness.

—Removing shoes when entering a house.

—Sitting on floor cushions around low tables.

—Using a kotatsu, hibachi, or small heater instead of a furnace.

—Using only a few pieces of furniture.

—Sleeping on floor mats.

—Wearing kimonos.

Japanese Homes and Customs

Karen Maki felt shy as she and her parents sat in her uncle's little blue car. Her uncle had just picked them up at the Matsuyama (mah tsoo YAH mah) airport on the island of Shikoku, and now they were going to his home. What would her aunt and her cousin be like? Karen's parents had moved to America soon after they were married. This was Karen's first visit to Japan.

Uncle Hisashi spoke rapidly to Karen's parents in Japanese. Karen caught some of what he was saying. He was thankful that God had given them a safe trip. He smiled at Karen. "Kiku will be

Japan

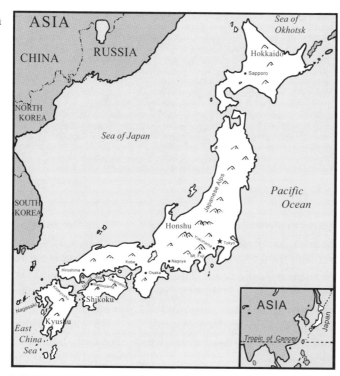

- **Japanese students study hard.** Many learn some English.

Note: In the Japanese language, each syllable receives the same amount of stress. But English-speaking people tend to accent certain syllables in Japanese words, and this is indicated in the pronunciations shown in the lesson. You may wish to have your students pronounce the words as the Japanese do, such as *hibachi* (hih bah chee), *kimono* (kuh moh nuh), and *kotatsu* (koh tah tsoo).

RELATED POINTS

- **Japan and the Philippines are similar in some ways but quite different in other ways.** Both countries are made up of islands and are off the east coast of Asia. Both do much trading with other nations. Both Japanese and Filipinos raise rice on terraces and catch fish in the seas around them.

However, Japan is in the Temperate Zone whereas the Philippines is in the Tropical Zone. Japan is a wealthy, modern nation that produces manufactured goods; but the Republic of the Philippines is a relatively poor nation with many farmers and fishermen who live much as their ancestors did.

These Japanese farmers are cutting their rice and hanging it up to dry.

happy to meet you," he told her in English. Karen returned the smile, not sure if she should reply or not.

Karen looked out the car window as they left the busy city and drove through the quieter countryside. She noticed orchards and what she guessed were rice fields.

In the villages the wooden houses, with their tile roofs, were small and close together. Short rows of vegetables were growing in the small spaces in front of many houses.

Finally they arrived at Uncle Hisashi's house, where they were warmly welcomed by Aunt

Lesson 26 193

Haruko and Kiku. Karen bowed politely. She was glad her parents had taught her some of the Japanese customs.

Karen removed her shoes as she entered the house. She looked around curiously. Instead of walls, sliding doors of rice paper divided the rooms. The floors were covered with thick straw mats called **tatami**.

Karen's cousin, Kiku, led her to a low table in the center of the next room. They knelt on floor cushions with their feet tucked under them. Karen noticed a square hole in the floor beneath the table. She asked, "Do you keep something under there?"

Uncle Hisashi explained, "That is a **kotatsu**. We keep hot coals in it during cool weather.

These Japanese are enjoying tea. The low table, the tatami mats, and the floor cushions are traditional. Also notice the sliding doors on the left. The electric heater is a modern addition.

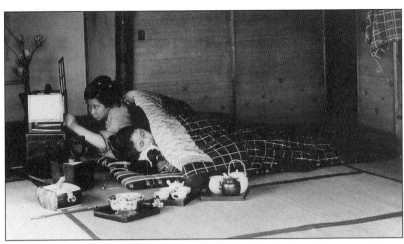

Traditional Japanese beds are padded mats placed on the floor. They are easily put away for the day so that the room can be used for other activities.

The coals help keep our feet warm while we are eating."

"Is that the only heat you use?" Karen asked.

"No, sometimes we use a **hibachi**, a small charcoal burner that we can move to any room in the house. And during the coldest months, we also use a gas heater. We don't have a furnace to heat the whole house."

The families thanked God for the meal. Then Kiku's mother placed a tray with small bowls of food in front of Karen. Karen was glad she had practiced eating with chopsticks at home. She held a bowl of rice in her left hand and began to eat.

"The rice and vegetables are delicious," Karen said. "But what is this?" she asked, pointing to a small bowl on her tray.

Aunt Haruko answered, "That is **miso soup**. It is made of soybean paste with vegetables and seaweed."

Mother laughed to see Karen's startled look. "Taste it," she urged. "It's good."

Karen observed the tidy room as she and Kiku sat sipping green tea from cups without handles. "They don't have many things in here," she thought. There was a nook in one wall where a scroll with a lovely painting and some Japanese writing was hung. A small stand beneath the scroll held a bamboo vase with a flowering branch. That was all that was in the room except the table and the floor cushions on which they sat.

When they rose from the table, Karen said politely, "*Goh-chee-soh sah-mah*" ("Thank you very much for the delicious meal").

Kiku looked surprised and pleased. "I didn't know you could speak Japanese."

"Father and Mother often use Japanese at home, so I have learned to speak some," Karen replied. "But I can't read or write any Japanese."

"I study English in school," said Kiku, "but since we don't use it much otherwise, it is hard for me to speak English very well."

"You must need to study a lot," Karen remarked. "I haven't learned any foreign language in school."

Karen's mother smiled. "Maybe Kiku will encourage you to do better with your school work. Students here in Japan need to study hard to keep up with their lessons."

"I'm sure your visit here will be good for both girls," said Aunt Haruko. "Kiku can practice speaking English, and Karen can practice speaking Japanese."

Karen followed Kiku into another room. "You will sleep in here with me," said Kiku.

Karen noticed that this room also contained very little furniture. "Where are our beds?" she asked.

Tea

Tea has been a favorite drink in Japan for hundreds of years. The Japanese often serve tea to their guests. They enjoy sipping the tea slowly while they visit. Sometimes they have special tea ceremonies.

The tea used in Japan is green tea, not reddish brown like the instant teas served in America. It is raised in the southern part of the Honshu island. Workers pick the leaves of the tea plants by hand. Then the leaves are steamed, rolled, dried, and sent to stores.

196   Unit 3, Chapter 6 Japan, Land of the Rising Sun

Kimonos are long, colorful robes traditionally worn by Japanese women. Most Japanese women today wear modern clothing.

"Right here," Kiku said with a laugh, opening a closet. "Some Japanese have beds like you have in America. But most of us still sleep on the floor. We put these padded mats down on the tatami, and then spread sheets and quilts on the pads. In the morning we put the bedding back into the closet. It isn't time for bed though. I want to give you a gift first."

Kiku put the bedding away and opened a nearby drawer. She pulled out a long, soft robe and held it out for Karen to see.

"A *kimono*!" exclaimed Karen. "Oh, thank you—it's lovely! I've never had a kimono of my own."

"I usually wear dresses like yours," Kiku said, "but sometimes I wear kimonos at home in the evenings. Maybe we can wear them some evening while you are here."

Lesson 26 Answers

Testing Your Understanding

A. 1. false
   2. true
   3. true
   4. true
   5. false
   6. true

—————— **Testing Your Understanding** ——————

A. *Write* true *or* false.

1. The islands of Japan lie off the coast of Africa.
2. Japan is in the Northern Temperate Zone and has four seasons.
3. Japan has four large islands and more than 3,500 small islands.
4. Small wooden houses are built close together in Japanese villages.
5. Aunt Haruko thought bowing was a strange American custom.
6. Karen removed her shoes before walking on the tatami.

7. At mealtime, the families sat on floor cushions and ate with chopsticks.

8. *Miso soup* is the Japanese term for noodle soup.

9. Students in Japan need to study hard to keep up with their school lessons.

10. The people of Japan have many pieces of furniture in their houses.

11. Many people in Japan sleep on bedding laid on the floor.

12. Children in Japan wear kimonos most of the time.

B. *Answer these questions.*

1. How far do the islands of Japan stretch from northeast to southwest?

2. What did Karen see growing in the small spaces in front of many houses?

3. What divided the rooms in Uncle Hisashi's house?

4. What three kinds of heaters did Uncle Hisashi's family use to warm their house?

5. What drink did Aunt Haruko serve?

Further Study

1. List the things Karen saw in the room where they ate.

2. The people of Japan are very polite. List several ways that Karen showed politeness to her uncle's family.

Map Exercises

1. Trace Map E in the map section.

2. Label the four large islands of Japan: Honshu, Hokkaido, Shikoku, and Kyushu.

---

7. true
8. false
9. true
10. false
11. true
12. false

B. 1. about 1,200 miles
2. short rows of vegetables
3. sliding doors of rice paper
4. a kotatsu, a hibachi, and a gas heater
5. (green) tea

Further Study

1. a nook in one wall; a scroll with a lovely painting and some Japanese writing; a small stand; a bamboo vase with a flowering branch; floor cushions; and a low table with trays, cups, and bowls of food; also, tatamis, sliding rice paper doors, and a kotatsu

2. (Sample answers)
   —She bowed when she met Aunt Haruko and Kiku.
   —She removed her shoes before entering the house.
   —She used chopsticks.
   —She said that the rice and vegetables were delicious.
   —She said "thank you" for the food and for the kimono.

Map Exercises

(Individual work. Check maps for accuracy and neatness.)

198   Unit 3, Chapter 6 Japan, Land of the Rising Sun

27. A Farm Village on Shikoku

Glossary Words

mandarin orange (MAN duh rihn) A small orange similar to a tangerine.

terrace (TAIR ihs) A level surface cut into the side of a hill, usually for raising crops.

Rice Paddies

The sun was just rising over the mountains that surrounded the village when Kiku and Karen got up the next morning. After a breakfast of rice, eggs, and miso soup, Aunt Haruko suggested that they pack a lunch and go for a hike up the mountains. Karen's father had gone along with Uncle

Small rice terraces on mountain slopes provide food for thousands of Japanese.

Hisashi to do carpenter work in a nearby town. Like many other farmers in Japan, Uncle Hisashi worked at another job when he was not busy with his crops.

Soon the girls and their mothers were walking through the farmland near the village. The land was divided into small fields. Between the fields were low dikes that held water in the fields when the rice was flooded. Small rice plants were already growing in a few of the fields.

"This is one of our rice paddies," Kiku said. She pointed to a piece of flooded land filled with neat rows of plants. "We set out the plants in the fields last week."

"It is smaller than most fields in America," commented Karen. "The paddies and farms that I saw yesterday were small too."

LESSON AIM

To give the students a glimpse of the farms of Japan and to show how differences in climate on the islands help determine what crops are raised.

MAIN POINTS

- **Farms and rice paddies in Japan are much smaller than those in North America.** [The average farm has only about 2½ acres.] Mountain terraces provide some additional rice paddies, but much of the land is too steep to farm. Forests cover about two-thirds of Japan.

- **Many Japanese farmers use modern machines for plowing, planting, and harvesting.**

- **Most Japanese follow the Shinto and Buddhist religions.**

- **The climate of each island helps determine**

which crops are raised. Rice is raised on all the main islands.

—Hokkaido is the coldest Japanese island. It is known for its cool-weather crops and its cattle.

—Honshu has cold winters in the north, but the southern coast is warmed by the Japan Current. Rice, fruits, and vegetables are grown there. Cities have taken over much of the good farmland.

—Shikoku and Kyushu are warmed by the Japan Current. In the warmest areas, two crops of rice can be grown each year. Mandarin oranges and other citrus fruits are also grown on these islands.

RELATED POINTS

- The farms on Hokkaido are larger than on the other islands because fewer people live there. The average farm on Hokkaido has about 25 acres.

"Most farms and rice paddies in Japan are small," Karen's mother explained. "Years ago when all the work was done by hand, they were even smaller. Now some paddies have been made larger so that farmers can use machines to do the plowing, transplanting, and harvesting."

As they neared the mountains surrounding the valley, Karen noticed that the rice paddies continued partway up the slopes. They were still level fields with dikes. But each paddy was up a little higher than the one below it.

"These fields look like giant steps," Karen commented. "Were they cut into the mountains?"

"Yes, these *terraces* were made to provide more level land for rice paddies," explained Aunt Haruko. "Paddies must be level so that they can be flooded. Orchards and fields that do not need to be flooded are planted on sloping fields. But much of Japan is too steep for any kind of farming. Forests cover about two-thirds of Japan."

Temples and Religions

The well-worn road narrowed to a winding, steep trail as the

Large rice paddies can be prepared and planted with machinery. Here the soil is being prepared with a rototiller.

This machine sets the young rice plants in the tilled and flooded paddy.

Small combines harvest several rows of rice in one pass.

hikers entered the forests above the fields. They stopped for a few minutes to admire a small waterfall. Then they climbed on until they reached a clearing near the top. From there they could see the villages and farms below.

"Is that a temple down there?" Karen asked, pointing toward a building in a nearby valley.

"Yes," Aunt Haruko answered. "There are many temples here in Japan. Very few Japanese are Christians. Most of them follow the Shinto (SHIHN toh) and Buddhist (BOO dihst) religions. These religions teach people to respect their elders and to be kind to others. But they do not teach that the Bible is God's Word or that Jesus died for our sins. We Christians try to help our neighbors find the true way to God, but it is hard for them to change from their ancient beliefs."

The girls and their mothers enjoyed a picnic lunch of ham and egg salad sandwiches, cucumber slices, tangerines, and cold tea. On their way back to the village, they stopped to chat with friends of Kiku and Aunt Haruko. Karen spoke politely to each one as she was introduced.

Mulberry Leaves and Silkworms

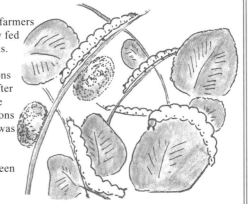

In the early 1900s, Japanese farmers grew many mulberry trees. They fed the mulberry leaves to silkworms. The silkworms grew until they were large enough to spin cocoons of silk thread for themselves. After the cocoons were completed, the worms were killed and the cocoons were unwound. The silk thread was used to make fine cloth.

Some silk is still produced in Japan, but today most silk has been replaced by manmade fibers.

Hokkaido is the northernmost large Japanese island. The winters on Hokkaido are cold and snowy, like northern United States. Notice the low clouds in front of the mountains.

"*Koh-nee-chee-wah*" ("Good afternoon") she said. "*Karen-toh moh-shee mah-soo*" ("My name is Karen").

Climates and Crops

That evening during supper, Kiku asked, "Does the United States have the same kind of weather that we have here in Japan?"

"That depends on which part of the United States you mean," answered Karen's father. "We live in Pennsylvania, which has cold winters and warm summers. States farther north have even colder winters. States in the south have very mild winters."

"Japan's climate varies too," Uncle Hisashi commented. "Hokkaido is the coldest of the four large islands. Its climate is like that of the state of Maine. Cold water currents flow by its coasts, and heavy snows fall during its long winters.

"The climate of Honshu is more like the climate in North Carolina, Virginia, or Pennsylvania.

Winters in northern Honshu are snowy and cold but not as long as on Hokkaido. Southern Honshu is warmed by the Japan Current, an ocean current that flows up from the south.

"The Shikoku and Kyushu islands have about the same climate as Georgia and Florida. The Japan Current helps keep these islands warm most of the year. They have mild, short winters and long, rainy summers."

"Is rice raised on all the large islands of Japan?" asked Karen.

"Yes, rice is our main crop. By tradition, rice is the most

These workers are harvesting Chinese cabbages on Honshu.

important food of Japan. But other crops have also become important in recent years."

"How do farmers decide what to raise on each island?" Kiku asked.

"The climate helps them decide," Uncle Hisashi answered. "Potatoes, sugar beets, and other cool-weather crops grow well on Hokkaido. Special kinds of rice that grow in cool weather are raised there. Hokkaido is also a good cattle and dairy region.

"Rice is the main crop on Honshu. Many fruits and vegetables are also grown, especially on farms near the cities. The cities of Honshu have taken over much of the good farmland. But crops are still raised on mountain terraces, in small valleys, on the edges of cities, and in the north where fewer people live.

"Kyushu and Shikoku have long growing seasons. In the warmest areas of these islands, it is possible to raise two crops of rice each year. Sometimes wheat or barley is raised between rice crops. ***Mandarin oranges*** and other citrus fruits grow well in the warm climate along the Pacific coast."

"I wish I could see more of Japan sometime," Kiku said. "I have been to many places here on Shikoku, but I have never been off this island."

"How would you like to travel to Honshu next week?" asked Uncle Hisashi, with a twinkle in his eyes.

"Next week!" exclaimed Kiku.

"Yes, next week. Mother and I have been wanting to show you more of Japan for some time. We have planned to take Karen and her parents to Tokyo (TOH kee oh), and from there they will fly back to America. We will cross the Inland Sea by boat. Then we can ride by train to Tokyo."

Testing Your Understanding

A. *Write the correct word(s) to complete each sentence. You will not use all the words.*

cattle	Hokkaido	Japan
cities	Honshu	rice
dikes	Kyushu	Shikoku
farmers	large	small
forests	machines	terraces

1. Many Japanese —— work at another job when they are not busy with their crops.

2. Low —— between the rice paddies hold in water.

3. Farms and rice paddies in Japan are usually ——.

4. Level steps called —— have been cut into some mountains to provide more land for growing rice.

5. Many Japanese farmers use —— for plowing, planting, and harvesting.

6. About two-thirds of Japan is covered with ——.

7. Japanese farmers raise —— on all the large islands.

8. —— is the coldest of the main Japanese islands. Special kinds of rice, cool-weather crops, and —— are raised there.

Lesson 27 Answers

Testing Your Understanding

A. 1. farmers
   2. dikes
   3. small
   4. terraces
   5. machines
   6. forests
   7. rice
   8. Hokkaido, cattle

9. —— is the largest island of Japan. Much of its good farmland has been taken over by ——.

10. —— and —— have long growing seasons. The —— Current helps keep them warm enough for growing citrus fruit.

B. *Answer these questions.*

1. Why have some of the rice paddies been made larger?
2. Why must rice be planted on level land rather than sloping land?
3. Which religions are followed by most of the Japanese?
4. What part of Honshu is the coldest?
5. What part of Honshu is warmed by an ocean current?

Further Study

1. Which Japanese island has a climate most like the climate where you live?
2. Why do Japanese farmers need to raise crops wherever they can?

Map Exercises

Use a map of Japan to answer these questions.

1. Which large Japanese island is farthest north?
2. Which large Japanese island lies in the southwest?
3. Which Japanese island is the largest?
4. Which large Japanese island lies between Honshu and Kyushu?

9. Honshu, cities
10. Kyushu, Shikoku, Japan

B. 1. so that farmers can use machines for plowing, planting, and harvesting
2. Paddies must be level so that they can be flooded with water.
3. the Shinto and Buddhist religions
4. the northern part
5. the southern part

Further Study

1. (Answer depends on your location. Use this opportunity to compare your climate with the climates of the four large Japanese islands.)
2. Much of Japan is covered with mountains and forests. Cities have taken over much of the good farmland.

Map Exercises

1. Hokkaido
2. Kyushu
3. Honshu
4. Shikoku

28. On the Inland Sea

Glossary Words

ferry

ferry (FEHR ee) A boat that makes regular trips to carry passengers and goods across a certain body of water.

raw materials Natural products such as iron ore or crude oil that are used to make finished products.

tsunami (tsoo NAH mee) A huge ocean wave caused by an earthquake or a volcano under the sea.

typhoon (ty FOON) A hurricane that occurs off the southeastern coast of Asia.

The Seas Around Japan

Karen and Kiku looked out over the Inland Sea as their ship left the dock. The families had taken an early morning train to Takamatsu (tah KAH mah tsoo), a city on the northeast coast of Shikoku. Now they were crossing the Inland Sea on a *ferry*. They were heading toward Kobe (KOH bee), a city on the large island of Honshu.

"Is traveling by boat or airplane the only way to get from one island to another?" asked Karen.

"It used to be," her father replied. "Now bridges and tunnels have been built between Honshu and the three other large islands. We decided to travel by ferry so that you could learn more about the seas around Japan."

Karen's father pulled out a map and unfolded it. "Notice the large bodies of water that surround the islands of Japan. We are here on the Inland Sea, which lies between Honshu, Shikoku, and Kyushu.

"Japan is separated from the mainland of Asia by three other seas: the East China Sea, the Sea of Japan, and the Sea of Okhotsk (oh KOTSK). East of Japan lies the huge Pacific Ocean."

LESSON AIM

To introduce the seas around Japan and the storms that threaten the coastline and to show the importance of fish, ports, and trade in Japan.

MAIN POINTS

- **The Japanese islands are surrounded by several seas.** The East China Sea, the Sea of Japan, and the Sea of Okhotsk lie between Japan and the mainland of Asia. The Pacific Ocean is east of Japan. The Inland Sea separates Honshu from Shikoku and Kyushu.

- **The Japanese fish in the seas around Japan and in other fishing areas around the world.** They also buy fish from other countries.

- **Typhoons and tsunamis cause destruction along the coasts of Japan.** [Tsunamis are also called tidal waves, though they have nothing to do with ocean tides.]

- **Much of Japan's coastline is crowded.** [This is especially true around the Inland Sea and near Tokyo.] New land has been gained by draining swamps, building dikes, and building small islands.

- **Japan is one of the major trading nations.** Raw materials and food are imported. Cars, electrical equipment, and other quality products are exported. Japan is a world leader in shipbuilding.

RELATED POINTS

- The seas around Japan have helped protect the Japanese from enemy nations. Only once have the Japanese been conquered by another nation. They surrendered at the close of World War II after the United States dropped atomic bombs on Hiroshima and Nagasaki.

206   Unit 3, Chapter 6 Japan, Land of the Rising Sun

Many ships and boats sail across the beautiful Inland Sea.

"Are those trees growing out of the water over there?" Karen asked.

Her father chuckled. "No, that is a small island just large enough for a few pine trees. God has placed hundreds of islands in this Inland Sea. Some are very small like that one. Others are several miles long."

Japanese Fishermen

Just then Uncle Hisashi joined the group. "What have you girls been learning?" he asked.

"Well, I know we are sailing across the Inland Sea between the islands of Shikoku and Honshu," Kiku replied.

"Good," replied Uncle Hisashi. "Do you know how the Japanese use the Inland Sea?"

"We haven't learned much about that," Karen admitted. "Do they fish here? I saw some fishing boats at the dock."

"Yes, that is one way this sea is used. Men have fished here for hundreds of years, and fish is still one of our favorite foods. Our country uses millions of tons of fish every year."

Japan's fishing industry uses many boats. At this fishing port the fishermen sell their catch, and work on their nets and other equipment.

"Do all those fish come from this sea?" Karen questioned.

"Oh, no; fish are caught in all the seas around Japan. Even all these seas together no longer supply enough fish for our country. Large Japanese fishing ships travel to fishing areas in many parts of the world. And some fish are bought from fishermen of other countries."

Typhoons and Tsunamis

As Uncle Hisashi spoke, the sky darkened and the wind began to blow. The ship rolled from side to side. "Let's go inside the cabin," Uncle Hisashi suggested.

Karen and Kiku watched out the windows as large raindrops began to fall. Soon the rain was pouring down. "I hope this isn't a *typhoon*," Kiku said.

"I don't think it is," Uncle Hisashi replied. "Typhoons do not often strike this early in the summer. This is likely just a heavy summer rain. Even if it were a typhoon, it would not hit as hard in this protected Inland

Sea as it would along the Pacific coast."

"What is a typhoon?" asked Karen.

"Typhoons are storms just like the hurricanes that strike the eastern coast of the United States. A typhoon has very strong winds that whirl around in a large circle perhaps 150 miles across. The whirling winds blow at speeds more than 75 miles per hour, and they do much damage. The winds also cause high waves that beat against the shores. Heavy rains fall and flood lowlands."

"I wouldn't want to be on the ocean when a typhoon hit," Karen decided.

"Typhoons have sunk many boats," agreed her father. "How-ever, a **tsunami** can be even worse."

"Is that something like a typhoon?"

"No, a tsunami is a huge wave caused by an earthquake or a volcano under the ocean. The sudden movement of the ocean floor makes waves like the waves made by throwing a rock into a pond. The waves race across the ocean until they reach land. There they pile up into walls of water as high as 50 feet or more."

The rain was still falling heavily, so Uncle Hisashi suggested that they eat lunch and tour the inside of the ship. A few hours later when they returned to the deck, the sun was shining again.

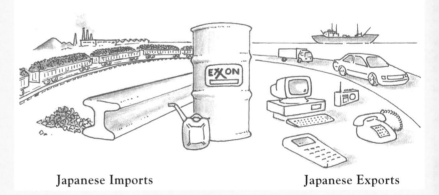

Japanese Imports   Japanese Exports

These cars are ready for exporting. Japan is a world leader in automobile exporting.

Imports and Exports

"Kobe, straight ahead," announced Uncle Hisashi. The city could easily be seen now. It was crowded between the sea and the mountains that rose behind it. Skyscrapers, great factories, huge oil tanks, and busy docks lined the coast in both directions as far as the girls could see. Rows of large ships were being loaded or unloaded. Other ships were sailing in toward the docks, bringing imports from foreign countries, and still others were leaving with loads of Japanese goods.

"The coast is crowded with buildings!" exclaimed Kiku.

"Yes," agreed Uncle Hisashi, "the shoreline has changed considerably since the first men settled these islands. First the level plains were built up. As the land became too crowded, new land was gained by draining swamps and building dikes to hold the water out. In recent years, large factories have been built on manmade islands near the shore. This port of Kobe was made larger by building an island off the coast and connecting it to the mainland with a bridge."

"Look, they're building new ships over there!" Karen observed.

"Japan is a world leader in shipbuilding," Uncle Hisashi replied. "The Japanese need more merchant ships and fishing boats than most other countries. They also make ships to sell to other countries."

"What do all those ships carry?" asked Kiku.

"Many kinds of products," answered Uncle Hisashi. "Japan is one of the major trading countries in the world. Our country needs to import some of its food, since we have so little farmland. Iron ore and coal are imported and used to make steel. Oil from other countries helps keep electric power plants, cars, trucks, and other machines running.

"The ships leaving Japan carry manufactured goods such as cars, trucks, electrical equipment, and steel products. We sell these exports to other countries. That gives us money to buy the *raw materials* and food we need to import."

Lesson 28 Answers

Testing Your Understanding

A. 1. Inland Sea
  2. east
  3. is not
  4. fish
  5. typhoon
  6. tsunami
  7. crowded
  8. shipbuilding
  9. imports
 10. exports

Testing Your Understanding

A. *Write the correct word(s) to complete each sentence.*

1. The (Sea of Japan, Inland Sea) lies between three large Japanese islands.

2. The Pacific Ocean lies (east, west) of Japan.

3. Traveling by boat (is, is not) the only way to get from one large Japanese island to another.

4. The people of Japan eat millions of tons of (beef, fish) every year.

5. A (typhoon, tsunami) is a severe storm.

6. A (typhoon, tsunami) is a huge wave.

7. Much of the coast of Japan is very (crowded, dry).

8. Japan is a world leader in (farming, shipbuilding).

9. Japan (imports, exports) food, iron ore, coal, and oil.

10. Japan (imports, exports) manufactured goods.

B. *Answer these questions.*

1. What three seas lie between Japan and the mainland of Asia?
2. Where do the people of Japan get the fish they need?
3. What causes a tsunami?
4. How has new land been gained around the coasts of Japan?
5. How do the people of Japan pay for the food and raw materials they need to buy from other countries?

Further Study

1. Name at least three ways to travel from one large Japanese island to another.
2. Why does Japan need more ships than most other countries do?

Map Exercises

1. On your map of Japan, label the Inland Sea, the East China Sea, the Sea of Japan, the Sea of Okhotsk, and the Pacific Ocean.
2. Label Matsuyama, Takamatsu, Kobe, and Tokyo.

B. 1. the East China Sea, the Sea of Japan, and the Sea of Okhotsk
2. from the seas around Japan, from fishing areas around the world, and from other countries (The Japanese also raise fish in ponds and fish hatcheries.)
3. an underwater earthquake or volcano
4. by draining swamps, building dikes, and building islands
5. by selling manufactured goods to other countries

Further Study
1. by ferry, by airplane, across bridges, through tunnels
2. Japan needs many ships to carry imports and exports, and many fishing boats to supply fish.

Map Exercises
(Individual work. Check maps for accuracy and neatness.)

29. A Train Ride to Tokyo

Glossary Words

bullet train One of the high-speed trains that carry passengers between large Japanese cities.

pulp Moist, ground-up wood that is used to make paper.

tremor (TREHM ur) A slight shaking of the earth; a small earthquake.

A Ride on the Bullet Train

The *bullet train* was nearly full. Kiku, Karen, and their parents were glad to find empty seats where they could sit together. Exactly on time, the train began moving. Soon they were speeding toward the city of Osaka (oh SAH kuh). Outside, mountains rose to their left and

Japan's bullet trains speed passengers from one large city to the next.

the Inland Sea lay to their right. Before long, they left the sea behind.

"This is the first time I've ridden on a bullet train," Kiku told her cousin. "But I've often traveled on the local trains near our village."

"A lot of Japanese must ride on trains," Karen observed. "Are they always this full?"

"Trains are often very busy," replied her father. "These bullet trains are popular because they travel quickly from one city to another. Even the regular trains are used much more than trains in the United States. Japan's highways are crowded, and the price of gasoline is high. The people of Japan often find it better to travel by trains or buses than by cars."

LESSON AIM

To give a glimpse of Japan's bullet trains, the Japanese Alps, and the large Japanese cities.

MAIN POINTS

- **Japan's trains are a fast, popular way to travel.** [Bullet trains run between the main cities. Slower trains connect the other parts of the country.] Bullet trains travel about 125 miles per hour.

- **Some of the large Japanese cities have grown together to make huge city areas.** [Each city that grows in this way becomes a mother city, or metropolis. Eventually the whole region becomes a metropolitan area.]

- **The highest mountain range in Japan is the Japanese Alps.** Japan's mountains limit the amount of farmland, but the mountain forests provide lumber and

paper pulp, and dams along the swift mountain rivers produce electricity.

- **Mount Fuji is the highest and most famous Japanese mountain.**

- **Japan is located along the Ring of Fire.** More than forty of Japan's volcanoes are considered active, and many earthquakes strike the islands.

  [You may want to research the strong earthquake that struck Kobe on January 24, 1995. The earthquake rated 7.2 on the Richter scale and lasted 20 seconds. It destroyed many structures thought to be earthquake proof, killed or injured thousands of people, and ruined over 46,000 buildings. One-fifth of the city's population was temporarily homeless and nearly a million households had no water.]

- **Tokyo is the capital of Japan and one of the largest cities in the world.** About one-fourth of the

Japan's crowded highways and high gasoline prices discourage traveling by car. Many people use trains instead.

"Will we ride on a bullet train all the way to Tokyo?" asked Kiku.

"We could," answered Uncle Hisashi, "but we plan to take a regular train from Kyoto (kee OH toh). That train will take us through the Japanese Alps, the highest mountain range in Japan. Bullet trains travel along the Pacific coast."

After a short stop at the Osaka station, the travelers were on their way again toward the city of Kyoto. The bullet train seemed to fly as it sped along about 125 miles an hour.

"This all looks like one big city," Karen said. "I can't tell where one city stops and the next one starts."

"These cities have grown so much that they have become like one big city," explained her father. "That is one reason we plan to travel through the Japanese Alps—we want to see more of the natural beauty of God's handiwork."

Japanese live in Tokyo and the surrounding cities. Most of the large Japanese cities are located in a line between Tokyo and the northern part of the Kyushu island.

RELATED POINTS

- A few comparisons will help to show how crowded Japan is.

    —Japan has about half as many people as the United States, but the United States has about twenty-five times as much land. Japan is about the size of Montana.

    —Since two-thirds of Japan is covered with forests, Japan's farms and cities cover less area than the state of New York.

    —As many people live in Tokyo and the surrounding cities as in the entire state of California.

214   Unit 3, Chapter 6 Japan, Land of the Rising Sun

The train soon arrived at Kyoto, where the travelers spent the night with friends of Uncle Hisashi. The next day they visited a palace and a castle that had been built while Kyoto was the capital of Japan.

Mountains of Japan

The following morning the families took a slower, regular train to the Japanese Alps. For a while the train traveled along Lake Biwa (BEE wah), Japan's largest lake. Gradually it left the busy city area and began winding through the mountains. A few rice paddies could be seen in the narrow valleys and on some terraces, but huge forests covered most of the mountains.

"These mountains are certainly a change from the crowded cities," Karen's mother observed.

"Japan must have a lot of mountains," Kiku stated. "There are mountains around our village, mountains near Kobe and Kyoto, and even higher mountains here."

"That's correct," Uncle Hisashi answered. "Mountains cover nearly all of Japan. That is why most people are crowded into large cities along the coast. The mountains also make farming difficult. Yet our country has learned to use its mountains. The mountain forests provide lumber for building and *pulp* to make paper. Dams have been built on many of the swift mountain rivers. Generators at these dams provide some of the electricity we use."

Late that afternoon, Kiku suddenly exclaimed, "Look, there's Mount Fuji (FOO jee)!"

"Oh, how beautiful!" Karen marveled. "Is Mount Fuji really the highest mountain in Japan?"

"Yes," replied Uncle Hisashi. "And Mount Fuji is also the most famous mountain in Japan, partly because of its lovely shape. It is a volcano, but it has not erupted since 1708."

"Have any volcanoes erupted in Japan recently?" Karen asked.

"Yes; Japan has more than forty volcanoes that are still considered active. Japan is located along the Ring of Fire that circles the Pacific Ocean. The Ring of Fire has many volcanoes and earthquakes. Japan has many small earthquake *tremors* every year. Once in a while there are large earthquakes that cause much damage."

Tokyo, Capital of Japan

"We must be getting close to Tokyo," Karen observed soon after they had passed Mount Fuji. The train was passing more houses and buildings again.

"Tokyo is still about 30 miles

Mount Fuji rises majestically behind a speeding bullet train and a rice field.

216   Unit 3, Chapter 6 Japan, Land of the Rising Sun

away," replied her father, "but all this area surrounding Tokyo is thickly settled. Tokyo became the capital of Japan more than one hundred years ago. Since then it has grown to become one of the largest cities in the world. As Tokyo became more crowded, many people who worked there moved to nearby cities and rode to work each day on trains. Now Tokyo and a large area around it is like one giant city."

Karen's father pulled out his map again. "Notice where the major cities of Japan are located. Tokyo is here near the center of the Japanese archipelago. About one-fourth of all the Japanese live in Tokyo or the cities around it. Most of the large Japanese cities are in a line between Tokyo and the northern part of the Kyushu island."

Late that evening the travelers arrived at the Tokyo station. They spent the next day touring the city. Then it was time for Karen and her parents to board a plane for their flight back to the United States.

As they parted, the two

Tokyo is one of the largest cities in the world.

families bowed to each other. "Come again," Kiku said to Karen.

"I'd like to," Karen replied. "Good-bye, and God bless you."

―――――――――― **Testing Your Understanding** ――――――――――

A. *Write* true *or* false *for each sentence. Copy each false sentence, and change one word in it to make it true.*

1. The people of Japan often travel by train.
2. Japan's regular trains travel about 125 miles per hour.
3. Kyoto was once the capital of Japan.
4. Lake Osaka is the largest lake in Japan.
5. Deserts cover nearly all of Japan.
6. Most of the people of Japan are crowded into large cities along the coast.
7. The highest mountain range in Japan is the Kyushu Alps.
8. Mount Fuji is the highest and most famous mountain in Japan.
9. Japan is located along the Ring of Fire.
10. Japan has few earthquakes and active volcanoes.
11. Kobe is the capital of Japan.
12. About one-tenth of the people of Japan live in Tokyo and the nearby cities.

B. *Write the correct word(s) to complete each sentence.*

1. The people of Japan often ride in trains instead of cars because the price of ――― is high and the ――― are crowded.
2. The forests of Japan provide ――― and ―――.
3. Some of Japan's electricity is generated at ――― that have been built on the rivers.
4. A ――― is a small earthquake.
5. Many ――― in Japan have become so large that they have grown together.

Lesson 29 Answers

Testing Your Understanding

A. 1. true
   2. false; Japan's ~~regular~~ bullet trains travel about 125 miles per hour.
   3. true
   4. false; Lake ~~Osaka~~ Biwa is the largest lake in Japan.
   5. false; ~~Deserts~~ Mountains (*or* Forests) cover nearly all of Japan.
   6. true
   7. false The highest mountain range in Japan is the ~~Kyushu~~ Japanese Alps.
   8. true
   9. true
  10. false; Japan has ~~few~~ many earthquakes and active volcanoes.
  11. false; ~~Kobe~~ Tokyo is the capital of Japan.
  12. false; About ~~one-tenth~~ one-fourth of the people of Japan live in Tokyo and the nearby cities.

B. 1. gasoline, highways
   2. lumber, pulp
   3. dams
   4. tremor
   5. cities

218   Unit 3, Chapter 6 Japan, Land of the Rising Sun

6. Tokyo
7. Tokyo, Kyushu

Further Study

1. the Philippines
2. Because of the many mountains in Japan, cities were built on the lowlands along the coast.
3. (Discuss facts in class.)
   a. (Figures will vary according to the date and source. If the whole metropolitan area is included, the figure is much higher.)
   b. Edo
   c. (Sample answers) Imperial Palace, National Diet Building, Tokyo Tower, Tokyo Railroad Station

Map Exercises

(Individual work. Check maps for accuracy and neatness.)

6. ——— is one of the largest cities in the world.
7. Most of the large cities in Japan are in a line between ——— and the northern part of ———.

Further Study

1. Which other country have you studied this year that is located along the Ring of Fire?
2. Why are most of the people in Japan crowded into large cities along the coasts?
3. Use an encyclopedia to find interesting facts about Tokyo. Here are a few questions to consider. Then try to find additional facts.
   a. How many people live in Tokyo?
   b. What was Tokyo called before it became the capital of Japan?
   c. What are some famous buildings in Tokyo?

Map Exercises

1. On your map of Japan, label the Japanese Alps, Lake Biwa, and Mount Fuji.
2. The map in this lesson shows where the largest cities of Japan are located. Add these cities to your map: Yokohama, Osaka, Nagoya, Kyoto, Sapporo, Hiroshima, and Kitakyushu.

30. Chapter 6 Review

============ Testing Your Understanding ============

A. *Write a glossary word for each definition.*

1. Straw floor mats.
2. A fast Japanese train.
3. A level surface cut into the side of a mountain.
4. A severe tropical storm.
5. A large group of islands.
6. A small earthquake.
7. A huge ocean wave.
8. A traditional Japanese robe.
9. Natural products that are used to make finished goods.

B. *Write the correct word(s) to complete each sentence.*

1. Japan includes ———— large islands and over ———— small islands.
2. Sliding doors made of ———— divide the rooms in traditional Japanese houses.
3. The people of Japan remove their ———— before entering a house.
4. Many Japanese farmers use ———— for plowing, planting, and harvesting.
5. Most Japanese follow the ———— and ———— religions.
6. ———— is the largest island of Japan.
7. ———— is the coldest large Japanese island.
8. Shikoku and Kyushu are warmed by the ———— Current.
9. ———— is raised on all the large islands of Japan.
10. Japan (imports, exports) raw materials and (imports, exports) manufactured goods.
11. Many of the large ———— of Japan are crowded together.
12. ———— is the capital of Japan. It is also one of the largest cities

Lesson 30 Answers

Testing Your Understanding

A. 1. tatami
2. bullet train
3. terrace
4. typhoon
5. archipelago
6. tremor
7. tsunami
8. kimono
9. raw materials

B. 1. four, 3,500
2. rice paper
3. shoes
4. machines
5. Shinto, Buddhist
6. Honshu
7. Hokkaido
8. Japan
9. Rice
10. imports, exports
11. cities
12. Tokyo, world

C. *Answer these questions.*

1. In which climate zone is Japan?
2. (*a*) How are traditional Japanese tables different from most American tables? (*b*) How are traditional Japanese beds different from American beds?
3. What helps the farmers on each island decide which crops to raise?
4. Where do the people of Japan get the fish they need?
5. Why are most of the people in Japan crowded into large cities along the coast?
6. How do the people of Japan use their mountains and forests?
7. Between what two places are most of the large Japanese cities located?

Map Exercises

Use your completed map of Japan to answer these questions.

1. What are the names of the four large Japanese islands?
2. What two seas lie between Japan and the mainland of Asia?
3. What sea lies between three of the large Japanese islands?
4. What ocean lies east of Japan?
5. What is the highest mountain in Japan?
6. Which of the large cities that you labeled is very close to Tokyo?

Review Study

1. Do you know the meaning of all the glossary words in Chapter 6?
2. Can you find Japan on a world map or a globe?
3. Do you know how houses in Japan are heated?
4. Do you know how farms in Japan are different from farms in North America?
5. Do you know where one-fourth of the people of Japan live?

C. 1. in the Northern Temperate Zone
2. a. Traditional Japanese tables are low. People sit on floor cushions around them.
   b. Traditional Japanese beds are made on the floor with pads and sheets.
3. the climate (There are also many other factors, such as supply and demand, and tradition; but climate is the main factor mentioned in the text.)
4. from the seas around Japan, from fishing areas around the world, and from other countries
5. Most of Japan is covered with mountains.
6. The forests provide lumber and pulp, and dams built on mountain rivers generate electricity. (Other uses could be mentioned, but these are the ones taught in the text.)
7. Tokyo and northern Kyushu

Map Exercises
1. Hokkaido, Honshu, Shikoku, and Kyushu
2. the East China Sea and the Sea of Japan
3. the Inland Sea
4. the Pacific Ocean
5. Mount Fuji
6. Yokohama

Review Study
1. (Review glossary words in class.)
2. (Have students point out Japan on a globe and a world map.)
3. with a kotatsu, a hibachi, or small gas heaters (Electric heaters are also used.)
4. Farms in Japan are much smaller than farms in North America.
5. in Tokyo and the surrounding cities

Extra Activity

A Japanese Meal

Ask your teacher or parents if you can help plan a Japanese meal for your class or family. You will need chopsticks, a low table, and food.

Some large department stores sell chopsticks. If you cannot find any there, you may be able to buy them from a Japanese or Chinese restaurant.

Chopsticks are held as shown in the diagram. The lower chopstick remains still while the upper one is moved up and down to grasp the food.

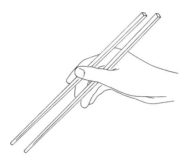

A low table can be made by placing a folded card table or a piece of plywood on blocks, buckets, or other supports. A large coffee table may also work. Sit on flat pillows or other cushions. Take your shoes off, and sit on your legs. Boys may place their knees several inches apart, but girls should keep their knees together.

For food, you may wish to serve boiled rice and pickled vegetables. Boil the rice just long enough to make it sticky so that it can be more easily eaten with chopsticks. Serve hot green tea with the meal. Remember to serve each kind of food in a separate bowl.

Extra Activity

(Do this activity together in class if possible. Since eating with chopsticks can be challenging, you may want to practice beforehand so that you can show your students how. Chopsticks make good "souvenirs" for your students after they have learned to use them.

In Japan, A simple soup would be served with rice and pickles. It would probably be made as follows:

Heat enough water to fill each soup bowl about two-thirds full. Add enough soy sauce to give it the color of weak coffee. Add several snow peas and a small amount of bean sprouts for each person. Cook together briefly; then add chopped chives or green onions, including the green tops. Bring to a boil again, and serve. Small cubes of tofu could also be added for protein.

This is not miso soup because it is made with soy sauce rather than soy paste. But this kind of soup is often served for lunch or supper. The Japanese eat the solid chunks with chopsticks, and then drink the remaining liquid from their soup bowls.)

So Far This Year

So Far This Year

1. a. Temperate Zone
   b. Frigid Zone
   c. Tropical Zone
2. fazendas
3. migrating, hibernating
4. Frigid
5. Sahara
6. delta
7. Carabaos
8. The Philippines, Japan
9. dry
10. artesian
11. aborigines
12. warm
13. an avalanche
14. Rhine
15. Switzerland, Japan
16. Terraces

1. Match the climate zones to the descriptions.
   a. A region of four seasons.   Tropical Zone
   b. A cold region around one of the poles. Temperate Zone
   c. A warm region along the equator   Frigid Zone

2. Much coffee comes from large (ranches, rain forests, fazendas) in Brazil.

3. Choose two: Some animals prepare for winter by (migrating, molting, hibernating, ruminating).

4. During summer in the (Tropical, Temperate, Frigid) Zone, the sun can be seen at midnight.

5. A great desert in northern Africa is the (Niger, Sahara, Fulani).

6. A deposit of soil at the mouth of a river is a (dam, delta, deluge).

7. (Horses, Oxen, Carabaos) are important farm animals in the Philippines.

8. Choose two: (Nigeria, The Philippines, Germany, Japan) are located along the Ring of Fire.

9. Most of Australia is (wet, dry).

10. Water flows out of an (artistic, artificial, artesian) well by its own pressure.

11. The people who first lived in Australia are known as (aborigines, abolitionists).

12. The Gulf Stream is a (warm, cold) ocean current that flows along the coasts of Europe.

13. A huge mass of swiftly sliding snow is (an avalanche, a blizzard, a glacier).

14. The (Basel, Rhine, Cologne) River is Switzerland's link to the sea.

15. Choose two: The countries of (Nigeria, Switzerland, Brazil, Japan) have few natural resources but many skilled workers.

16. (Locks, Dikes, Terraces) are level steps cut into hillsides to provide more land for farming.

Seals and penguins are two of the animals that live in cold climates. These seals and penguins are making themselves at home on South Georgia Island, north of Antarctica and east of South America's southern tip.

UNIT FOUR
Cold, High, and Dry Lands

"He giveth snow like wool: he scattereth the hoarfrost like ashes. He casteth forth his ice like morsels: who can stand before his cold? He sendeth out his word, and melteth them: he causeth his wind to blow, and the waters flow" (Psalm 147:16–18).

31. Greenland, a Danish Delight

Glossary Words

fiord (FYAWRD) A long, narrow arm of the sea running between high rocky cliffs or banks. (*Fiord* can also be spelled *fjord*.)

glacier (GLAY shur) A large mass of ice, moving slowly down a slope.

iceberg A large, floating chunk of ice that has broken away from a glacier.

ice cap A deep layer of snow and ice that covers a large area and does not melt during the summer.

The World's Largest Island

The world's largest island is Greenland. It is about the same size as the states of Alaska and Texas together.

Greenland reaches farther north than any other land. Its northernmost point, Cape Morris Jesup, is only 440 miles from the North Pole. Almost the whole island is north of the Arctic Circle, in the Northern Frigid Zone.

Notice on the map that most of the towns of Greenland are on the southern and southwestern coast.

*   *   *   *

"Did you say Greenland? What's green about it?" Ray Tarent asked his father. They were on a ship that was approaching the port of Godthåb (GAWT hawp), the capital of Greenland.

"There's not much green to be seen now. Really, there is not much green on Greenland anytime. God has covered most of this huge island with an *ice cap*, a deep, permanent layer of ice and snow. Around the south and southwest coast, the land is green with grass, bushes, and scrub trees during the short growing season."

"Then why is it called Greenland?"

"Explorers gave it that name hundreds of years ago so that it would sound appealing to settlers," replied Ray's father. "Would you like to go ashore while our ship stops here?"

LESSON AIM

To introduce students to the geography and climate of Greenland.

MAIN POINTS

- **Size and location of Greenland.** Greenland is the world's largest island. It is about the size of Alaska and Texas together. Greenland has the northernmost land in the world.

- **Most of Greenland is covered with an ice cap.** Plants grow along the southern and southwestern coast during the summer.

- **Fishing is the main industry of Greenland.** Other occupations include farming and working at weather stations, airports, and military bases.

- **Greenland belongs to the small country of Denmark.**

- **Severe weather limits winter activities.** The people spend much of their winters at home. Most harbors freeze shut, but Godthåb, the capital, has an ice-free harbor year round.

- **Most of the people of Greenland are a mixture of Eskimo and Danish descent.** Eskimos of the North still hunt for their food. Most of the people live in villages or towns.

- **Icebergs break off from glaciers and float out into the sea.**

RELATED POINTS

- Godthåb is the capital of Greenland because of its ice-free harbor. What does this mean to the people of Greenland? It means that food and other necessities can be shipped in at any time. It also means that the products of Greenland can be shipped out. In a cold land, an ice-free port is the heart of the country.

Occupations in Greenland

Father and son watched for a while as the ship took on cargo. Then Ray asked, "What is being loaded onto our ship?"

"We're loading you up with fish!" answered one of the workers on the dock. "Frozen fish, canned fish, salted and dried fish."

"People must fish a lot here," Ray commented.

"Fishing is the main industry of Greenland. More than a third of our people are employed with either catching fish or processing them for export. There are several fish-processing plants in Holsteinsborg (HUHL stynz borg) and a shrimp-processing plant in Christianshâb (KRIHS tyahns hawp)."

Ray and his father strolled along the street of Godthâb. "Where do the people get wood to build their houses if trees don't grow in Greenland?" asked Ray.

"The wood must be shipped in," answered Father. "Whole houses are prepared in Denmark and shipped here to be assembled. Denmark is the little country that Greenland belongs to. Greenland is fifty times larger than Denmark, but Denmark has one

Greenland

hundred times as many people as Greenland."

As father and son walked back toward the dock, they were joined by a Greenlander boarding the ship for a journey. Mr. Hastings was glad to introduce himself, and they continued visiting as the ship left harbor. "Are you a fisherman?" asked Ray.

"No," replied Mr. Hastings, "I am a farmer. We raise sheep along

The fishing industry employs many of Greenland's people. Notice the houses set high on the rocky shore.

the coast here. During summer the sheep can graze on grass, and we harvest hay for winter feed. Potatoes and other vegetables that like cool weather also grow well. Now the winter season is approaching, and the ice and snow will stop most of the farm work for a while."

"How else does winter affect life on Greenland?" asked Ray's father.

"Ice and snowstorms discourage traveling. People stay in their own settlements. Families save fuel by spending most of their time in one room, which they keep warmer than the rest of the house. Much of the shipping stops because most ports freeze shut over winter. But Godthåb is kept ice-free all year by warm ocean currents from the south."

The People of Greenland

Mr. Hastings pointed to a small kayak that slipped by their ship. "There is an example of the Eskimo culture of northern Greenland. The people there still live by hunting seals, polar bears, and whales. They build their winter homes of earth and stone. Their summer homes are tents. The Eskimos lived here before any people from Iceland or Denmark arrived.

"Most people in Greenland are a mixture of Eskimo and Danish descent. There are nearly 60,000 people in Greenland. Most of them live in villages or towns. The largest town is the capital that we just left, which has about 10,000 people."

"It must be hard to survive in such a cold land. Why do people live here at all?" asked Ray.

"Some important things are done in Greenland that could not be done anywhere else. We have not mentioned the weather stations, airports, and military bases that provide other jobs for Greenlanders. By studying the weather here, scientists can forecast storms on the North Atlantic Ocean. Airports provide stopping places for flights between Denmark and the western United

Sheep can be raised on the southern coast of Greenland. This hay will be used to feed the sheep during the long winter.

230   Unit 4, Chapter 7 Cold Lands, Small and Great

States or Japan. The radar station at the military base enables governments to observe what is going on in other parts of the world."

"*Icebergs*!" exclaimed Ray, pointing at several huge mounds of ice floating in the sea. "How do they freeze in such large chunks?"

"They come from the land," explained Mr. Hastings. "All but the very edge of Greenland is heaped with ice and snow, as high as two miles in some places. This ice cap gradually pushes out toward the edges of the island. Large bodies of slowly moving ice, called *glaciers*, are formed as the ice pushes down toward the sea. Chunks of ice break off where the glaciers meet the water in the *fiords*. These huge chunks float out into the sea as icebergs."

Jakobshavn is one of the largest towns in Greenland, with 3,500 inhabitants. Near this town is the world's most productive glacier, which discharges an iceberg into the fiord every five minutes.

"The fiords we passed looked like beautiful places to explore," remarked Ray.

"They are beautiful. The channels are lined with rugged cliffs. With the sea reaching far into the land like that, Greenland has a long coastline."

Testing Your Understanding

A. *Write the correct word(s) to complete each sentence.*

1. Greenland is the largest ——— in the world.
2. Cape ——— is the northernmost point of land in the world.
3. Most of Greenland is north of the ———, which is the boundary of the Northern Frigid Zone.
4. The layer of snow and ice that covers Greenland is called an ———.

Lesson 31 Answers

Testing Your Understanding
A. 1. island
   2. Morris Jesup
   3. Arctic Circle
   4. ice cap

5. Godthåb

6. Denmark

7. fishing

8. Eskimos, whales

B. 1. The port is kept ice-free all year by warm ocean currents from the south.

2. Scientists can forecast storms on the North Atlantic Ocean by studying the weather of Greenland.

3. Icebergs form as glaciers slide into the sea and huge chunks of ice break off.

Further Study

1. Explorers called it Greenland so that it would sound appealing to settlers.

2. (Sample answers)
   —Most of the farm work stops.
   —People stay in their own settlements.
   —Families spend most of their time in one room.
   —Much of the shipping stops.
   —Eskimos of the North build homes of earth and stone.

Map Exercises

1. (Individual work.)

2. a. Atlantic Ocean
   b. Godthåb
   c. Holsteinsborg, Christianshåb
   d. Cape Morris Jesup

(Check maps for accuracy and neatness.)

5. The capital of Greenland is ———.

6. Greenland belongs to the country of ———.

7. The main industry of Greenland is ———.

8. The ——— of northern Greenland live on seals, polar bears, and ———.

B. *Answer these questions.*

1. Why does the port at Godthåb never freeze?

2. Why do scientists study the weather of Greenland?

3. How do icebergs form?

Further Study

1. How did Greenland get its name?

2. How does winter affect the people of Greenland?

Map Exercises

1. Trace Map F in the map section.

2. Use the map at the beginning of this lesson to help you label these things on your map.
   a. The ocean to the south of Greenland.
   b. The capital of Greenland.
   c. Two other towns that have seafood-processing plants.
   d. The northernmost point of Greenland.

32. Siberia, the Russian Frontier

Glossary Words

digging peat

mineral (MIHN ur uhl) Something taken from the earth that is neither plant nor animal.

peat Partly decayed plant matter found in swamps, which can be dried and used for fuel.

plateau (pla TOH) An area of high, level land.

steppe (STEHP) A vast, rolling plain covered with grass.

taiga (TY guh) The forest region of Siberia.

Siberia, Sleeping Land

Siberia is a vast, cold region of eastern Russia. Siberia covers the northern part of Asia and lies partly within the Arctic Circle. The Ural Mountains divide Siberia from western Russia, which is in Europe. The Ural Mountains also form a boundary between the continents of Europe and Asia.

Siberia means "Sleeping Land" in one of the Asian languages. But Siberia is slowly waking up. The Russian government encourages people to move into this cold land to develop the resources there. Let us ride along with the Ivan Pavlov family on a journey to visit relatives at the coal mines of Kutulik near Lake Baikal (by KAHL).

Siberia From West to East

"Why are we riding a train to Kutulik instead of going by bus?" Olna asked her older brother.

"It is too far to take a bus," answered Eric. "We are going a long, long way, and the buses do not make regular trips that far. Most people would probably fly to get there faster, but Father wants us to see more of the country."

"It all looks the same," commented Chuna. "Since we left the Ural Mountains, all we've seen is *taiga*. There's nothing very inspiring about swamps and trees."

LESSON AIM

To give a glimpse of Siberia, a forbidding land that has been developed and exploited only in recent times.

MAIN POINTS

- **Siberia is a large, cold region in northern Asia.** The Russian government is trying to develop the rich resources that are found there.

- **Siberia from West to East.** A large plain stretches across western Siberia from the Ural Mountains to the Yenisey River. The forests in the west are the wet taiga.

  A plateau lies between the Yenisey River and the Lena River. [This higher region is better drained than the western lowlands. Some mountains are in this region, especially along the southern border.] The Lena River is the largest river in Siberia. Lake Baikal, the deepest lake in the world, is also located in this area.

Mountains fill the Siberian Highlands east of the Lena River. Volcanoes line the Pacific coast. This is the coldest region in the Northern Hemisphere.

- **Siberia from South to North.** The treeless steppe is in southern Siberia. This is a wheat-growing area. [The steppe is found mainly in the southwest, since mountains run along much of the southeastern border.]

  Forests are north of the steppe. They make a wide strip across the country.

  The tundra lies north of the tree line. The permafrost of the tundra extends to a depth of more than 1,000 feet in some areas. Eskimos and other wandering groups of people live off the animals found there. [These people are nomads who hunt rather than nomads who tend flocks or herds.] Some fur farms have been established in northern Siberia.

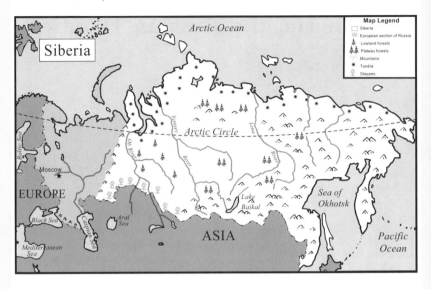

"The swamps are worth more than you think," Father said. "**Peat** is harvested from them and dried for fuel. Russia is the world leader in producing peat."

"Think of all the lumber that could be cut from those trees," suggested Eric. "There are a few places where logging operations can be seen. And if you watch closely, you may see some wildlife. The forest is full of animals."

"Bears?" asked Olna.

"Yes, brown bears. And reindeer, elk, red foxes, lynxes, sables, and ermines."

"We're coming to a river!" exclaimed Olna.

"Is it the Ob River?" asked Eric.

"We have already crossed the Ob," answered Father. "This is the Yenisey River (yehn ih SAY). The Yenisey marks the edge of the taiga plains, so you will see different scenery now. The land east of here is higher. It is a **plateau** that stretches for miles and miles to the Lena River. That is the largest river in Siberia, and it marks the next division of the land.

"East of the Lena River, mountains fill the Siberian Highlands.

- **Siberia is rich in mineral resources.** For many years, free labor was provided by prisoners sent into exile there. Now a new image of the region is emerging. Hopes are high that Siberia will make a great economic contribution to the nation of Russia.

RELATED POINTS

- **Soviet Union, Russia, and Siberia.** *Soviet Union* is a shortened name for the former *Union of Soviet Socialist Republics* (USSR), which was dissolved in 1989. It included the area known as the Russian Empire before 1917.

Russia is commonly used in referring to the Soviet Union. But it refers more specifically to the largest and most important republic, the Russian Soviet Federated Socialist Republic (RSFSR). Russia is still the largest political unit in the world, even though the Soviet Union no longer exists.

Siberia is the Asian part of Russia (the RSFSR). The name Siberia refers to a geographic region rather than a political unit. Though Siberia is only part of the vast republic of Russia, it is about 400,000 square miles larger than all of Canada, the second largest country in the world.

The Trans-Siberian Express trains carry passengers long distances in Siberia. Trains are also used to haul Siberian minerals and forest products.

In this mountain region is the very coldest part of the Northern Hemisphere, colder even than the North Pole region. The average January temperature there is 58 degrees below zero [Fahrenheit]. Far to the east along the Pacific Ocean is a line of volcanoes. One of them is the highest mountain in eastern Asia."

Siberia From South to North

"We would see even more variation if we were traveling from south to north instead of eastward across the land," explained Father. "If we could begin at the southern border of Siberia, we would see acres and acres of grassland. The dry *steppes* are a very good region for growing wheat and other crops that do not need much rain. Huge farms spread across the steppes.

"Traveling north, we would soon come to an area with more rainfall and more trees. The forests make a wide strip across the country. The farther north you go, the wetter you find it, as you

236   Unit 4, Chapter 7 Cold Lands, Small and Great

Ermine, Sable, and Lynx

The ermine is a small, hot-tempered animal with a beautiful fur coat. It belongs to the weasel family. Ermines have brown coats in the summer, but they are best known for their white winter coats. At one time, only kings, queens, and other important leaders were allowed to wear this fine white fur.

The sable is another fur-bearing animal found in Siberia. It also belongs to the weasel family, and it is much like the marten of North America. Sables have beautiful dark brown or black fur, with a light-colored patch on the throat. The fur is not used much any more because sables have become rare.

The lynx is a wild cat with thick, soft fur. It has a short tail, long legs, heavy paws, and a tuft of hair at the tip of each ear. A full-grown lynx may be as much as three feet long.

saw in the marshy taiga we traveled through.

"But it also gets colder as you go farther north. Evergreen trees take the place of birch, aspen, and willow. Soon you would find the forest thinning out to tundra, a cold treeless plain. Most of the tundra lies north of the Arctic Circle, in the Frigid Zone. The soil of the tundra is frozen solid over 1,000 feet deep in some areas. Deeply frozen soil like this is called permafrost. Even in the warmest summers, the soil thaws to a depth of only one or two feet."

"Does anybody live there?" asked Chuna.

"Oh, yes," answered Father. "Eskimos and some other groups of people live in the Far North. They travel around and live off the polar bears, whales, and seals that they hunt. There are also some settlements where fur farms have been established. The tundra is a good place to raise animals for fur because they grow heavier, warmer coats in this cold climate."

Siberian Minerals

"Why do you live in cold Siberia?" Eric asked Alexander during their visit.

The dry steppes of southern Siberia are a good region for growing wheat and other small grains.

"My father was sent to Siberia as a young man," answered Alexander. "He was a prisoner because of his faith in God. The government sent multitudes of prisoners to Siberia to build cities and work in the forests and coal mines. After he was released, my father stayed in Siberia, married, and raised his family here. I also have a job working in the coal mines."

"Is there much coal in this land?" asked Eric.

"Yes, Siberia is rich in

Beautiful Lake Baikal is the deepest lake in the world.

mineral resources. Some other minerals found here are iron ore, aluminum, nickel, diamonds, gold, natural gas, and petroleum."

"Do you ship all those things by railroad?"

"Most of them go by train, but not all of them. A pipeline carries oil and natural gas west to Europe. When the rivers are open, we ship many goods by boat, and some logs are floated down the rivers. But most of the Siberian rivers flow north and are frozen eight or nine months of the year."

"Does Lake Baikal freeze in the winter?"

"It does. The ice grows strong enough to drive across the lake. Lake Baikal is the deepest lake in the world—over a mile deep."

Testing Your Understanding

A. *Write the correct word for each description.*

plateau	permafrost	steppe
peat	tundra	mineral
taiga		

1. Decayed plants that can be used for fuel.
2. Grassy plain.
3. Heavily forested region.
4. Something mined from the earth.
5. Soil that is frozen year round.
6. Level highland.
7. Cold, treeless land.

Lesson 32 Answers

Testing Your Understanding

A. 1. peat
   2. steppe
   3. taiga
   4. mineral
   5. permafrost
   6. plateau
   7. tundra

B. *Choose the correct words.*

1. A good word to describe Siberia's climate is (cold, dry, wet, hot).
2. Siberia is on the continent of (Europe, Asia, Africa).
3. The (Lena, Yenisey, Ural) Mountains divide Siberia from the rest of Russia.
4. The most wild animals are found in the (tundra, taiga, steppes).
5. The (Ob, Baikal, Lena) River is the largest river in Siberia.
6. The (mountains, plateaus) of Siberia have the coldest temperatures in the Northern Hemisphere.
7. Many Russian (farmers, Eskimos, prisoners) were sent to Siberia to work.
8. Most of the minerals from Siberia are carried by (boats, trains, trucks) to other places.

Further Study

1. Describe the three main regions of Siberia from west to east.
2. Describe the three main regions of Siberia from south to north.

Map Exercises

Trace Map G in the map section, and heavily outline the part called Siberia. Then follow the directions below.

1. Label these things on your map.
   a. The river that divides the plains from the plateau.
   b. The river that divides the plateau from the mountains.
   c. The deepest lake in the world.
2. Label and color the following areas as shown below.
   TUNDRA (brown)
   TAIGA (green)
   STEPPES (yellow)

B. 1. cold
2. Asia
3. Ural
4. taiga
5. Lena
6. mountains
7. prisoners
8. trains

Further Study

1. A large plain stretches eastward from the Ural Mountains to the Yenisey River. The forests in the west are the wet taiga. A plateau lies between the Yenisey River and the Lena River, which is the largest river in Siberia. Lake Baikal, the deepest lake in the world, is also located in this area. A mountainous region called the Siberian Highlands extends eastward from the Lena River to a line of volcanoes along the Pacific coast. This is the coldest region in the Northern Hemisphere.
2. Treeless steppes are in southern Siberia. This is a good wheat-growing area. Forests are north of the steppe. They make a wide strip across the country. The tundra lies north of the tree line. The permafrost of the tundra extends to a depth of more than 1,000 feet in some areas. Eskimos and other wandering groups of people live off the animals found there.

Map Exercises

1. a. Yenisey River
   b. Lena River
   c. Lake Baikal
2. (Individual work. Check maps for accuracy and neatness.)

33. Iceland, Steppingstone Between Two Worlds

Glossary Words

fillet (fih LAY) A strip of boneless meat or fish.
geothermal (jee oh THUR muhl) Having to do with the earth's heat.
geyser (GY zur) A spring that shoots hot water into the air.
reinforced concrete (ree ihn FAWRST) Concrete that has steel bars in it for extra strength.

Geography Quiz

Einar Jokulsson pedaled his bicycle along beside Jon Sigfusson, on the way to spend the night at his friend's house. "Are you ready for the geography test tomorrow?" asked Jon.

"I reviewed some, but I'm not sure I know it as well as I should," confessed Einar.

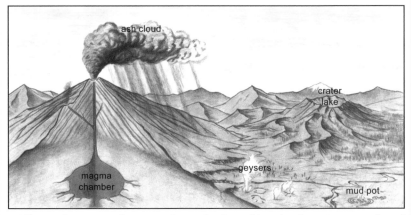

When a volcano erupts, hot magma from under the earth's surface forces its way out through a weak spot in the earth's crust. The ashes and molten rock that fall from an erupting volcano choke rivers and kill plant life. When a volcano is no longer active, a lake may form in the crater. Geysers and mud pots are also heated by hot magma, but they may be quite a distance from an actual volcano.

LESSON AIM

To show the importance of Iceland, a small island nation.

MAIN POINTS

- **Iceland is an island between Greenland and Europe.** It is considered a part of Europe, even though it is closer to Greenland. [Greenland is considered a part of North America.] The northern tips of Iceland almost touch the Arctic Circle. Reykjavík is the capital city.

- **Iceland is warmed by an ocean current.** Average temperatures in Iceland are higher than in most areas near the Arctic Circle.

- **Iceland is called the Land of Ice and Fire.** Glaciers cover one-eighth of Iceland. Volcanoes, hot springs, and geysers bring up heat from within the earth. [Because of the harsh interior,] most Icelanders live around the edges of the island.

- **Hot springs and waterfalls provide heat and electricity.** Geothermal heat is used to warm nearly all the buildings in Reykjavík. Electric generators at waterfalls provide cheap electricity.

- **Occupations of Icelanders**
  —Fishing and fish processing is the largest industry.
  —Farmers raise cattle, sheep, hay, potatoes, and turnips. Warm-weather crops are raised in greenhouses that are heated with water from the hot springs.
  —[In recent years, more Icelanders have begun working in factories.]

- **Earthquake tremors are frequent.** Reinforced concrete buildings can withstand most tremors and earthquakes.

Iceland

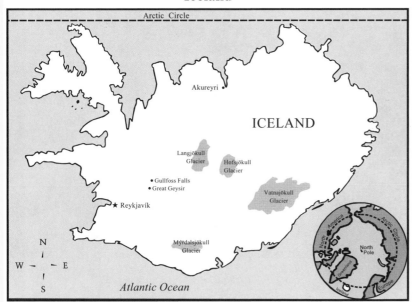

"We could quiz each other on the way home," suggested Jon. "Where is Iceland?"

"Right here!" said Einar with a laugh. "Iceland is an island between Greenland and Europe. It is considered part of Europe, even though it is closer to Greenland. The northern points just about touch the Arctic Circle. Now I have a question. Is Iceland colder than Greenland?"

"No. Greenland is much colder than Iceland, even though the name *Greenland* sounds warmer than *Iceland*. An ocean current from the south keeps Iceland warmer than most lands near the Arctic Circle. But Iceland still has a cool climate with long summer days and long winter nights. Where do most Icelanders live?"

"Icelanders live around the edges of the island. Over half of them live in the area of Reykjavík (RAY kyuh veek), the capital of Iceland. What is the middle of the island like?"

RELATED POINTS

- Vikings from Norway began settling Iceland in 874. They governed themselves for the first several hundred years, and then came under the rule of Norway and later Denmark. Iceland regained its independence in 1944.

- Iceland has many fissure volcanoes. Lava from fissure volcanoes flows out of numerous openings along a crack in the earth rather than out of just one main vent.

- Volcanoes occasionally erupt under the ocean around Iceland. The small island of Surtsey was formed during a submarine eruption in 1963.

Reykjavík is the capital and largest city of Iceland. It lies on Iceland's southwest coast, and more than half of Iceland's people live in or near Reykjavík.

"In the middle there are mountains, glaciers, and barren lava fields. Glaciers cover one-eighth of Iceland. The largest glacier, Vatnajökull (VAHT nah yoh kyool), covers about 8,300 square kilometers [3,200 square miles] and is one kilometer thick (over one-half mile). It is larger than all the other glaciers of Europe put together. Why is Iceland called the Land of Ice and Fire?"

"You told about the ice part. The fire is the volcanoes, hot springs, and **geysers**. More than two hundred volcanoes have erupted in Iceland. Some of them are still active. Iceland has more hot springs than any other country in the world. Some of the hot springs are geysers, which shoot hot water into the air. The word *geyser* comes from the name of the most famous one in Iceland—Great Geysir. Did you ever see Great Geysir?"

"Yes," replied Jon. "Our family took a trip there last summer. It was a great sight to see that steaming water shoot up almost 200 feet into the air. We also visited Gullfoss Falls. Such beauty! And such waterpower!

"Here we are at home already. So much for the geography quiz. I will need to feed and bed the sheep. You may come along and watch or help as you please."

Occupations in Iceland

"I don't know much about farming because my father is a fisherman," Einar stated as the boys began the chores. "What crops do you raise?"

"Our main crop is hay for our sheep. Grass and hay grow quickly during the summer, when the sun shines nearly all the time. Some farmers raise potatoes and turnips. These crops also grow well in our cool climate."

"I'm certainly glad for the farmers here in our country," commented Einar. "We can enjoy meat, milk, and other fresh farm products without importing them

The main farm crop in Iceland is hay. Grass can grow better than grain in cool temperatures and short summers. The hay machine behind the tractor is called a tedder. *A tedder spreads the mown grass to help the grass dry faster.*

from other lands. We can always make use of wool for clothing, and we can sell some too."

"We are just as glad for the fishermen!" replied Jon. "What is better than a tasty **fillet** of fresh fish? Fish are a very important part of our industry. Lots of people would be out of jobs if it were not for fishing and processing fish. Iceland exports more fish and fish products than anything else."

"Our neighbors have a greenhouse business," commented Einar. "They are expanding and will be putting up another greenhouse this winter."

"What do they raise?" asked Jon.

"They raise lots of vegetables, tomatoes, grapes, and flowers. They are even trying bananas."

"They probably warm their

The fishing industry employs many of Iceland's people. On the left, fishermen haul in two large nets full of fish. On the right, workers prepare the fillets and place them in small tin cans.

Like Greenland, Iceland has many fiords along its coast.

greenhouses with ***geothermal*** heat."

"Oh, yes," answered Einar. "It is most practical to use the natural heat that God has put right here for us in the hot springs. I suppose all of Reykjavík uses geothermal heat to warm their homes and businesses. Those great pipes that run from the springs to the city carry a lot of hot water."

"Some power plants use steam from hot springs to run generators that produce electricity," said Jon. "But most of our electricity is produced by generators at waterfalls on our rushing rivers.

"Say, we've finished the chores early. Thanks for your help. Maybe we'll have time for a swim before supper, to make use of some geothermal heat ourselves."

Earthquakes

The two boys came to supper with hearty appetites. "Your meal is very good," said Einar with appreciation. "At home we eat fish quite often. Mutton is a treat for me."

As Einar spoke, the earth

seemed to speak too. There was a rumbling and shaking until the house and furniture trembled. Jon looked at his father and asked, "Is it going to—," but just then everything settled down again.

"That was a little harder than some tremors," said Father, "but not serious enough to be alarmed about."

"I'm glad this is a new house!" exclaimed Jon. "It would take a pretty hard earthquake to damage *reinforced concrete*."

Testing Your Understanding

A. *Write* true *or* false.

1. Iceland belongs to Greenland.
2. Iceland is south of the Arctic Circle.
3. Reykjavík is the capital of Iceland.
4. Iceland is colder than Greenland.
5. During the winter, Iceland has long nights.
6. Most Icelanders live near the coast.
7. Glaciers shoot hot water into the air.
8. Some volcanoes in Iceland are still active.
9. Iceland exports fish products.
10. Most homes in Reykjavík are heated by electricity.
11. Some farmers in Iceland raise tomatoes in large fields.
12. Reinforced concrete is used to make strong buildings.

B. *Answer these questions.*

1. Why does Iceland have a warmer climate than most other lands near the Arctic Circle?
2. (*a*) How much of Iceland is covered by glaciers? (*b*) What is the name of the largest glacier?
3. How is most of the electricity generated in Iceland?
4. How do Icelanders use God's gifts to heat their homes and businesses?

Lesson 33 Answers

Testing Your Understanding

A. 1. false
   2. true
   3. true
   4. false
   5. true
   6. true
   7. false
   8. true
   9. true
  10. false
  11. false
  12. true

B. 1. Iceland is warmed by an ocean current from the south.
   2. a. one-eighth
      b. Vatnajökull
   3. by waterpower (at waterfalls on rushing rivers)
   4. They use hot water from the hot springs for heating.

Further Study

1. Why is Iceland called the Land of Ice and Fire?
2. Where does the word *geyser* come from?
3. Why are greenhouses needed in Iceland but not in the Philippines?

Map Exercises.

Use the map of Iceland to answer these questions.

1. Is Europe east or west of Iceland?
2. What large ocean is south of Iceland?
3. Is the glacier Vatnajökull on the eastern half or the western half of Iceland?
4. What important line is just north of Iceland?

Further Study

1. Iceland is a land of ice because of its glaciers. It is a land of fire because of its volcanoes, hot springs, and geysers.
2. The word geyser comes from Great Geysir, the name of the most famous geyser in Iceland.
3. Greenhouses are needed in Iceland because few crops can be raised in the cool climate, and the growing season is short. Many crops can be raised year round in the warm Philippine climate.

Map Exercises

1. east
2. Atlantic Ocean
3. on the eastern half
4. Arctic Circle

34. Antarctica, the Frozen Continent

Glossary Words

icebreaker

penguins

blizzard (BLIHZ urd) A violent storm of wind and snow.

icebreaker A sturdy ship used to break through ice-covered waters.

ice pack A large mass of floating ice chunks packed together.

ice shelf A large, thick layer of solid ice extending from land out into the sea.

penguin (PEHN gwihn) A sea bird that cannot fly, which lives in the cool regions of the Southern Hemisphere.

treaty (TREE tee) An agreement between two or more nations.

Antarctic Animals

David and Cyrus Meer hurried on their way home from school. A friend of Father's was with their family for the day. Charles Fisher had just returned from a visit to Antarctica, and the boys were eager to hear about his trip.

"What do you boys know about Antarctica?" asked Charles as he drew a stack of pictures from a large envelope.

"It's at the South Pole," volunteered David, "and terribly cold."

"*Penguins* live there," offered Cyrus. "Did you see any?"

"Yes," replied Charles, "and I have pictures of some. There are several kinds of penguins. The emperor penguins are the largest. They stand about 4 feet tall. But the Adélie (uh DAY lee) penguins are more amusing. They seem to like being around people, and they are very entertaining with their clumsy waddle."

"Their fur makes them look as

LESSON AIM

To introduce the students to Antarctica, the world's coldest continent.

MAIN POINTS

- **Antarctica is a cold, bleak continent surrounding the South Pole.**

- **Penguins and a few other animals live on Antarctica.** Many animals live in the surrounding seas. No native people inhabit the continent.

- **A great ice cap covers Antarctica.** Scientists study the ice to learn more about past conditions in the world. Land can be seen where mountains rise above the ice cap. Few plants live there.

- **Antarctica has the coldest temperatures in the world.** It is also the windiest place on earth. Antarctica has winter while countries in the Northern Hemisphere have summer.

- **The United States and other nations have agreed to study Antarctica without claiming it.**

- **An ice pack freezes around Antarctica during winter.**

- **The South Pole is surrounded by land and is therefore colder than the North Pole.**

if they're dressed in black and white suits," said Cyrus.

"That's feathers," corrected Charles. "Penguins are actually birds. They cannot fly, but they use their wings as flippers for swimming—and they can swim fast! Their short, thick feathers make a waterproof coat, and thick layers of fat keep them warm."

"Do other animals live in Antarctica?" asked David.

"Yes, petrels, skuas, and a few other birds live there. The only land animals are a few kinds of insects and spiders. But God has filled the sea around Antarctica with life. Seals, whales, and fish abound in the waters."

The albatross is a large sea bird that builds a mud nest for its young. Albatrosses nest on many islands in the South Pacific Ocean and on the coast of Antarctica.

Adélie penguins gather in large groups to raise their young. Sometimes over 200,000 penguins will gather at one spot. Adélie penguins are found only in Antarctica.

RELATED POINTS

- Antarctica has a large percent of the world's ice. If the ice cap melted, the ocean level around the world could rise as much as 200 feet.

- Antarctica has only recently been discovered and explored. The first recorded sighting of the continent was in the early 1800s. Amundsen reached the pole in 1911. Much of the continent was unknown until airplanes were used to explore it in the mid-1900s.

Antarctica

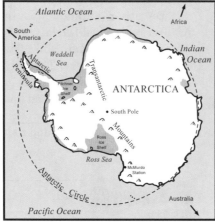

"No polar bears or reindeer?" asked David.

"None whatsoever. And no Eskimos. No people but the men who go there for scientific study or exploration. It seems that God did not plan for people to live in Antarctica."

The Antarctic Ice Cap

"What do the men study?" asked Cyrus.

"They study the most common thing there—ice. Most of Antarctica is a great ice cap. It keeps building up as snow is added to it. Most of the snow does not melt. It packs into ice that keeps pushing slowly toward the sea. There, huge chunks of ice break off and form icebergs.

"Scientists dig deep into the ice and learn interesting things about the layers. They have found traces of particles that were trapped in the snow long ago. The particles came from volcanoes or other things that affected large areas of the earth. Studying conditions in Antarctica helps the scientists to understand world-wide weather patterns.

"Some people also study the land under the snow. They are exploring for mineral resources."

"Is there any land that is not covered with ice and snow?" asked Cyrus.

"Not much. Here, let's look at my map. God placed mountains around the edge of Antarctica and across the continent from the Ross Sea to the Weddell Sea. Only where the mountains stick out of the ice cap can land be seen."

"Does anything grow there?"

"Only a few lichens, mosses, and grasses that can stand the long, cold winters and grow quickly in the long summer days. In the summer it warms up to about 32 degrees [Fahrenheit] along the coast. In the middle of the continent, summer temperatures are more like 20 degrees below zero."

"Warms up!" exclaimed David. "What's it like in the winter?"

"Cold!" Charles shivered. "And dark. The lowest temperature ever recorded on earth was nearly 130 degrees [Fahrenheit] below zero on the high inland ice cap. A more normal winter temperature along the coast is 76 degrees below zero.

"See the Antarctic Circle on the map? All the land inside that circle has no daylight at the beginning of winter, which is in June. Then there are some weeks of dawn, and finally day and night with the days growing longer and longer. By December the sun does not set at all, and summer is beginning in Antarctica."

The South Pole

Later when the family was all together, Charles began telling about his travels. "We flew to McMurdo, the largest community in Antarctica. The runway there is ice. And the wind! Antarctica is the windiest place on earth. At some places people avoid the wind by using tunnels through the snow to go from their living quarters to their work places.

"We flew from McMurdo across the Transantarctic Mountains to the South Pole. The scientific

Penguins do not seem to mind the ice and icy waters of cold Antarctica. Their feathers form a waterproof coat, and their thick layers of fat keep them warm.

Flippers and webbed feet make penguins excellent swimmers. They dive into the water from icy cliffs and swim rapidly in leaps and dives across the surface of the water.

Airplanes are vital to the scientific stations in Antarctica.

station there is named Amundsen-Scott in honor of the explorers who first reached the place. It is hard to imagine the hardships they faced in that challenge. Roald Amundsen led a group, with skis and dog sleds, across those mountains. And there was no station there to shelter them when they got to the Pole. Robert F. Scott also led a party to the Pole, but they never made it back. They died in a **blizzard** when they were almost back to their place of supplies."

"Who operates the station at the South Pole?" asked Father.

"The United States established the base," answered Charles. "Nobody owns Antarctica.

Twelve nations have signed a **treaty** that they will work together there without claiming the land for any of their countries. They share plans and scientific information, and they work together peacefully."

"How big is Antarctica?" asked Father.

"That depends on the time of year. The land covers about five and a half million square miles, which is about twice as big as Australia. In winter Antarctica becomes almost twice as large because of the **ice shelf** around the coast. In summer the coastline shrinks as the **ice pack** breaks up and fills the sea with icebergs.

Strong ships called *icebreakers* help to keep passages open through the floating ice. But about half of the Ross Sea is covered with an ice shelf even in summer."

North and South Poles

"How is the South Pole different from the North Pole?" Mother asked.

"The North Pole is in the Arctic Ocean. Water moves and carries heat, so the North Pole is not as cold as the South Pole. Because the South Pole is inland, its climate is much harsher than in the north. No animals or plants live at the South Pole.

The sun shines on the South Pole from September to March, and during that time it cannot be seen from the North Pole. Then from March to September, it shines on the North Pole and cannot be seen from the South Pole. But it is not completely dark for six months. The light is like dusk that slowly grows darker until there is full darkness in winter. Then the dusk slowly becomes lighter until the sun rises again on the first day of spring."

"Are there real poles there?" asked David.

"No, the poles are just two points on the earth. The earth is turning like a ball on a rod that goes through its center. The poles are where the two ends of the rod would come through. People have found where the poles are by studying the movement of the earth in relation to the sun and the stars."

=========== Testing Your Understanding ===========

A. *Copy the names of things that are found on Antarctica or in the waters around it.*

penguins	South Pole	polar bears
petrels	seals	reindeer
scientists	Eskimos	ice cap
farms	insects	Arctic Ocean
icebergs	palm trees	mountains
moss	lichens	nations
cities	blizzards	whales
ice pack	scientific stations	

Lesson 34 Answers

Testing Your Understanding

A. penguins, petrels, scientists, icebergs, moss, ice pack, South Pole, seals, insects, lichens, blizzards, scientific stations, ice cap, mountains, whales

B. *Write* true *or* false *for each sentence. Copy each false sentence, and change one word in it to make it true.*

1. Penguins are birds that can swim but cannot fly.
2. Antarctica has many kinds of wildlife.
3. Some Eskimos live in Antarctica.
4. Scientists study the geysers of Antarctica.
5. Antarctica is the coldest, windiest continent on earth.
6. Antarctica has winter while North America has summer.
7. Antarctica is about half as big as Australia.
8. Icebreakers keep open passages through the ice pack.
9. During the winter, about half of the Ross Sea is covered with ice.
10. The South Pole is in the Arctic Ocean.

Further Study

1. What is the lowest temperature ever recorded on earth?
2. Give two reasons that areas along the coast of Antarctica are not as cold as the inland areas. (Review the last section of Lesson 1.)
3. Explain why people do not make their homes in Antarctica.

Map Exercises

Use the map of Antarctica to complete these exercises.

1. Name the peninsula that reaches farthest north.
2. Name the two seas that extend in toward the South Pole.

Use a globe to answer these questions.

3. Is Antarctica at the top or the bottom of a globe?
4. Which three oceans surround Antarctica?
5. Which continent is closest to Antarctica?

B. 1. true
2. false; Antarctica has ~~many~~ few kinds of wildlife.
3. false; ~~Some~~ No Eskimos live in Antarctica.
4. false; Scientists study the ~~geysers~~ ice (cap) of Antarctica.
5. true
6. true
7. false; Antarctica is about ~~half~~ twice as big as Australia.
8. true
9. false; During the ~~winter~~ summer, about half of the Ross Sea is covered with ice.
10. false; The ~~South~~ North Pole is in the Arctic Ocean.

Further Discussion

1. nearly 130° Fahrenheit below zero
2. (Any two) The coast of Antarctica is closer to the equator. Oceans keep the coast warmer. Much of the inland area is higher than the coastal area.
3. Antarctica is a cold, barren land. Winters are long and dark, and even the summers are too cold for most plants to grow. Almost all the food and other supplies would have to be imported. God apparently did not plan for people to live in Antarctica.

Map Exercises

1. Antarctic Peninsula
2. Ross Sea, Weddell Sea
3. at the bottom
4. Pacific Ocean, Atlantic Ocean, Indian Ocean
5. South America

35. Chapter 7 Review

================ Testing Your Understanding ================

A. *Write a glossary word for each definition.*

1. A large, grass-covered plain.
2. A long arm of the sea between two cliffs.
3. The forests of Siberia.
4. An agreement between countries.
5. High, level land.
6. A spring that shoots out hot water.
7. A ship that breaks through an ice pack.
8. Decayed plant matter found in swamps.
9. A deep layer of ice that covers a large area and does not melt during the summer.
10. A thick layer of ice extending from land out into the sea.
11. A large mass of ice moving slowly down a slope.
12. Having to do with heat from the earth.

B. *Write the correct word(s) to complete each sentence.*

1. Most of Greenland lies (north, south) of the Arctic Circle.
2. —— live in the northern parts of Greenland and Siberia.
3. —— is an important industry in Greenland and Iceland.
4. Ice caps cover most of Greenland and ——.
5. Siberia is on the continent of ——.
6. Many valuable —— are mined in Siberia.
7. —— is soil that is frozen all year.
8. Lake —— is the deepest lake in the world.
9. Iceland is considered a part of (Europe, North America).
10. —— is the capital of Iceland.
11. The coast of Iceland is warmed by an ——.

Lesson 35 Answers

Testing Your Understanding

A. 1. steppe
   2. fiords
   3. taiga
   4. treaty
   5. plateau
   6. geyser
   7. icebreaker
   8. peat
   9. ice cap
   10. ice shelf
   11. glacier
   12. geothermal

B. 1. north
   2. Eskimos
   3. Fishing
   4. Antarctica
   5. Asia
   6. minerals
   7. Permafrost
   8. Baikal
   9. Europe
   10. Reykjavík
   11. ocean current

12. Glaciers
13. Ice, Fire
14. Antarctica

C. 1. a warm ocean current
  2. in the mountains of eastern Siberia
  3. to warm their homes and greenhouses
  4. Icelanders live around the edges of their island. Over half of them live in the area of Reykjavík.
  5. The North Pole is kept warmer by water currents in the Arctic Ocean, but the South Pole is inland. (The South Pole is also at a higher elevation [9,000 feet] due to the ice cap.)

Map Exercises
1. Atlantic Ocean
2. Cape Morris Jesup
3. taiga (forests)
4. Yenisey River
5. the Arctic Circle
6. west
7. Pacific Ocean, Atlantic Ocean, Indian Ocean

Review Study
(Individual work. Review the glossary words in class. Have students point out each of the four areas they studied in this chapter.)

---

12. —— cover one-eighth of Iceland.
13. Iceland is called the Land of —— and ——.
14. —— is the coldest, windiest continent on earth.

C. *Answer these questions.*

1. In Greenland, what helps to keep the harbor of Godthåb open year round?
2. Where is the coldest region in the Northern Hemisphere?
3. How do Icelanders use their hot springs?
4. Where do most Icelanders live?
5. Why is the North Pole not as cold as the South Pole?

Map Exercises

Use your completed maps of Greenland and Siberia to answer these questions.

1. What ocean is south of Greenland?
2. What is the northernmost point of Greenland?
3. What lies between the steppes and the tundra of Siberia?
4. What river divides the plains of Siberia from the plateau region?

Answer these questions about Iceland and Antarctica. You may need to use a globe or a world map.

5. What line is just north of Iceland?
6. Is Greenland east or west of Iceland?
7. Which three oceans surround Antarctica?

Review Study

1. Do you know the meaning of all the glossary words in Chapter 7?
2. Can you find Greenland, Siberia, Iceland, and Antarctica on a world map or a globe?

So Far This Year

1. Give the number of the correct climate zone for each place. Answers may be used more than once.
   - a. Nigeria
   - b. Ohio
   - c. Most of Greenland
   - d. Australia (two zones)
   - e. Baffin Island
   - f. Most of Europe
   - g. Most of Brazil
   - h. Japan
   - i. Siberia (two zones)
   - j. Antarctica
   - k. Philippines
   - l. Iceland

   1. Northern Frigid Zone
   2. Northern Temperate Zone
   3. Tropical Zone
   4. Southern Temperate Zone
   5. Southern Frigid Zone

2. The sunrise, sunset, and daily temperatures stay about the same year round in lands near the (equator, poles, ocean).

3. Dams help to provide all the following benefits except (fishing, irrigation, electricity, climate control, flood control).

4. Choose two: Along the Ring of Fire, there are many (earthquakes, tornadoes, forest fires, volcanoes).

5. An (import, export) is brought into a country, and an (import, export) is shipped out of a country.

6. When the Northern Hemisphere has summer, the Southern Hemisphere has (spring, summer, autumn, winter).

7. The first European settlers in Australia were (criminals, debtors, heretics).

8. Europe is connected to the continent of (Asia, Africa, Australia).

9. The (Alps, Andes, Appalachians) are some of the highest mountains in Europe.

10. The first book that Gutenberg printed on his new printing press was the ———.

So Far This Year

1. a. 3
   b. 2
   c. 1
   d. 3, 4
   e. 1
   f. 2
   g. 3
   h. 2
   i. 1, 2
   j. 5
   k. 3
   l. 2
2. equator
3. climate control
4. earthquakes, volcanoes
5. import, export
6. winter
7. debtors
8. Asia
9. Alps
10. Bible

11. Menno Simons
12. shaking hands
13. small
14. Trains
15. Greenland
16. Asia
17. south
18. colder

11. (Felix Manz, Pilgram Marpeck, Menno Simons) was an important leader of the Anabaptists in the Netherlands.

12. All the following are Japanese customs except (bowing, shaking hands, sitting on the floor, wearing kimonos).

13. Most farms in Japan are (large, small).

14. (Buses, Trains, Jeepneys) provide a fast way to travel between large cities in Japan.

15. The largest island in the world is (Australia, Greenland, Iceland).

16. Siberia is a large, cold region in northern (Africa, Europe, Asia).

17. Iceland is (north, south) of the Arctic Circle.

18. Because the South Pole is surrounded by land, it is (warmer, colder) than the North Pole.

Like rain in the desert, a center pivot irrigation system brings green life to the barren wastes of the Sahara.

CHAPTER 8

HIGH LANDS AND DRY LANDS

"Before the mountains were brought forth, or ever thou hadst formed the earth and the world, even from everlasting to everlasting, thou art God" (Psalm 90:2).

36. Ecuador, Land of Many Climates

Glossary Words

sucre

altitude (AL tih tood) Height above the level of the oceans.

sea level The level of the oceans.

sucre (SOO kray) The unit of money in Ecuador.

The Andes Mountains

Find the continent of South America on a globe or a world map. If your globe or map shows mountains, you will notice a system of mountains running north and south along the entire western coast of South America. These are the Andes, the longest chain of mountains in the world. The Andes are also very high. Some of the peaks are over 4 miles above *sea level*! That is higher than the Alps in Europe or the Rocky Mountains in North America. Only a few mountain ranges in Asia are higher than the Andes.

Look again at the globe or world map. Follow the Andes mountain range north or south until you reach the equator. Here you will see the small country of Ecuador. You have learned that lands near the equator are usually warmer than lands farther from the equator. What kind of climate would you expect Ecuador to have?

The lowlands of Ecuador have a hot tropical climate like most other lands along the equator. But the climate is cooler on the mountain slopes. And the highest peaks are covered with snow year round!

Tropical Lowlands

Sharon and Delbert were excited. The airplane was preparing to land, and they could see the city of Guayaquil (gwah yah KEEL). Their father was a minister, and he was taking his

LESSON AIM

To introduce the students to the country of Ecuador and to show how altitude affects climate.

MAIN POINTS

- **The Andes are a high mountain system in South America.** They make up the longest mountain chain on earth. [Some mountain chains under the oceans are longer than the Andes.]

- **The country of Ecuador is located where the Andes Mountains cross the equator.** Ecuador has a variety of climates from the tropical rain forests of the lowlands to the cold, barren peaks of high mountains. The peaks of the highest mountains are covered with snow year round.

- **The equator is an invisible line around the earth, halfway between the North Pole and the South Pole.** It is not a physical feature that can be seen.

- **Tropical crops are raised in the warm lowlands.** People use sucres, the Ecuador unit of money, to buy them in local markets. [Large amounts of tropical produce are exported.] Bananas are one of Ecuador's most important crops.

- **The air becomes thinner and colder as altitude increases.** Breathing is difficult at very high altitudes.

RELATED POINTS

- Point out the highest mountains and some of the major mountain systems on each continent. The students should be able to name the ones they studied earlier this year.

family along to visit missionaries at a few places in Ecuador. Father had told them that the name of the country was Ecuador because the equator ran through it.

"Can we see the equator?" asked Delbert, peering out the airplane window.

"No, the equator is not a physical feature like a mountain or a river," Father answered. "The equator is known by the way the earth spins. If a ball were spinning in the air, you could say it had top and bottom spinning points. The part around the middle between those points would be its equator, even though there is nothing to mark it."

"Oh, it's hot here!" exclaimed Sharon as they walked down the stairs from the plane. "I knew they don't have winter at the equator, but I wasn't ready for this."

"It is certainly a change from

Guayaquil is Ecuador's largest city and one of the most important seaports on the South American Pacific coast.

the cold weather we have had at home," commented Father. "You can be glad the Pacific Ocean helps keep this part of Ecuador from being even warmer than it is. Lands near the equator receive the direct rays of the sun year round."

The family was soon swatting at mosquitoes and gnats. "I wasn't ready for this either," said Mother. "We will probably appreciate some of the advantages of wintertime more after this trip."

The Dolmans were waiting for their luggage to go through

customs when Father saw the mission family who had come to the airport to meet them. Soon they were sharing warm greetings and plans for the day. The Mussers wanted to shop at a market while they were in the city.

"That will be interesting," Sharon said eagerly. "I'm curious about what you can see at a tropical market."

"Lots of food, for one thing," offered Barbara Musser. "We want to get some oranges and bananas. And there are many craft items like straw hats and fans and pottery. I have some *sucres*. Let's decide together how to spend them."

At the market, the girls followed their mothers past rows of people who had their goods spread out on the ground for sale. Many of them had a bit of cloth stretched above their heads to shade them from the hot sun. Mrs. Musser selected some fresh fruit and treated the Dolmans to sweet oranges.

"What is that?" asked Sharon, pointing toward a basket of something that looked like white sweet potatoes.

"Cassava," answered Barbara. "It grows under the ground like potatoes. Sweet cassava can be eaten raw, but usually it is cooked or ground into flour. Bitter cassava is poisonous if eaten raw, but it loses its poison when it is heated. Cassava is also used to make tapioca."

After all the business was done, they left Guayaquil and

This equatorial monument marks the equator line, just a few miles from Quito. Tourists like to pose here with a foot in each hemisphere.

drove a few hours to the mission station. The Dolmans spent several days there, visiting the Christians and delivering gifts and messages from friends and relatives in the United States. Then they traveled by railroad to another mission station in the highlands of Ecuador.

The markets at Quito hum with activity. The markets sell crafts and souvenirs to tourists, as well as many practical goods for native households.

"Look at all those banana plants!" Sharon commented as their train crossed the lowland plains on its way toward the mountains.

"Bananas are one of the most important crops in Ecuador," Father replied. "Cacao, sugar cane, citrus fruits, coffee, and other tropical crops also grow well in these warm lowland areas. But we will soon leave this tropical region behind. Bananas don't grow on the high slopes of the Andes!"

Higher Altitudes

"My ears feel funny!" exclaimed Delbert awhile later as the train slowly climbed the steep mountain track.

"That is because we are going up so high," Father explained. "Things change as you go up a mountain. The air is thinner. The air pressure around your body is less than what you are used to. The funny feeling is from the extra pressure inside your ears. It is usually helpful to open your mouth wide or swallow."

"It is cooler here too," commented Mother. "This weather is pleasant."

Mount Everest

Mount Everest is the highest mountain in the world. It is located on the border between Tibet, a region of China, and the small country of Nepal. Mount Everest is in the great Himalaya mountain range. Its peak is 29,028 feet above sea level. That means it is nearly 5½ miles high!

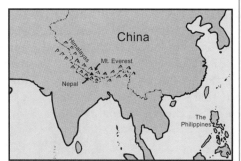

"Is that snow on the mountain peaks?" asked Sharon. "Is it really that cold here near the equator?"

"Yes, that is snow," assured Father. "The higher you go, the colder it is. A town on the mountain a mile above the lowlands will generally have temperatures

15 to 20 degrees [Fahrenheit] cooler than the lowland towns."

"Then I'd live up here," declared Delbert. "And when I wanted to play in the snow, I'd take a trip to the top of the mountains."

"I don't think you'd play much up there," said Father. "Remember, the air keeps getting thinner as you go higher. If you are very active at high *altitudes*, you soon are out of breath. Instead of the funny feeling in your ears, you might feel dizzy or get a headache. That is called mountain sickness. But if people stay at high altitudes, they usually adjust to the thin air in a few days."

Testing Your Understanding

A. *Write the correct word(s) for each description.*

Andes	bananas	Asia
sucre	cassava	sea level
equator	altitude	hot climate
Ecuador	Guayaquil	cool climate

1. Longest mountain chain.
2. Continent with the highest mountains in the world.
3. The level of the oceans.
4. A small country in South America.
5. An imaginary line running around the world.
6. A city in the lowlands of Ecuador.
7. The unit of money used in Ecuador.
8. A tropical plant that can be made into tapioca.
9. One of the most important crops in Ecuador.
10. The height above sea level.
11. The type of climate in the lowlands of Ecuador.
12. The type of climate in the highlands of Ecuador.

Lesson 36 Answers

Testing Your Understanding

A. 1. Andes
   2. Asia
   3. sea level
   4. Ecuador
   5. equator
   6. Guayaquil
   7. sucre
   8. cassava
   9. bananas
  10. altitude
  11. hot climate
  12. cool climate

B. *Answer these questions.*

1. How high are the highest mountains in the Andes mountain system?
2. What kind of climate do most lands near the equator have?
3. What kind of crops are raised in the lowlands of Ecuador?
4. Why does a person sometimes get a strange feeling in his ears when he goes up a mountain?
5. What covers the peaks of the highest mountains in Ecuador?
6. What is mountain sickness?

Further Study

1. List some advantages of winter.
2. (*a*) If the temperature in a lowland town is 90 degrees Fahrenheit, what would the temperature likely be at a nearby town that is one mile above sea level? (*b*) What would the temperature be at another place nearby that is two miles above sea level?

Map Exercises

1. Trace Map H in the map section.
2. Label Ecuador, Peru, Colombia, and the Pacific Ocean.
3. Label Guayaquil.
4. Draw mountain symbols to show the Andes.

B. 1. over 4 miles high
2. a hot tropical climate
3. tropical crops (bananas, cassava, cacao, sugar cane, citrus fruits, coffee, and others)
4. There is extra pressure inside the ears because the air outside is becoming thinner.
5. snow
6. sickness caused by being out of breath because of thin air at high altitudes

Further Study
1. (Sample answers)
   —relief from the heat of summer
   —relief from mosquitoes, gnats, and many other pests
2. a. 70°–75°F.
   b. 50°–60°F.

Map Exercises
(Individual answers. Check maps for accuracy and neatness.)

37. The Highlands of Ecuador

Glossary Word

mestizo (mehs TEE zoh) A person who is part Indian and part Spanish.

Climate of the Highlands

The train stopped at Riobamba (ree oo BAHM buh). What pleasant weather and what beautiful scenery met the Dolmans as they left the train! They were in a broad valley between snowy mountain peaks. Mr. and Mrs. Lansing from the highland mission station were waiting to meet them. They loaded the luggage on the back of a little old

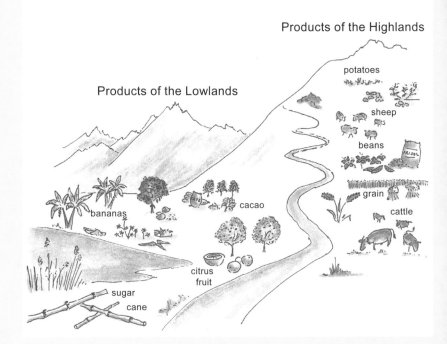

Products of the Highlands

potatoes

sheep

beans

grain

cattle

Products of the Lowlands

bananas

cacao

citrus fruit

sugar cane

LESSON AIM

To expand the students' knowledge of the highlands of Ecuador and to reinforce the concept that highlands have cool or cold climates even though they are near the equator.

MAIN POINTS

- **The highlands of Ecuador have springlike weather year round.** Quito, the capital city, has cool weather in spite of its location a few miles south of the equator. [Quito has an elevation of about 9,350 feet.] The thin mountain air cools quickly during the night.

- **Indians live in the highlands.** Indians and mestizos (part-Indian people) make up most of the population in Ecuador. The mestizos live in the lowlands; most Indians live in the highlands. Many of the Indians farm as their ancestors have for centuries.

- **Highland farmers raise cool-weather crops and some livestock.**

- **Ecuador has very high mountain peaks.** Chimborazo, the highest mountain in Ecuador, is higher than any mountain in the United States or Canada. Cotopaxi is one of the highest active volcanoes in the world. Aconcagua, in Argentina, is the highest mountain outside Asia.

To prepare their ground for crops, the Indians of Ecuador often use wooden farm tools pulled by oxen.

pickup truck. Then Father got into the cab with Brother Lansing, and the rest of them climbed up to ride on the back.

"No bugs to make us swat and scratch!" announced Delbert. "And nice cool weather. It's hard to believe we are still close to the equator. Is it always so pleasant here?"

"We have springlike weather most of the time," answered Sister Lansing. "Sometimes it is rainy. And it gets quite cool at night. The air is so thin here that when the sun goes down, the heat soon disappears.

"Quito (KEE toh), the capital of Ecuador, is only a few miles south of the equator. Yet it has cool weather year round because it is high above sea level."

Indians of the Highlands

They passed an Indian family working in a small field by the road. The Indians waved, and Mother asked, "Do the

RELATED POINTS

- A large lowland area called the Oriente lies east of the Ecuador mountains. Only a few Indians live in this tropical rain forest. The streams that rush down the eastern side of the Andes join to form rivers that empty into the Amazon River.

  More people have moved into this area since oil was found there. A 300-mile pipeline has been built to carry oil over the mountains and down to ships on the Pacific coast.

272   Unit 4, Chapter 8 High Lands and Dry Lands

Indians gladly receive your teaching?"

"That was a family that comes to church frequently," answered Sister Lansing. "Their youngest boy was very sick a year ago. We saved his life by taking him to the doctor, and they have shown their appreciation ever since. But receiving Bible teaching comes slowly for them. These people are not quick to change their ways or their thinking."

"They surely don't have modern farming ways," commented Sharon. "Do they all use cows and simple wooden plows, or whatever that was?"

"That is a very typical sight," replied Sister Lansing. "Tractors are unheard of. Hardly anyone has cars. They simply live as their ancestors have for centuries."

"What do they grow up here?" asked Delbert.

"Potatoes, beans, and grain are suitable crops for these cool highlands," replied Sister Lansing.

Snow-capped Mount Chimborazo rises 20,703 feet. Mount Chimborazo lies in the Tropical Zone, but because of the cool temperatures at high altitudes, the snow on the top of the mountain does not melt.

"A good bit of grazing is done too. The cattle and sheep raised on these mountains provide dairy products, meat, and wool."

"Are there many occupations besides farming?" asked Mother.

"The Indians have been skilled weavers for many generations. Some of them make pottery. But more of Ecuador's people are farmers than anything else."

"Most of the people in the highlands must be Indians," Sharon observed.

"Yes, most of Ecuador's population is Indian or mixed descendants of Indians. Many of the **mestizos**, who are part Indian, live on the coastal plain. Most of the Indians live here in the Andes. Because of the mountains, it is not easy to travel and to trade a great deal with people in other areas. Each village seems to stand alone, with its people taking care of all their own needs."

High Mountain Peaks

"Here is our village!" Sister Lansing announced as Brother Lansing parked the truck. Soon the families were walking the

Mount Cotopaxi, at 19,700 feet, is the second highest mountain in Ecuador and one of the tallest active volcanoes in the world. Notice the small fields on the mountainside.

short distance up to the mission station.

" 'Thy righteousness is like the great mountains,' " quoted Father. He had paused to look across a wide valley toward a majestic, snowcapped peak. "What a great God we serve!"

"Yes," replied Brother Lansing, "His faithfulness 'reacheth unto the clouds.' That high mountain is Chimborazo (chihm buh RAH zoh), the highest mountain in Ecuador. It is higher than any mountain in the United States or Canada. Some of the Andes peaks in the countries south of here are even higher. Aconcagua (ah kahn KAH gwah), in the country of Argentina, is the highest peak in the Andes mountain chain."

"Does Ecuador have any volcanoes?" asked Delbert.

"Yes. Many of the volcanoes of Ecuador have erupted in the past. Three of them are still considered active. Cotopaxi (koh tuh PAK see), the second highest mountain in Ecuador, is one of the highest active volcanoes in the world."

Sister Lansing opened the door of the mission. "Welcome to our home," she said warmly. "We hope you will enjoy your stay here in the cool highlands of Ecuador."

Testing Your Understanding

Lesson 37 Answers

Testing Your Understanding

A. 1. weather
   2. cool
   3. Quito
   4. Cattle, sheep
   5. mestizos
   6. farmers
   7. mountains
   8. Chimborazo
   9. Aconcagua
  10. Cotopaxi

A. *Write the correct word(s) to complete each sentence.*

1. The highlands of Ecuador have pleasant —— year round.
2. Because of the thin air, the highlands become —— at night.
3. —— is the capital city of Ecuador.
4. —— and —— provide dairy products, meat, and wool.
5. Indians and —— make up most of the population of Ecuador.
6. Some of the Indians are weavers or potters, but most are ——.
7. The —— make it difficult for the Indians to travel.
8. —— is the highest mountain in Ecuador.
9. —— is the highest mountain of the Andes.
10. —— is one of the highest active volcanoes in the world.

B. *Answer these questions.*

1. How far is Quito from the equator?
2. What kind of crops are raised in the highlands?
3. Where do most of the Indians of Ecuador live?
4. How are mestizos different from Indians?
5. How many active volcanoes does Ecuador have?

Further Study

1. Name some ways that the mountain peaks of Ecuador are like most of Greenland.
2. Name some ways that the mountain peaks of Ecuador are different from Greenland.

Map Exercises

1. On your map of Ecuador, label Quito and Riobamba.
2. Mark both Chimborazo and Cotopaxi with a ▲ sign, and then label them.

B. 1. a few miles
  2. cool-weather crops (potatoes, beans, and grain)
  3. in the mountains
  4. The mestizos are part Indian (and part Spanish).
  5. three

Further Study
1. They have cold temperatures and are covered with snow.
2. —The air is not thin on Greenland.
  —Greenland has long summer days and short winter days; the mountain peaks in Ecuador have about the same amount of sunlight the year round.

Map Exercises
(Individual answers. Check maps for accuracy and neatness.)

276   Unit 4, Chapter 8 High Lands and Dry Lands

38. Life in a Desert

Glossary Words

burnoose

burnoose (bur NOOS) A hooded robe worn by Arabs.

caravan (KAR uh van) A group of desert travelers.

dune (DOON) A hill of sand that has been piled up by wind.

oasis (oh AY sihs) A green, watered place surrounded by a desert.

sheik (SHEEK) The leader of an Arab tribe.

caravan

Deserts of the World

The dry lands of the world are called deserts. Many deserts are found in the warm regions near the Tropic of Cancer and the Tropic of Capricorn. Other deserts, like the Gobi Desert (GOH bee) in central Asia, are farther from the equator. These deserts have hot summers and very cold winters.

Some deserts cover only a small area. Others cover vast regions. The largest desert of all is the Sahara in northern Africa.

Not all deserts are full of sand *dunes*. God also placed rocks, mountains, and hardy desert plants in some deserts. But all deserts have one thing in common—they receive very little rainfall.

Let us visit Ahab as he travels with his tribe in the Sahara.

At Home in a Tent

Ahab herded the sheep and the goats toward his father's tent. There had not been much food for

LESSON AIM

To introduce the students to the deserts of the world and to show how some desert dwellers live.

MAIN POINTS

- **The dry lands of the world are called deserts.** Many deserts are found near the Tropics of Cancer and Capricorn. Others are located farther from the equator.

- **The Sahara is the largest desert in the world.** [It is not usually called the "Sahara Desert" because Sahara comes from the Arabic word for *desert*.]

- **Desert lands may be covered with sand dunes, rocks, mountains, or desert plants.** Sandy areas occasionally have sandstorms.

- **Sheep, goats, and camels are raised on the sparse desert plants.**

- **Deserts are often hot during the day and cold at night.**

- **Many desert dwellers live in tents and wander from place to place.** Leaders of Arab tribes are called sheiks. (The term *nomad* was introduced in Lesson 6. It will be reviewed in Lesson 39.)

- **Camels are especially well suited for desert life.** Because of their ability to go for days without food and water, they are the main pack animals in caravans. [They are also valued for their rich, sweet milk.]

the animals that day. It was getting harder and harder to find grass and shrubs near this camp. He was glad that they would soon be moving on to another *oasis*.

Ahab watched the setting sun as it sank toward the great sand dunes on the western horizon. Their journey would take them away from this area of the shifting dunes and their ever-changing pattern of landscape. Winds carried sand up one side of a dune and dumped it on the other side. Thus the sand hills seemed to creep and move around the desert with a strange kind of beauty.

Suddenly Ahab saw a dusty cloud that made him hurry the flock. A sandstorm was coming! He unwound the end of the cloth that he wore wrapped around his head. He would use it to cover his face if the sandstorm struck before he was in the tent.

The animals would be safe. Near the tents, the camels would lie down with their backs to the wind. The sheep and the goats would huddle in the shelter of the camels' bodies and wait through the fury of flying sand. In a sandstorm the air can be so thick with sand that it is impossible for a person to see where he is going. The strong wind throws the sand with stinging force. A storm might last a few hours or a few days.

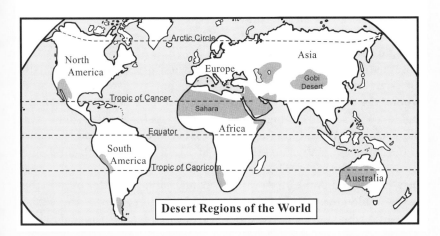

Desert Regions of the World

RELATED POINTS

- The Bible refers to camel caravans in many Old Testament accounts. Abraham's servant traveled with camels (Genesis 24:10, 11, 19, 20, 32, 63, 64); it was a camel caravan that brought Joseph into Egypt (Genesis 37:25); and the Queen of Sheba used camels to bring gifts to Solomon (1 Kings 10:2). Many other passages mention camels, deserts, and the life of shepherds and nomads.

Desert shrubs are the only plants that can survive in the dry, rocky ground of the eastern Sahara.

When Ahab reached the tent, he helped his mother let down and fasten the black goat-hair curtains at the sides of the tent. His parents and brothers and sisters stayed in the tent while the swirling wind piled sand around the outside. Sand drifted inside too. It settled on them and their food. Ahab and his family drank cups of sweet tea and then lay down for the night. The night grew cold, and Ahab drew his heavy woolen ***burnoose*** around himself to keep warm. He fell asleep to the sound of howling wind and swishing sand.

Traveling in a Desert

When Ahab woke early the next morning, the air was still. His parents were up and preparing to move. Some of the family helped take down the goat-hair curtains and the poles of their tent. Ahab and his brother Benjamin took two camels and the water bags to the well at the center of the oasis. What little grass that had been left was now buried in drifts of sand.

The boys filled their goatskin bags with water and loaded them on the camels. When they returned to the camp, the tent pieces were folded and loaded on other camels. Everything was packed and ready to move when the word was given. The other families about them were also making final preparations for the journey. At last their *sheik* mounted his camel and led the way across the sands toward another oasis that he thought would be a good place for their next stay.

As the day wore on, the heat grew more intense. Ahab took off his burnoose and walked in his light cotton robe. Though it was hot, Ahab kept his skin well covered to protect it from the burning sun. He also kept the cloth veil on his head for shade.

When it was nearly midday and the sun was beating down its hottest, the sheik called a halt. The mothers served goat cheese and figs, and the animals found a few desert shrubs on which to graze. The tribe relaxed through the hottest hours of the day. In a

Sand dunes creep across an Egyptian highway. In some places, trucks plow the sand off the highways much as trucks in cold areas plow snow.

few hours, they packed up and traveled another stretch before stopping for the night.

During the second morning, Ahab saw small, barren hills in the distance. The *caravan* began to cross areas of hard, rocky ground. Gradually the large sand dunes were left behind.

Later that day, Father pointed out to Ahab a dark hump on the horizon. It was the tops of palm trees at the next oasis! Everyone was glad to see that they were near the end of their journey. Even the animals seemed to sense that water was near, and they pressed on more eagerly.

The sheep and the goats needed water more than the camels did. God has made the camels especially suited to desert life. They are able to live on the tough scrub bushes of the desert. Good feeding and sufficient water help a camel build up a great fatty hump on its back that serves as a storehouse. The camel can travel across the desert for days or even

The Mongols of the Gobi Desert

The Gobi Desert is a large desert in central Asia. The people who live there are called Mongols. They raise sheep and live in round shelters called yurts. Yurts are made with wooden frames covered with fur or wool cloth, which helps keep the Mongols warm during the cold winters. The Mongols wear warm sheepskin clothes.

Mongols use horses and ponies much more than the nomads of the Sahara do. They also have camels, but their camels have two humps instead of one hump like the Sahara camels. These two-hump camels have longer wool and are better suited for cold weather.

A Mongol and his yurt

weeks without food or water. In a sandstorm, the camel can close its nostrils tightly and cover its eyes with three sets of eyelids. Loose sand makes no problem for the camel in walking. The two-hoofed toes on each foot spread when the camel steps, and a broad cush-ioned pad keeps the foot from sinking into the sand.

Notice that the camel's nostrils are slits. This helps to keep flying sand out as the camel breathes.

Testing Your Understanding

A. *Write* true *or* false *for each sentence. Copy each false sentence, and change one word in it to make it true.*

1. Many deserts are found near the Tropic of Cancer and the Tropic of Capricorn.
2. The largest desert in the world is the Gobi.
3. The Sahara is in southern Africa.
4. Some deserts are covered with rocks or desert plants.
5. A dune is a strong wind that blows sand with stinging force.
6. Ahab and his family lived in a burnoose made of black goat-hair curtains.
7. Sheep, goats, and camels eat grass and desert shrubs.
8. The Sahara is much warmer during the day than at night.
9. A caravan is a group of desert travelers.
10. Camels need water more often than sheep and goats.

Lesson 38 Answers

Testing Your Understanding

A. 1. true
2. false; The largest desert in the world is the ~~Gobi~~ Sahara.
3. false; The Sahara is in ~~southern~~ northern Africa.
4. true
5. false; A ~~dune~~ sandstorm is a strong wind that blows sand with stinging force.
6. false; Ahab and his family lived in a ~~burnoose~~ tent made of black goat-hair curtains.
7. true
8. true
9. true
10. false; Camels need water ~~more~~ less often than sheep and goats.

B. 1. All deserts receive very little rainfall.
2. Winds blow the sand.
3. The goats and camels had eaten most of the grass and shrubs near their camp.
4. He could cover his face with the cloth he wore on his head.
5. They filled their goatskin bags with water and loaded them on the camels.
6. the sheik
7. their fatty humps

Further Study

1. (Sample answers)
—Travelers can lose their way in the blinding storms.
—The stinging sand could cause injury to people or animals.
2. Wells are scarce and far apart in the desert. Camels can go without water for a while, but other animals and people need it daily.
3. rocky ground (and barren hills)

Map Exercises

1. Mauritania, Mali, Niger, Chad, Sudan, Egypt, Libya, Tunisia, Algeria, Morocco, (Western Sahara)
Note: Only a small part of Morocco is in the Sahara. At the time of this writing, Morocco claimed the area called Western Sahara.
2. Atlas Mountains
3. Ahaggar Mountains
4. Aïr, Tibesti Mountains

B. *Write answers to these questions.*

1. How are all deserts alike?
2. How do sand dunes move?
3. Why did Ahab's tribe need to move on to another place?
4. How could Ahab protect his face from flying sand outside the tent?
5. What did Ahab and Benjamin do just before they started their journey?
6. Who decided where the tribe would go next?
7. What serves as a storehouse for camels?

Further Study

1. Why is it dangerous to travel during a sandstorm?
2. Why was it important for the caravan to take bags of water along?
3. What type of land did the caravan cross after it left the large sand dunes?

Map Exercises

Use the map on page 283 to complete these exercises.

1. Write the names of all the countries that are partly in the Sahara.
2. Name the mountain region that is northwest of the Sahara.
3. Name the mountain region that is near the center of the Sahara.
4. Name the mountain regions that are in Niger and Chad.

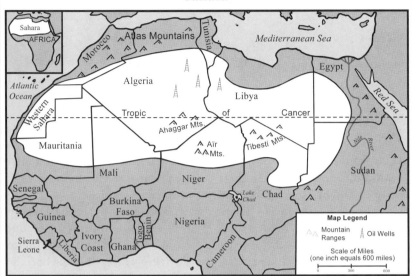

Sahara

39. A Desert Oasis

Glossary Words

haggle (HAG uhl) To discuss prices in an effort to come to an agreement; bargain.

nomads (NOH madz) People who live in movable dwellings and move frequently from one place to another.

At the Oasis

Ahab's caravan pitched their tents on the dry ground beyond the edge of the great oasis. There was enough water here to support many trees and fields of crops, but no one would think of living in the lush watered space. Even the permanent dwellers at the oasis built their houses in a small town out on the desert. Every bit of watered land must be used for growing plants.

Low fences surrounded much of the oasis. Inside the fence, irrigation streams carried water to plots of beans, grapes, peppers, cucumbers, and squash. Fields of barley provided a valuable grain supply. And there were trees! The shade looked inviting, yet Ahab knew the delicious fruit of the trees was even more important. Most of them were date palm trees. Orange, apricot, and olive trees were growing between some of the date palms.

The sandy soil of the desert is rich enough to grow trees and crops. The hot sunshine helps them grow fast. Only the need for water keeps the vast stretches of desert barren.

Bargaining With Merchants

One day Ahab and Benjamin went into the town with their father. Father wanted to sell some goatskins and camel hair. He showed a merchant the fine quality of hair and told him how much he wanted for them. The merchant seemed shocked at such a price and offered a much lower sum. Father shook his head and said it would not be worth his time to keep the animals for that amount. He asked another

LESSON AIM

To give a glimpse of life at a desert oasis and to briefly show how the discovery of oil has changed the lives of some desert dwellers.

MAIN POINTS

- **Oases are found wherever there is water in the deserts.** The amount of water available determines the amount of land that can be irrigated for trees and crops. Towns are often built near large oases.

- **Desert nomads buy and sell products at the oasis towns.** Merchants and customers haggle over prices until they reach an agreement.

- **Houses in the desert towns are built with sun-dried mud bricks.** The thick earthen walls help keep the temperature inside comfortable.

- **The discovery of oil has changed the lives of some desert dwellers.** The men who work at oil wells can afford better houses, and some buy vehicles. But other desert men are still nomads who live much as their tribes have lived for hundreds of years.

RELATED POINTS

- The country of Egypt contains a large oasis that is watered by the Nile River. Most of Egypt lies in the northeastern part of the Sahara.

- Wells are frequently mentioned in the Bible. Following are a few references you may want to discuss with your students. Genesis 21:14–19, 25, 31, 33; 25:11; 26:1, 6, 12–25; Exodus 15:22, 23, 27.

An oasis town in the Sahara. Notice how the town is built back from the trees and plants that flourish near the well.

amount a bit lower than his first price. The merchant shook his head and said he still could not afford it. Then he offered an amount a bit higher than his first offer. Father came down a bit more. The merchant came up a bit more, and finally they agreed on a price that satisfied both of them.

Next Father went to a farmer who was selling raisins and dried dates. At first the farmer asked a price that was much too high for the food. Father disagreed and offered a very low price. Then they **haggled** over the price until they reached an agreement.

Houses at the Oasis

Father and the boys walked back through town with their supply of raisins and dates. As Ahab and Benjamin looked down one street, they saw a crowd of people. "Father," Benjamin asked, "what are they doing?"

"It looks as if they are building a new house," Father

The camel and the jeep are the two main ways of transportation in the Sahara.

replied. He led the boys down the street where they could see the activity. The houses in town were not goat-hair tents. They had permanent walls of sun-dried mud bricks. This house was nearly finished. The walls were done, and the roof was being made. Strong men were placing logs from palm tree trunks across the walls. A pile of palm leaves was ready to spread over the logs. Beside the house some boys were tramping around in a hollow filled with mud. The earth and water they were mixing would be plastered over the palm leaves on the roof, where it would dry into a hard surface.

"That is how they make the bricks too," Father told the boys. "They mix mud and shape it into blocks, and then let it dry hard."

Ahab looked at the new house. "I don't see any blocks."

"After they lay the blocks, they coat the walls with mud," explained Father. "These earth walls help to keep the houses cooler during the hot days. And at night, they are warmer than a tent."

Jeeps and Oil Wells

"Look, Father!" exclaimed Ahab as they left the town and started toward their camp. "What is coming?" Far across the desert, they could see something speeding toward them.

"That is a jeep," Father answered. "Workers from one of the oil wells near here are probably coming to town."

Ahab and Benjamin waved as the men in the jeep passed them. "I haven't seen a jeep for a long time! Why don't we get one, Father?" Ahab asked.

"Jeeps work fine for some people, but camels are much better for us. Jeeps can break down or run out of gasoline far out in the desert. Camels don't need gasoline. They give us milk to drink and hair for cloth. Their hides provide leather. Jeeps can travel faster, but if we traveled fast, the sheep and the goats could not keep up.

"Life has changed since oil was found in the desert. Many men have moved near the oil wells, where they can earn more money. There they can have nice houses and drive cars or jeeps. But I like our life better. We **nomads** are free to come and go as we please."

Back at their camp that evening, Ahab sat by the tent and watched the stars come out. The dry desert air lost its heat quickly, and the night winds were beginning to feel cold. Ahab pulled his warm burnoose around himself. "Houses and jeeps are all right for some people," he thought, "but give me the beauty of the wide-open desert spaces. I want to be a nomad like my father."

=========== Testing Your Understanding ===========

A. *Write the correct word(s) to complete each sentence.*

1. Most areas of a desert do not have enough —— for crops and trees to grow.

2. Most of the trees grown in the Sahara are —— trees.

3. Father took —— and —— hair to sell at the market.

4. Father and the merchants —— over prices until they reached an agreement.

Lesson 39 Answers

Testing Your Understanding

A. 1. water
   2. date palm
   3. goatskins, camel
   4. haggled

5. raisins, dates
6. houses
7. mud bricks
8. palm trees
9. oil wells
10. nomads

B. 1. Every bit of watered land must be used for growing plants.
2. Oases are the only spots in deserts with enough water for crops and trees to grow.
3. The towns provide a place for the nomads to sell their products and buy what they need.
4. The walls keep the houses cooler during the day and warmer at night.
5. mud

Further Study
1. Nomads need shelters that can be easily moved, since they travel from place to place with their flocks.
2. (Sample answers)
—Camels do not need gasoline or any other special fuel.
—Camels do not break down or run out of fuel.
—Camels provide milk, hair, and hides. (They also provide meat, but it is eaten only on special occasions or when an animal must be killed—such as when it breaks a leg.)
—Camels travel slowly enough for sheep and goats.

Map Exercises
1. a. about 5 inches
   b. about 3,000 miles
2. Libya and Algeria

5. Father bought —— and —— while he was in town.
6. In the oasis towns, people live in —— instead of tents.
7. The walls of the houses are made of sun-dried ——.
8. The roofs are made with the trunks and leaves of ——.
9. The men who work at the —— earn more money than the nomads do.
10. People who are —— can come and go as they please.

B. *Answer these questions.*
1. Why did the nomads pitch their tents on the dry ground outside the oasis?
2. Why do crops and trees grow in an oasis but not in the surrounding desert?
3. How do towns help the nomads?
4. How do the mud walls of the houses help keep them comfortable?
5. What is used to make a hard surface on the roof?

Further Study
1. Why do the nomads live in tents instead of houses?
2. Why is it better for the nomads to use camels rather than jeeps? (Give several reasons.)

Map Exercises
Use the map on page 283 to complete these exercises.
1. Notice the scale of miles at the bottom of the map. It tells you that on this map, one inch represents 600 miles. Use a ruler to measure the number of inches between the Atlantic Ocean and the Nile River. Then multiply the number of inches by 600 to find how wide the Sahara is.
   a. About how many inches wide is this area on the map?
   b. About how many miles wide is the Sahara?
2. In which countries are most of the Sahara oil wells found?

40. Chapter 8 Review

―――――――――― Testing Your Understanding ――――――――――

A. *Write a glossary word for each definition.*

1. A group of desert travelers.
2. A person who is part Indian and part Spanish.
3. The level of the oceans.
4. A hill of sand.
5. People who move from place to place.
6. A green, watered spot in the desert.
7. The unit of money used in Ecuador.
8. The leader of an Arab tribe.
9. The height above the level of the oceans.
10. A hooded robe worn by some desert nomads.

B. *Write* true *or* false *for each sentence. Copy each false sentence, and change one word in it to make it true.*

1. The Andes are high mountains in North America.
2. The equator runs through Ecuador.
3. Tropical crops are grown in the highlands of Ecuador.
4. The city of Guayaquil has cool weather year round.
5. Quito is the capital of Niger.
6. Mount Everest is one of the highest active volcanoes in the world.
7. Many deserts are found near the Tropic of Cancer.
8. The Sahara is the largest desert in the world.
9. Desert nomads raise camels, sheep, and goats.
10. Goats can go without water for many days.
11. Oases are found wherever soil is available.
12. People who live in desert towns usually have houses instead of tents.

Lesson 40 Answers

Testing Your Understanding

A. 1. caravan
2. mestizo
3. sea level
4. dune
5. nomads
6. oasis
7. sucre
8. sheik
9. altitude
10. burnoose

B. 1. false; The Andes are high mountains in ~~North~~ South America.
2. true
3. false; Tropical crops are grown in the ~~highlands~~ lowlands of Ecuador.
4. false; The city of ~~Guayaquil~~ Quito has cool weather year round. or The city of Guayaquil has ~~cool~~ hot (or warm) weather year round.
5. false; Quito is the capital of ~~Niger~~ Ecuador.
6. false; Mount ~~Everest~~ Cotopaxi is one of the highest active volcanoes in the world.
7. true
8. true
9. true
10. false; ~~Goats~~ Camels can go without water for many days.
11. false; Oases are found wherever ~~soil~~ water is available.
12. true

C. 1. (Sample answers)
  —The highlands are cooler than the lowlands.
  —Tropical crops are raised in the low-lands; cool-weather crops are raised in the highlands.
  —The air in the highlands is thinner than the air in the lowlands.
  —The mountains of the highlands make travel more difficult.
  —Indians live in the highlands; mestizos live in the lowlands.
  —The highlands do not have as many insect pests.
2. the thin air at high altitudes
3. Chimborazo
4. to find grazing for their herds
5. Nomads are free to come and go as they please.

Map Exercises
1. Pacific Ocean
2. Peru, Colombia
3. Guayaquil, Riobamba, Quito
4. Ahaggar Mountains
5. Egypt
6. about 3,000 miles

Review Study
1. (Review glossary words in class.)
2. (Have students point out Ecuador and the Sahara.)
3. Asia
4. on the tops of the Andes Mountains (Snowcapped mountains are also found near the equator in Africa.)

C. *Answer these questions.*

1. How are the highlands of Ecuador different from the lowlands of Ecuador? (List at least three ways.)
2. What causes mountain sickness?
3. What is the highest mountain in Ecuador?
4. Why do desert nomads need to move from place to place?
5. Why do some nomads continue living in the desert rather than working for more money in a town or at an oil well?

Map Exercises

Use your completed map of Ecuador to answer these questions.

1. What ocean is west of Ecuador?
2. What two countries border Ecuador?
3. What three cities of Ecuador are mentioned in the text?

Use a map of the Sahara to answer these questions.

4. What Sahara mountain region is in the country of Algeria?
5. What country is in the northeast corner of the Sahara?
6. About how wide is the Sahara?

Review Study

1. Do you know the meaning of all the glossary words in Chapter 8?
2. Can you find Ecuador and the Sahara on a world map?
3. Do you know which continent has the highest mountains in the world?
4. Do you know where snow can be found near the equator?

So Far This Year

1. The largest river in the world is the (Amazon, Nile, Rhine) River in Brazil.
2. Choose two: Some animals prepare for winter by (migrating, molting, hibernating, ruminating).
3. During (summer, winter) in the Frigid Zone, the sun can be seen at midnight.
4. The largest desert in the world is the (Niger, Sahara, Gobi) in northern Africa.
5. A game reserve is (a safe place for playing games, a place of safety for wild animals).
6. A large group of islands is an (arena, archipelago, architect).
7. (Carabaos, Horses, Oxen) are important farm animals in the Philippines.
8. The smallest continent is (Africa, Europe, Australia, Asia).
9. All (mammals, marsupials, marmots) carry their young in a pouch.
10. Water flows out of an (artistic, artificial, artesian) well by its own pressure.
11. The Gulf Stream is a (warm, cold) ocean current that flows along the coasts of Europe.
12. (Locks, Dams, Dikes) are used to raise or lower ships from one water level to another.
13. The autobahn is a large (highway, railroad) in Germany.
14. The Netherlands is known for all the following except (tulips, windmills, watches, wooden shoes).
15. (Locks, Dikes, Terraces) are level steps cut into hillsides to provide more land for farming.
16. Choose two: The countries of (Nigeria, Switzerland, Brazil, Japan) have few natural resources but many skilled workers.
17. The main business in Greenland is (farming, fishing, lumbering).

So Far This Year
1. Amazon
2. migrating, hibernating
3. summer
4. Sahara
5. a place of safety for wild animals
6. archipelago
7. Carabaos
8. Australia
9. marsupials
10. artesian
11. warm
12. Locks
13. highway
14. watches
15. Terraces
16. Switzerland, Japan
17. fishing

18. glaciers
19. steppe
20. hurricanes
21. people
22. springlike weather year round
23. hogs

18. Icebergs break off from (avalanches, blizzards, glaciers) and float out into the sea.

19. A (plateau, steppe, tundra) is a large, grassy plain in Siberia.

20. All the following are common in Iceland except (volcanoes, geysers, hot springs, hurricanes, earthquakes).

21. All the following creatures make their homes in Antarctica except (insects, penguins, petrels, people, seals).

22. The highlands of Ecuador have (four seasons, a rainy season and a dry season, springlike weather year round).

23. People of the desert raise all the following animals except (sheep, hogs, goats, camels).

UNIT FIVE
Neighboring Lands

Beautiful Mt. Hood, in the Cascade Range in Oregon, casts a sharp reflection in clear blue waters.

CHAPTER 9

NORTH AMERICAN HOMELANDS

"For all the law is fulfilled in one word, even in this; Thou shalt love thy neighbor as thyself" (Galatians 5:14).

41. Regions of the United States

Glossary Words

Continental Divide (kahn tuh NEHN tuhl) A ridge of mountains that separates streams flowing into the Pacific Ocean from streams flowing into the Atlantic Ocean.

state One of the divisions of land in some countries, such as the United States of America.

The United States of America is a nation of fifty *states*. What kind of land is found in the United States? Find this country on a world map or globe. Most of the United States is in the southern part of the Northern Temperate Zone. What kind of

United States

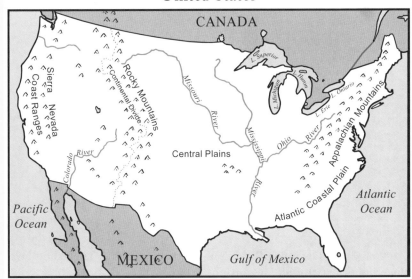

LESSON AIM

To introduce the students to the geography and climates of the United States.

MAIN POINTS

- **Most of the United States is in the southern part of the Northern Temperate Zone.** It has a variety of climates.

- **Farming and manufacturing are important along the Atlantic Coast.** More manufacturing is done in the North, and more farming is done in the South.

- **The Appalachian Mountains stretch from Alabama to Canada.**

- **The Central Plains are a good farming region.** The Mississippi River and its tributaries drain into the Gulf of Mexico. The eastern part of the Central Plains has plenty of rainfall, but the western part, or Great Plains, receives less rainfall. Products are shipped down the Mississippi River and from ports on the Great Lakes.

- **The western mountain region has chains of mountains running north and south.** The Continental Divide separates the streams that flow into the Pacific Ocean from the streams that flow into the Atlantic Ocean. Some areas of the West have plenty of rainfall, but other areas are deserts.

- **Alaska and Hawaii are separate from the other states.** Part of Alaska is in the Northern Frigid Zone. Hawaii is a group of islands in the Tropical Zone.

climate do you think the United States has?

God has blessed much of the United States with a pleasant, temperate climate. But the country has a variety of climates, from tropical to frigid and from dry deserts to well-watered crop-lands.

Eastern United States

Coastal plains lie near the Atlantic Ocean. This is a good area for farming as well as for manufacturing. Harbors along the coast make it easy to do business with other nations. Merchants import goods for the factories, and they export manufactured products. More manufacturing is done in the North, where winters are longer and colder. More farming is done in the South, where the growing season is longer. Since the South is near the Tropical Zone, the climate there is nearly tropical. Produce from southern farms is shipped north, and manufactured goods from northern factories are shipped south.

West of the coastal plains rise rolling hills and wooded mountains. This is the Appalachian

The Atlantic coastal plain is a good place to grow produce. This field of onions is in Georgia.

Highland region. The Appalachian Mountains stretch from Alabama all the way to Canada.

The next region is the Central Plains. Great areas of flat land stretch for miles and miles. The mighty Mississippi River and its tributaries drain rainfall from this area into the Gulf of Mexico in the south. Find the Ohio River

RELATED POINTS

- Trace the boundaries of the United States. Notice which countries and oceans border it. Use a globe to show how far Alaska and Hawaii are from the other forty-eight states.

- **The United States is the fourth largest country in the world.** Only Russia, Canada, and China are larger.

Large cities have developed in the United States, especially along the coasts and on the Great Lakes. This is Chicago, a giant industrial city at the south end of Lake Michigan.

and the Missouri River on the map. They bring water from the mountains in both directions to the Central Plains.

The eastern part of the Central Plains receives plenty of rainfall. Corn is an important crop. Large cities have been built around the Great Lakes and along the main rivers. Find the five Great Lakes. Which is the only one that does not touch Canada?

The western part of the Central Plains are called the Great Plains. This region is sometimes called the Breadbasket of America. The Great Plains are a good farming area, and vast fields of wheat provide bread for many people. Some of the wheat is shipped down the Mississippi River and on to other countries of the world. Some of it is shipped from ports on the Great Lakes. The Great Plains are somewhat drier than the plains east of the Mississippi, but wheat does not need as much water as some other crops do. This is also an excellent area for raising hay and cattle.

Western United States

There is one more important region in the United States. Between the Great Plains and the Pacific Ocean is a wide area of high mountains, plateaus, and valleys. The Rocky Mountains, the Sierra Nevada Mountains, and the Coast Ranges are chains of mountains that run north and south through the western part of the country. The ***Continental Divide*** is a line in the Rocky Mountains. All the water on one side of this line runs into rivers that empty into the Pacific Ocean. All the water on the other side of the line runs into the Atlantic Ocean or the Gulf of Mexico, which joins the Atlantic.

The West Coast is a good growing region with a pleasant climate. Clouds from the ocean

Wheat grows in the dry Great Plains. Farmers often plant their wheat in strips as this picture shows. Each year, only half of the field is planted. This helps to conserve moisture. Next year, the dark brown strips will be planted and this year's wheat strips will lie empty. That way, each crop of wheat benefits from two years' worth of moisture.

The Location of Alaska
and Hawaii

bring plentiful rainfall. But the clouds lose most of their moisture as they pass over the high mountain peaks. Some of the valley regions in the west are very dry. Some valleys are very hot, especially in the southern part of this region. There you will find the deserts of the United States. In the western mountain ranges, you will also find the cold climate of the highlands. Some of the mountains are covered with snow all year round.

The United States has an even colder region—the state of Alaska. Alaska is separate from the main part of the country. It lies far to the northwest, beside Canada. Part of Alaska is north of the Arctic Circle.

The most tropical part of the United States is also separate from the main part of the country. Far away in the Pacific Ocean is a group of islands that forms the state of Hawaii. The islands are tops of volcanic mountains, and some of the volcanoes are active. Hawaii is in the Tropical Zone and has a pleasant climate year round.

Lesson 41 Answers

Testing Your Understanding
A. 1. Northern Temperate Zone
   2. coastal plains
   3. factories
   4. west

Testing Your Understanding

A. *Choose the correct answer.*

1. Most of the United States is in the (Tropical Zone, Northern Temperate Zone, Frigid Zone).
2. A region of (highlands, plateaus, coastal plains) lies along the Atlantic Ocean.
3. The North has more (factories, farms, warm weather) than the South.
4. The Appalachian Mountains are (west, east, south) of the coastal plains.

5. The Mississippi River and its tributaries drain the (Gulf of Mexico, Central Plains, Great Lakes).

6. The (Sierra Nevada, West Coast, Continental Divide) separates the rivers flowing into the Pacific Ocean from the rivers flowing into the Atlantic Ocean.

7. Clouds from the Pacific Ocean lose moisture as they pass over (deserts, high mountains, the Gulf of Mexico).

8. The coldest part of the United States is (Alaska, the Rocky Mountains, the West Coast).

9. Part of Alaska lies north of the (Atlantic Ocean, Arctic Circle, Frigid Zone).

10. Hawaii is (a cold state, a region of plains, a group of islands).

B. *Answer these questions.*

1. How far north and south do the Appalachian Mountains stretch?

2. Why are the Great Plains sometimes called the Breadbasket of America?

3. What three main mountain chains run north and south through the western United States?

4. Are the deserts of the United States in the East or in the West?

Further Study

Use a map of the United States to answer these questions.

1. Name the five Great Lakes.

2. Which one of the Great Lakes does not touch Canada?

3. What country lies south of the western United States?

Map Exercises

1. Trace Map I in the map section. Notice that Alaska and Hawaii are not shown on the map.

5. Central Plains
6. Continental Divide
7. high mountains
8. Alaska
9. Arctic Circle
10. a group of islands

B. 1. from Alabama to Canada
2. Wheat from the Great Plains provides bread for many people.
3. the Rocky Mountains, the Sierra Nevada, and the Coast Ranges
4. in the West

Further Study
1. Lake Ontario, Lake Erie, Lake Huron, Lake Michigan, Lake Superior
2. Lake Michigan
3. Mexico

Map Exercises
(Individual work. Check maps for accuracy and neatness.)

(Individual work. Check maps for accuracy and neatness.)

4. a. Russia
   b. Canada
   c. Pacific Ocean
   d. Asia

2. Label the Mississippi River, the Missouri River, the Ohio River, and Lake Michigan.

3. Label the Atlantic Coastal Plain, the Appalachian Mountains, and the Central Plains. Then label the Rocky Mountains, the Sierra Nevada, and the Coast Ranges.

4. Find Alaska and Hawaii on a globe or world map, and answer these questions.
   a. Which country is west of Alaska?
   b. Which country is east of Alaska?
   c. In what ocean is Hawaii?
   d. What great continent is west of Hawaii?

42. A Nation of Fifty States

Glossary Words

Congress (KAHNG grihs) The group of people who make laws for the United States.

county seat The town or city that is the center of county government.

government The people who rule a country or part of a country.

governor The highest leader in a state.

population (pahp yoo LAY shun) The number of people living at a certain place.

president The highest leader in the United States.

tax Money that people pay to their government.

The United States Government

A nation is much more than land and mountains and rivers. A nation is the people and their actions and ideas. People in a nation must work together in agreement.

Different parts of a nation provide things that are needed in the other parts. Oranges grow in Florida. Wheat is raised in Kansas. Cars are made in Michigan. People use trucks, ships, and railroads to exchange these things with each other.

Laws are an important part of a nation. Laws give us freedom to worship God without being persecuted. Some laws tell how to drive safely. Some laws tell how much *tax* to pay. Laws help people to treat each other fairly.

Each nation has a capital city as its headquarters. The capital is where laws are made and other national business is conducted. The capital of the United States is Washington, D.C.

The leader of the nation is called the *president*. A president is chosen by the votes of the people. He is president four years at a time. During that time he lives in a special home in Washington, D.C. called the White House.

LESSON AIM

To introduce the students to the government and the states within the United States.

MAIN POINTS

- **Laws help people to work together.**
- **Washington, D.C. is the capital of the United States.**
- **The United States government has three parts: the president, Congress, and judges.**
- **The United States has fifty states.** Each state has its own government and capital city.
- **The states are divided into counties.** The business of the county is centered in the county seat. [See note in Answer Key, Testing Your Understanding, Part B.]
- **The states vary in size and population.** Alaska is the largest state but has the smallest population.

Rhode Island is the smallest state. California has the largest population.

- **States have nicknames and state birds, flowers, trees, and other special symbols.**

RELATED POINTS

- Discuss reasons why some areas are more populated than others. Point out that frigid, desert, and mountainous lands usually have fewer people. Also notice that most large cities are located along oceans, rivers, or large lakes.
- If your school is in the United States, discuss how the factories and farms in your area benefit other parts of the country.
- Remember: *capital* means city; *capitol* means legislative building.

The White House is home for the president and his family.

The president does not rule the nation all by himself. He has to work with ***Congress***. Congress is a group of people who discuss and plan laws for the nation. They cannot do much without the president's approval, and the president cannot do much without the approval of Congress. They must work together for the good of the nation. Judges help to decide how the laws shall be obeyed. The president, Congress, and the judges are three main parts of the United States ***government***.

The Fifty States

The United States is a nation of fifty states united under one main government. But each state also has its own ***governor*** and other officials, who take care of smaller matters within that state. Each state has a capital city. What is the capital of your state?

Each state is further divided into sections called counties. The main city in a county is called the ***county seat***. It has offices to take care of the government business for that area. Do you know the

Washington, D.C.

The capital of the United States is Washington, D.C. The initials *D.C.* stand for District of Columbia. The city of Washington is in a special little district that is not part of any state. This district is between Maryland and Virginia on the Potomac River. Find Washington, D.C. on the map on page 307.

The long building with the tall, columned dome is the Capitol of the United States.

Each state has its own capital city. This is the capitol building of Vermont.

name of the county where you live? What is the name of the county seat?

Some states are very large, and some are much smaller. Alaska is the largest state. It is almost five hundred times as large as Rhode Island, the smallest state. On a map, different colors are often used to show where the different states are. But the actual land is not those colors. The states are divided by invisible lines that people have agreed on for boundaries. Like friendly neighbors who agree where their property lines are, the states do not need fences to mark their boundaries. Sometimes the boundaries follow a mountain range or a river.

The states do not have the same number of people. More people live in the big state of California than in any other state. But some of the large western states have fewer people than many of the small eastern states. And even though Alaska is the largest in size, it has one of the smallest **populations** of any state. Most Americans prefer living in states farther south where the climate is warmer.

Each state has a nickname that tells something about that state. Delaware is called the First State. Can you guess why? Do you know why Arizona is called the Grand Canyon State? Some state nicknames come from plants or animals in those states. The Pine Tree State is Maine, and the Sunflower State is Kansas. Louisiana is the Pelican State, Michigan is the Wolverine State,

Minnesota is the Gopher State, and Oregon is the Beaver State.

Each state has also chosen a certain bird to be a symbol of that state. The Baltimore oriole is the state bird of Maryland, where the city of Baltimore is found. Rhode Island Red is the name of a kind of chicken. Which state do you think has chosen that bird? Some birds have been chosen by more than one state. Illinois, Indiana, Kentucky, North Carolina, Ohio, Virginia, and West Virginia all

The United States

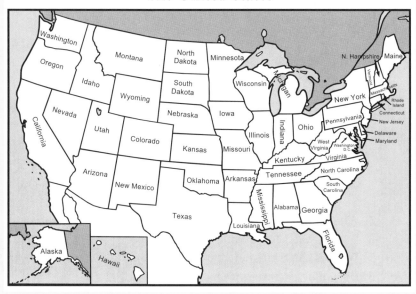

claim the cardinal as their state bird!

The states have other special symbols too. Do you know the state flower and the state tree for your state?

─────── **Testing Your Understanding** ───────

A. *Write the correct word(s) to complete each sentence.*

1. —— give us freedoms and tell us how much tax to pay.
2. —— is the capital city of the United States.
3. The —— is the leader of the United States.
4. A group of people called —— helps to make laws.
5. —— help to decide how laws shall be obeyed.
6. Each state has a —— of its own to take care of smaller matters.
7. States are divided into ——.
8. —— is the largest state, but it has a small population.
9. —— has the largest population of any state.
10. The —— of a state tells something about the state.

B. *If you live in the United States, answer these questions about your state and your county. If you live in another country, choose a state that you think is interesting and answer questions 1–8. Use an encyclopedia or another reference book to find the information.*

1. How large is the state? (Give your answer in square miles.)
2. What states are next to it?
3. What is the capital city?
4. Who is the governor of the state? (Your teacher may need to help you.)
5. When did it become a state?
6. What is the population of the state?
7. What is the state nickname, bird, flower, and tree?
8. How many counties are in the state?

Lesson 42 Answers

Testing Your Understanding

A. 1. Laws
2. Washington, D.C.
3. president
4. Congress
5. Judges
6. governor (government)
7. counties
8. Alaska
9. California
10. nickname

B. (Individual work. Answers depend on states and counties chosen. *Note:* Louisiana is divided into parishes rather than counties, and Alaska has boroughs and municipalities. In New England states, the towns have more responsibility for local government than the counties have.)

9. What is the name of your county?

10. What is the name of your county seat?

Further Study

1. Does any boundary of your state (or the state you chose for Part B) follow a mountain, a river, or a large body of water? If so, tell what that boundary is.

2. Why do more people live in Hawaii than in Alaska?

Map Exercises

1. Trace a map of your state (or the state you chose for Part B).

2. Trace and label the main rivers in the state. Also label any large bodies of water.

3. Mark the capital with a star, and label it. If you live in the state, mark your hometown or city with a dot, and label it. Also mark and label other important cities in the state.

Further Study

1. (Individual work. Answers depend on states chosen.)

2. The climate in Hawaii is much more pleasant than the climate in Alaska.

Map Exercises

(Individual work. Maps depend on states chosen.)

43. Regions of Canada

Glossary Word

Canadian Shield (kuh NAY dee uhn) A large area of Canada that has only a thin layer of soil.

A Large Northern Country

North America has a large nation that is even larger than the United States. Canada is the second largest nation in the world. Only Russia has more land space than Canada.

Canada touches three oceans.

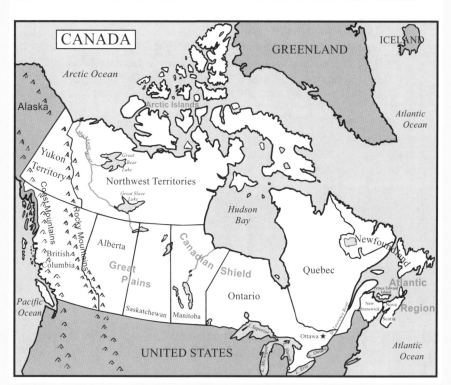

LESSON AIM

To introduce the students to the geography and climates of Canada.

MAIN POINTS

- **Canada is a large nation in North America.** Only Russia is larger. Most of Canada lies in the northern part of the Northern Temperate Zone. The Arctic islands [and some of the mainland] are in the Northern Frigid Zone. Most Canadians live in the South because the northern parts of the country are very cold.

- **The Atlantic region of Canada is milder than most other parts of the country.** Many people live near the St. Lawrence River and the Great Lakes.

- **The Canadian Shield is a cold, rugged land around the Hudson Bay.** The area is rich in minerals, forests, and wildlife, but few people live there.

- **The Great Plains of Canada are valuable for their grain fields and grasslands.** Forests grow in the northern part.

- **Western Canada is mountainous.**

- **The Arctic islands have a very cold climate.**

- **Canada has many lakes and rivers.** The Great Lakes and the St. Lawrence River allow ships from the Atlantic Ocean to sail hundreds of miles into the continent. The Mackenzie River and its tributaries form the greatest river system in Canada.

The Arctic Ocean of the North Pole reaches the islands and coastline of northern Canada. What are the other two oceans that border Canada? What country borders Canada on the south?

Most of Canada is in the northern part of the Northern Temperate Zone. The Arctic islands lie north of the Arctic Circle in the Northern Frigid Zone. Most Canadians live near the southern border because God has given northern Canada a very cold climate.

Regions of Canada

Canada has different land regions. Some of them are part of the same regions that are found in the United States.

A small section in the East is called the Atlantic region. This area has a milder climate than most other places in Canada. The Atlantic Ocean nearby keeps the climate from being severely cold. More people live near the St. Lawrence River and the Great Lakes than in any other part of Canada.

The next main land region is a great horseshoe shape around

Some of Canada's eastern seacoast is mountainous. Fishing and tourism help to provide a living for coastal towns.

the Hudson Bay called the **Canadian Shield**. God has filled this cold, rugged land with forests, hills, lakes, and rivers. Not many people live in the Canadian Shield, but the area is rich in valuable minerals and timber. Deer, elk, moose, wolves, and many smaller animals live there. The northern part of the Canadian Shield is too

RELATED POINTS

• Compare Canada with Siberia. Both lands cover most of the northern part of a continent. Both have tundra in the north and farmland in the south. Their arctic lands are across the North Pole from each other. But Siberia is colder, partly because it has more inland area that is not warmed by large bodies of water.

The farmers near Arborg, Manitoba, grow a variety of crops. The yellow fields are canola, from which cooking oil is made. On the right side of the photo, a blooming alfalfa field is green with a purple cast. Between the two empty fields, a crop of oats is growing. The white specks on the left are beehives.

cold for trees. Here frozen tundra stretches across the empty miles.

West of the Canadian Shield lies a region of great plains. Huge fields of grain stretch for miles and miles across the southern part. Grasslands used for grazing cover some areas of the prairie. North of the grain fields and grasslands are forests of evergreen trees.

Western Canada is a mountainous region. The Rocky Mountains extend from the United States north into Canada. The Coast Mountains run along the Pacific Ocean. Between the Rockies and the Coast Mountains are plateaus, valleys, and more mountains. Even the islands off the west coast of Canada are the tops of mountains sticking out of the ocean.

The Arctic islands north of the mainland are also part of Canada. Few people live on these cold islands, and no trees grow there.

But many beautiful flowers bloom during the short summers when there is daylight around the clock. This is the Land of the Midnight Sun.

Rivers and Lakes of Canada

Canada shares four of the five Great Lakes with the United States. Because of these lakes and the St. Lawrence River, ships from the Atlantic Ocean can sail hundreds of miles into the continent.

Canada's longest river, the Mackenzie, flows through the Northwest Territories to the Arctic Ocean. Barges carry cargo on this river during the summer months when it is not frozen.

Niagara Falls

Niagara Falls is among the best-known waterfalls in the world. The falls are located between Lake Ontario and Lake Erie on the Niagara River. One section, called the Horseshoe Falls, is in Canada. The other section, the American Falls, is in the United States.

Logging in the western Canadian forests provides employment for many people in British Columbia. The steep mountains make logging a hard and dangerous job. To get the logs out of many places, loggers have to bulldoze roads in the forest and construct temporary log bridges over creeks and gorges.

The Great Bear Lake and Great Slave Lake are two large lakes in northern Canada connected to the Mackenzie River. The land is dotted with many, many other lakes and rivers.

─────────── **Testing Your Understanding** ───────────

A. *Write* true *or* false *for each sentence. Copy each false sentence, and change one word in it to make it true.*

1. The only country larger than Canada is China.
2. Most of Canada is in the Northern Frigid Zone.
3. Most Canadians live in southern Canada.
4. The Atlantic region has a colder climate than most other parts of Canada.
5. Many people live near the St. Lawrence River and the Great Lakes.
6. The Canadian Shield is a large area around Alaska.

Lesson 43 Answers

Testing Your Understanding

A. 1. false; The only country larger than Canada is ~~China~~ Russia.
   2. false; Most of Canada is in the Northern ~~Frigid~~ Temperate Zone. [*or*] ~~Most~~ Part of Canada is in the Northern Frigid Zone.
   3. true
   4. false; The Atlantic region has a ~~colder~~ milder (warmer) climate than most other parts of Canada.
   5. true
   6. false; The Canadian Shield is a large area around ~~Alaska~~ Hudson Bay.

7. Huge fields of grain are raised in the northern parts of the Great Plains.

8. The western region of Canada has mountain ranges.

9. During the summer, the Arctic islands have daylight twenty-four hours a day.

10. The Mackenzie River flows into the Pacific Ocean.

B. *Answer these questions.*

1. What country borders Canada on the south? (You may use a map to find the answer.)

2. What helps keep the eastern part of Canada from being severely cold?

3. What lies just north of the grain fields and grasslands of the Great Plains?

4. Why do few people live on the Arctic islands?

5. What makes it possible for ships to sail from the Atlantic Ocean hundreds of miles into North America?

Further Study

1. Which Arctic island of Canada did you study in Chapter 1?

2. What makes the Canadian Shield valuable?

3. Why do barges use the Mackenzie River only during the summer?

Map Exercises

1. Trace Map J in the map section, including the outlines of the Great Lakes that are partly in Canada. Label the Great Lakes.

2. Trace and label the St. Lawrence River, the Mackenzie River, the Great Bear Lake, and the Great Slave Lake.

3. Label the Hudson Bay and the three oceans that border Canada.

4. Label the Atlantic region, the Canadian Shield, the Great Plains, the Rocky Mountains, the Coast Mountains, and the Arctic islands.

7. false; Huge fields of grain are raised in the ~~northern~~ southern parts of the Great Plains.

8. true

9. true

10. false; The Mackenzie River flows into the ~~Pacific~~ Arctic Ocean.

B. 1. the United States

2. the Atlantic Ocean (also, the Great Lakes)

3. forests

4. The climate is very cold.

5. the St. Lawrence River and the Great Lakes

Further Study

1. Baffin Island

2. minerals, forests, and animals

3. It is frozen during the rest of the year.

Map Exercises

(Individual work. Check maps for accuracy and neatness.)

44. A Nation of Provinces and Territories

Glossary Words

Parliament (PAHR luh muhnt) The group of people who make laws for Canada.

premier (PREE mee ur) The highest leader in a Canadian province.

prime minister The highest leader in Canada.

province (PRAHV ihns) One of the divisions of land in some countries, such as Canada.

territory (TEHR ih tawr ee) A part of a country that is not a state or a province, but has some government of its own.

Government of Canada

The nation of Canada is much like the United States in the way people live and work together. They have many similar laws and freedoms.

The capital city of Canada is Ottawa, along the Ottawa River in Ontario. The head of government for the nation is called the *prime minister*. He works with a group of lawmakers called the *Parliament*. Canadians also consider the king or queen of England as their official head, but the ruler in England has little to do with the government of Canada.

Provinces and Territories

Canada is not divided into states, but into ten areas called *provinces*. Each province has a capital city. The head of the government in each province is called a *premier*. Like the prime minister, he works with a group of lawmakers.

The Atlantic provinces are Newfoundland, New Brunswick, Nova Scotia, and Prince Edward Island. They are the four smallest provinces in Canada. Smallest of all is Prince Edward Island.

The largest province is Quebec. It includes most of the eastern part of Canada, and it has

LESSON AIM

To introduce the government, provinces, and territories of Canada.

MAIN POINTS

- **The laws and freedoms in Canada are much like those in the United States.**

- **Ottawa is the capital of Canada.**

- **The Canadian government is headed by a prime minister and the Parliament.** The king or queen of England is the official head, but he or she has little to do with the actual governing of Canada.

- **Canada has ten provinces.** Each province has a capital city and is governed by a premier and a group of lawmakers.

The four Atlantic provinces are the smallest: Newfoundland, New Brunswick, Nova Scotia, and Prince Edward Island. Quebec is the largest province, but Ontario has the most people. [About one out of three Canadians lives in Ontario.] Manitoba, Saskatchewan, and Alberta are prairie provinces. The mountainous province of British Columbia is bordered by the Pacific Ocean.

Note: In 2001, Canada's Parliament changed the official name of the province of Newfoundland to Newfoundland and Labrador.

- **The Yukon Territory and the Northwest Territories lie north of the provinces.** The territories have capital cities. They make some of their own laws, but they are governed more directly by the national government than the provinces are. [Territories do not have representatives in the national government as provinces or states do.]

over 250 times as much land as Prince Edward Island. The capital city of this province is also called Quebec. It is the oldest city in Canada. French explorers started a settlement there in the early 1600s.

Next to Quebec is Ontario, the second largest province. Ontario has more people than any of the other provinces. The small area lying between the Great Lakes is the southernmost part of Canada. Most of Ontario's people live in this heartland of Canada. It is a great farming and manufacturing region.

Manitoba, Saskatchewan, and Alberta are prairie provinces. Most of Canada's grain and cattle are raised in the southern part of these provinces. The colder northern part is a land of lakes and evergreen forests.

The province of British Columbia is bordered by the Pacific Ocean. Because of warm ocean currents, the land along the coast has one of the mildest climates in all of Canada. High mountains cover much of the province, but good farmland is found in some valleys. Forests cover about half of British Columbia.

The Parliament building in Ottawa, Ontario, is where Canadian government leaders meet to make laws.

Note: As of April 1, 1999, the Northwest Territories has divided into two territories. The western part is called the Northwest Territories and has its capital at Yellowknife, as before. The eastern part is called Nunavut, with its capital at Iqaluit.

- **The Royal Canadian Mounted Police is a famous police force of Canada.**
- **English and French are the official languages of Canada.** Most of the French-speaking people live in Quebec.

RELATED POINTS

- Briefly explain the difference between the governments of Canada and the United States. The method of choosing prime ministers or presidents is one main difference. A prime minister in Canada is chosen by Parliament and stays in office as long as he is supported by a majority of Parliament members. Presidents of the United States are elected by the people and serve a maximum of two four-year terms.

Fields of young wheat in Saskatchewan will feed people around the world. Alberta and Manitoba also produce much wheat. Canada exports millions of bushels of wheat to other countries.

Canada also has two large *territories* besides the ten provinces. The Yukon Territory lies next to Alaska. The Northwest Territories includes the tundra region and the many Arctic islands. Each territory has a capital city and makes some of its own laws. But the territories are governed more directly by the national government than the provinces are.

Mounted Police

The Royal Canadian Mounted Police is a famous police force of Canada. Their work was established in the days of the fur traders and pioneers who settled Canada. They were called mounted police because they traveled on horses. Today they ride horses in special ceremonies, but they use cars and snowmobiles for their police work. In the thinly populated northern areas, they travel from place to place in airplanes.

Languages of Canada

Canada has two official languages. French and English words are printed on all Canadian money. In some schools, students can take classes in French or in English. Some people can speak both languages, but most Canadians know only one. Most of the French people live in the province of Quebec where the early French settlers lived.

Smoke rolls from the stack of a gold-mining operation in the Northwest Territories.
Even in cold northern lands, God has placed valuable resources in the ground.

=========== **Testing Your Understanding** ===========

A. *Write the correct word(s) to complete each sentence.*

1. Canada and the ——— have similar laws and freedoms.
2. ——— is the capital city of Canada.
3. The ——— is the highest leader in Canada.
4. A group of leaders called ——— make laws for Canada.
5. Canada is divided into ——— instead of states.
6. The ——— provinces are the smallest provinces in Canada.
7. ——— is the largest Canadian province.
8. ——— has more people than any other province.
9. ———, ———, and ——— are the prairie provinces.
10. ——— is a mountainous western province.
11. The two territories of Canada are the ——— and the ———.
12. The two official languages of Canada are ——— and ———.

Lesson 44 Answers

Testing Your Understanding
A. 1. United States
   2. Ottawa
   3. prime minister
   4. Parliament
   5. provinces
   6. Atlantic
   7. Quebec
   8. Ontario
   9. Manitoba, Saskatchewan, Alberta
  10. British Columbia
  11. Yukon Territory, Northwest Territories
  12. English, French

B. (Individual work. Answers depend on provinces chosen.)

B. *If you live in Canada, answer these questions about your province. If you live in another country, choose a province that you think is interesting and answer these questions about it. Use an encyclopedia or another reference book to find the information.*

1. How large is the province? (Give your answer in square kilometers or square miles.)
2. What provinces are next to it?
3. Does it border another country or any large bodies of water? If so, write their names.
4. What is the capital city?
5. Who is the premier of the province? (Your teacher may need to help you.)
6. When did it become a province?
7. What is the population of the province?
8. What is the provincial flower? Also give the motto, bird, and nickname of the province if it has any.

Further Study

1. the king or queen of England
2. Quebec
3. between the Great Lakes in southern Ontario
4. in the days of the fur traders and pioneers who settled Canada

Further Study

1. Who is the official head of the Canadian government, yet has little to do with it?
2. What is the oldest city in Canada?
3. Where is the heartland of Canada?
4. When was the Royal Canadian Mounted Police force established?

Map Exercises

(Individual work. Maps depend on provinces chosen.)

Map Exercises

1. Trace a map of your province (or the province you chose for Part B).
2. Trace and label the main rivers in the province. Also label any large lakes, bays, or oceans within the province or along the borders.
3. Mark the capital with a star, and label it. If you live in the province, mark your hometown or city with a dot and label it. Also mark and label other important cities in the province.

45. Chapter 9 Review

=========== Testing Your Understanding ===========

A. *Write a glossary word for each definition.*

1. The highest leader in Canada.
2. The highest leader in the United States.
3. The highest leader in a state.
4. The highest leader in a province of Canada.
5. A group of people who make laws for the United States.
6. A group of people who make laws for Canada.
7. Money that people pay to their government.
8. Mountains that divide the flow of water.
9. A large, rocky area of Canada.
10. One of the large sections of Canada that makes many of its own laws.
11. The center of county government.
12. A part of a country that is not a state or a province.

B. *Write the correct word(s) to complete each sentence.*

Alaska	Frigid	Appalachian
Canada	laws	Great Lakes
Hawaii	nickname	Temperate
Ottawa	mountains	Washington, D.C.

1. Most of the United States is in the Northern —— Zone.
2. The —— Mountains stretch from Alabama to Canada.
3. —— is the largest state, but it has a small population.
4. —— is the capital of the United States.
5. —— is the capital of Canada.
6. The state of —— is made up of islands.
7. A state —— tells something about the state.
8. The United States and Canada share four of the five ——.
9. The northern islands of Canada are in the Northern —— Zone.

Lesson 45 Answers

Testing Your Understanding

A. 1. prime minister
2. president
3. governor
4. premier
5. Congress
6. Parliament
7. tax
8. Continental Divide
9. Canadian Shield
10. province
11. county seat
12. territory

B. 1. Temperate
2. Appalachian
3. Alaska
4. Washington, D.C.
5. Ottawa
6. Hawaii
7. nickname
8. Great Lakes
9. Frigid

10. mountains
11. Canada
12. laws

C. 1. the Mississippi River (and its tributaries)
2. in the West
3. a. fifty
   b. ten
4. Southern Canada has a milder climate than northern Canada.
5. Royal Canadian Mounted Police
6. English and French

Map Exercises
1. Atlantic Coastal Plain, Appalachian Mountains, Central Plains, Rocky Mountains, Sierra Nevada, Coast Ranges
2. a. Atlantic Region, Canadian Shield, Great Plains, Rocky Mountains, Coast Mountains
   b. Arctic islands
3. Lake Michigan
4. Lake Superior, Lake Huron, Lake Erie, Lake Ontario

Review Study
1. (Review glossary words in class.)
2. Hawaii
3. the Mackenzie River
4. (Have students point out the United States and Canada on a globe and a world map.)

10. The western regions of the United States and Canada have many ———.
11. ——— is the second largest country in the world.
12. Canada and the United States have similar ——— and freedoms.

C. *Answer the following questions.*
1. What large river system drains the Central Plains of the United States?
2. Are the deserts of the United States in the East or in the West?
3. (*a*) How many states are in the United States? (*b*) How many provinces are in Canada?
4. Why do most Canadians live in the southern part of their country?
5. What is the name of the famous Canadian police force?
6. What are the two official languages of Canada?

Map Exercises

Use your maps of the United States and Canada to complete these exercises.

1. Name the six main regions of the United States from east to west.
2. (*a*) Name five main regions of Canada from east to west. (*b*) What makes up the land farthest north in Canada?
3. Which one of the Great Lakes lies entirely within the United States?
4. Name the four Great Lakes that are shared by the United States and Canada.

Review Study

1. Do you know the meaning of all the glossary words in Chapter 9?
2. Do you know which state is in the Tropical Zone?
3. Do you know which Canadian river is the longest?
4. Can you find the United States and Canada on a globe or a world map?

So Far This Year

1. Write the number of the correct climate zone for each place. Answers may be used more than once.

   a. Most of Brazil
   b. Ohio
   c. Nigeria
   d. Australia (two zones)
   e. Baffin Island
   f. Philippines
   g. Most of the United States
   h. Siberia (two zones)
   i. Japan
   j. Most of Greenland
   k. Iceland
   l. Ecuador
   m. Antarctica
   n. Most of Europe
   o. Canada (two zones)

   1. Northern Frigid Zone
   2. Northern Temperate Zone
   3. Tropical Zone
   4. Southern Temperate Zone
   5. Southern Frigid Zone

2. The sunrise, sunset, and daily temperatures stay about the same year round in lands near the (equator, poles, ocean).

3. A deposit of soil at the mouth of a river is a (dike, delta, deluge).

4. Choose two: The countries of (Nigeria, the Philippines, the Netherlands, Japan) are archipelagos.

5. Choose two: Along the Ring of Fire, there are many (earthquakes, tornadoes, forest fires, volcanoes).

6. The largest range of mountains in Australia is the (Great Dividing Range, Great Barrier Reef).

7. When the Northern Hemisphere has winter, the Southern Hemisphere has (spring, summer, autumn, winter).

8. The (Alps, Andes, Appalachians) are some of the highest mountains in Europe.

9. The (Basel, Rhine, Cologne) River is Switzerland's link to the sea.

So Far This Year

1. a. 3
   b. 2
   c. 3
   d. 3, 4
   e. 1
   f. 3
   g. 2
   h. 1, 2
   i. 2
   j. 1
   k. 2
   l. 3
   m. 5
   n. 2
   o. 1, 2
2. equator
3. delta
4. the Philippines, Japan
5. earthquakes, volcanoes
6. Great Dividing Range
7. summer
8. Alps
9. Rhine

10. Bible
11. Menno Simons
12. small
13. Trains
14. Greenland
15. Asia
16. typhoons
17. South Pole
18. equator
19. thinner, colder
20. forests
21. an oasis
22. Andes Mountains
23. Sierra Nevada

10. The first book that Gutenberg printed on his new printing press was the ———.

11. (Felix Manz, Pilgram Marpeck, Menno Simons) was an important leader of the Anabaptists in the Netherlands.

12. Most farms in Japan are (large, small).

13. (Buses, Trains, Jeepneys) provide a fast way to travel between large cities in Japan.

14. The largest island in the world is (Australia, Greenland, Iceland).

15. Siberia is a large, cold region in northern (Africa, Europe, Asia).

16. All the following are common in Iceland except (volcanoes, geysers, typhoons, hot springs, earthquakes).

17. Antarctica is a cold continent around the (North Pole, South Pole).

18. The (equator, Tropic of Capricorn, Antarctic Circle) crosses Ecuador.

19. At high altitudes, the air becomes (denser, thinner) and (warmer, colder).

20. Desert land may be covered with any of the following except (sand, rocks, forests, mountains).

21. A watered place in a desert is (a nomad, a caravan, an oasis).

22. All the following are in the United States except the (Appalachian Mountains, Mississippi River, Andes Mountains, Central Plains, Rocky Mountains).

23. All the following are in Canada except the (Canadian Shield, Great Plains, Rocky Mountains, Mackenzie River, Sierra Nevada, Arctic islands).

Rules for Drawing Neat Maps

1. Use printing, not cursive writing, for all words on the map.
2. Print all words horizontally except the names of rivers and mountain ranges. A river or mountain range name should follow the course of the river or mountain range.
3. Use all capital letters for the names of countries, states, provinces, and large bodies of water. Capitalize only the first letter of each word for cities, lakes, rivers, and land regions.
4. Color bodies of water blue. Make all coloring strokes horizontal, not vertical or in different directions.
5. To color countries, states, or provinces, use a color that is different from the color of any area beside it. Do not use any color that is too dark for the lettering to show.

Table of Contents

Map A Nigeria (Lessons 6, 7, 8, 9, 10)

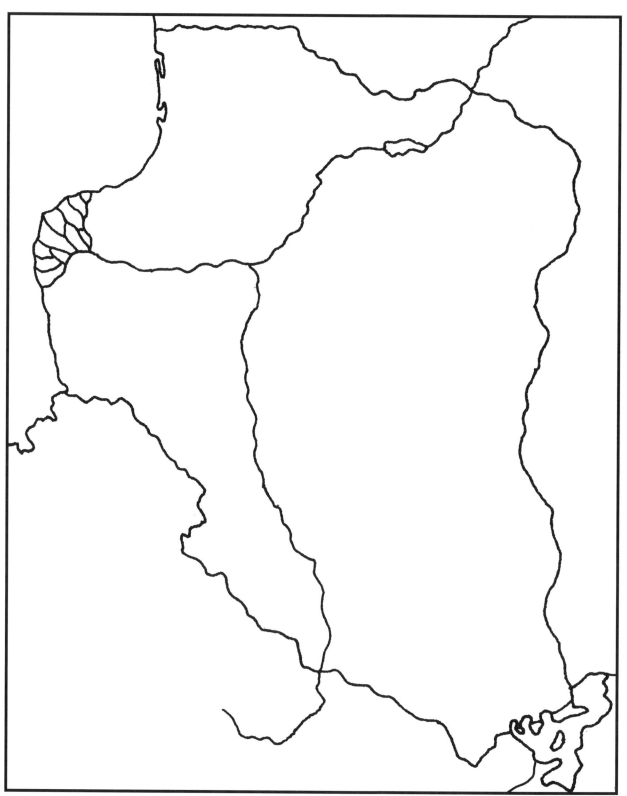

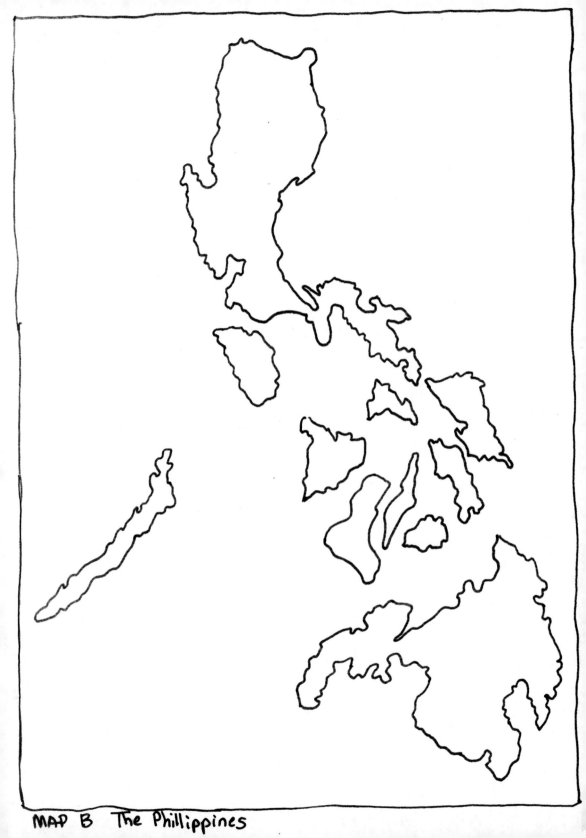

MAP B The Phillippines

Map B   The Philippines (Lessons 11, 12, 13, 14, 15)

Map C Australia (Lessons 16, 17, 18, 19, 20)

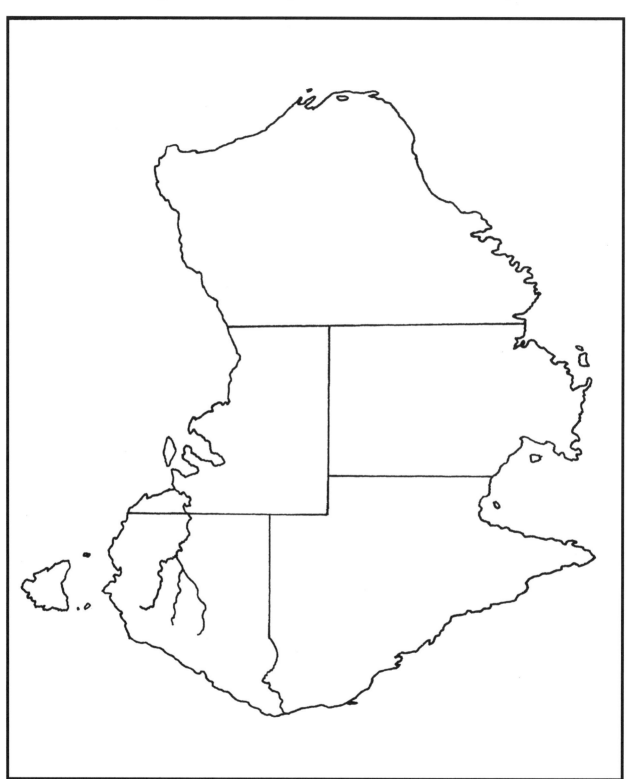

Map C Australia

Map D Northwestern Europe (Lessons 21, 22, 23, 24, 25)

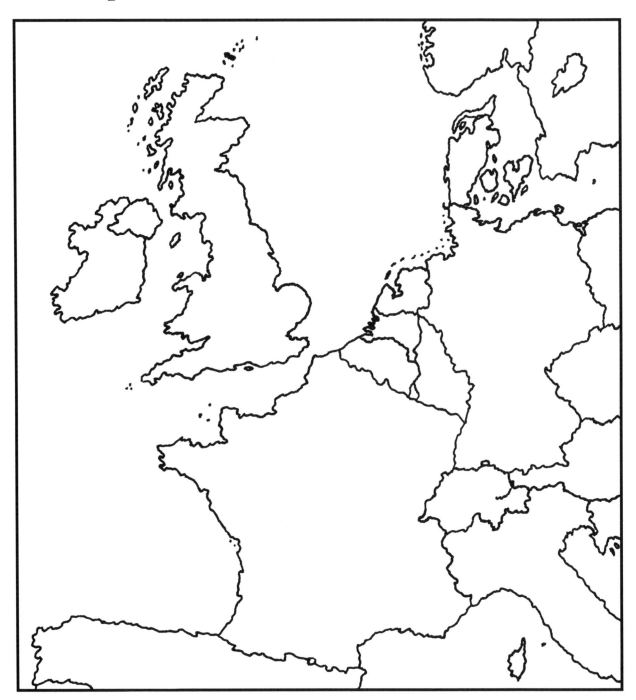

Map E   Japan (Lessons 26, 28, 29, 30)

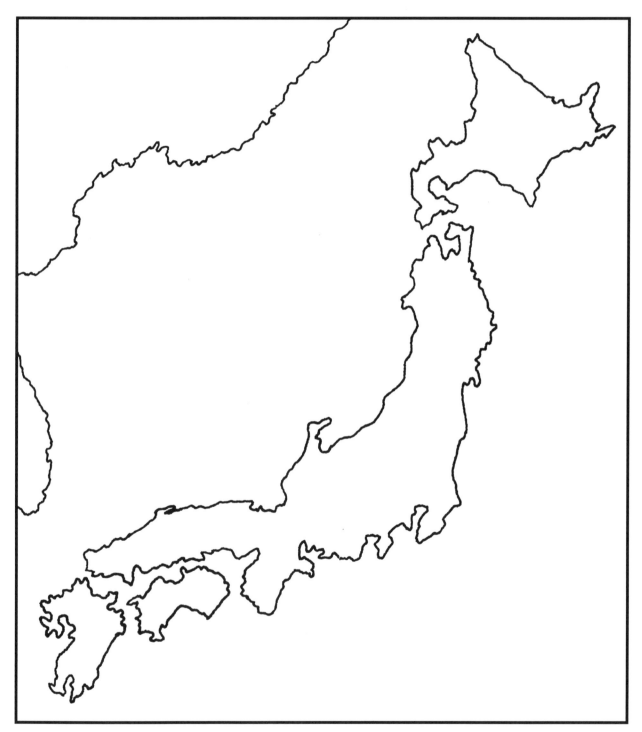

Map F   Greenland (Lessons 31, 35)

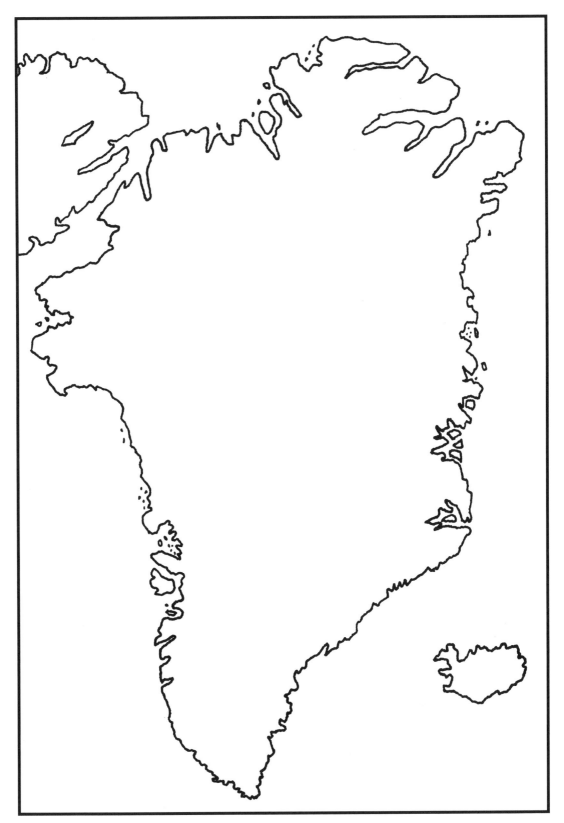

Map G Russia (Lessons 32, 35)

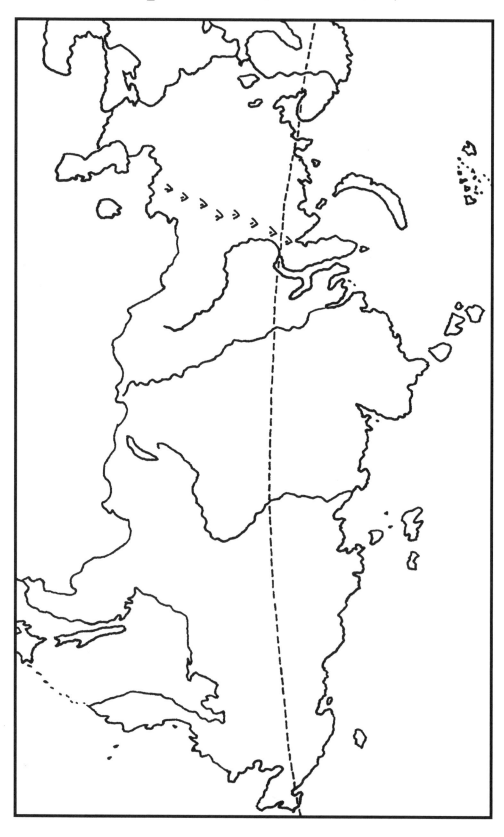

Map H   Ecuador (Lessons 36, 37, 40)

Map I   The United States (Lessons 41, 45)

Map J Canada (Lessons 43, 45)

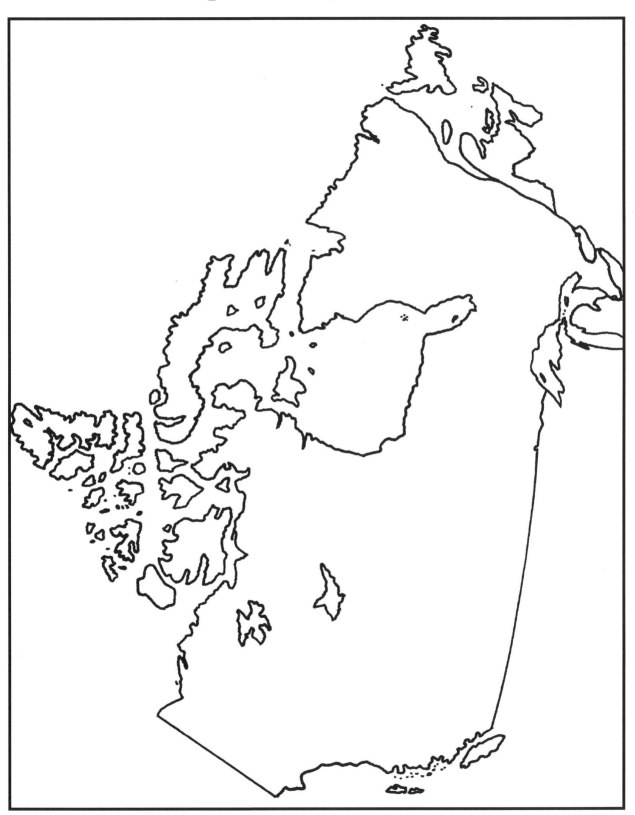

Homelands Around the World

Chapter 1 Test   Score _____

Name _____ Date _____

A. *Write* **true** *or* **false** *for each sentence.*

_____true_____   1. The imaginary line running around the middle of the earth is called the equator.

_____false_____   2. An area of land completely surrounded by water is a peninsula.

_____false_____   3. The Amazon River is a large river in North America.

_____true_____   4. Two trees that grow in tropical forests are rubber trees and kapok trees.

_____false_____   5. The two seasons in the temperate zone are the wet season and the dry season.

_____false_____   6. Animals that hibernate travel to a warmer place for the winter.

_____true_____   7. Climate affects the way people live.

_____true_____   8. There may be different climates in the same climate zone.

_____true_____   9. Coffee trees grow well only if there is a wet season and a dry season.

_____true_____   10. The seasons change because the earth's axis is tilted in relation to its orbit around the sun.

B. *Write the letter of the word(s) that fit in each blank below. You will not use all the letters.*

a. port   g. continent   m. Antarctic Circle

b. sledge   h. tributary   n. Tropic of Cancer

c. igloo   i. hemisphere   o. Tropic of Capricorn

d. fazenda   j. trading post   p. Tropical Zone

e. globe   k. Amazon River   q. Frigid Zones

f. legend   l. Arctic Circle   r. Temperate Zones

_c_ 11. An Eskimo house made from blocks of ice or snow.

_j_ 12. A place where furs and other supplies may be bought, sold, or traded.

_h_ 13. A river that flows into a larger river.

_i_ 14. Half of the earth.

_d_ 15. A plantation of South America where coffee or sugar is raised.

_a_ 16. A place where ships load and unload cargoes.

_g_ 17. One of the seven large landmasses of the earth.

_r_ 18. Lands in the ——— have four seasons.

_f_ 19. A ——— shows what map symbols mean.

_o_ 20. The ——— is the boundary between the Tropical Zone and the Southern Temperate Zone.

_b_ 21. A ——— is a heavy sled, sometimes pulled by dogs over ice and snow.

_l_ 22. The ——— is the boundary between the Northern Frigid Zone and the Northern Temperate Zone.

C. *Do these exercises.*

23. Write the names of these climate zones in order from warmest to coldest: Frigid Zone, Tropical Zone, Temperate Zone. _Tropical Zone, Temperate Zone, Frigid Zone_

24. The four main directions are north, south, east, and west. Write them at the proper place on the blanks around this map.

<u>   *north*   </u>

<u>*west*   </u>

<u>   *east*</u>

<u>   *south*   </u>

D. *Write the answers in complete sentences.*

25. What is climate? <u>*the usual weather of an area*</u>

26. Why are there no trees in the frigid zones? <u>*The frigid zones are too cold*</u>
<u>*for trees to grow.*</u>

27. When an animal hibernates, what does it live on? <u>*the fat stored in its*</u>
<u>*body*</u>

28. The Northern Frigid Zone is sometimes called the Land of the Midnight Sun. Why? <u>*During summer, the sun can be seen night and day for a while.*</u>

Homelands Around the World

Chapter 2 Test   Score _____

Name _____   Date _____

A. *Write* **true** *or* **false** *for each sentence.*

_____*false*_____   1. Most people in the large cities of Nigeria wear traditional Nige-
                      rian clothes.

_____*true*_____   2. About half of the Nigerians are Muslims.

_____*true*_____   3. Many tropical animals could not live in lands that have cold
                      winters.

_____*false*_____   4. In northern Nigeria, there is little difference between daytime
                      and nighttime temperatures.

_____*false*_____   5. Mangrove trees are known for their beautiful wood.

B. *Write* **north**, **south**, *or* **both** *to tell whether these descriptions fit northern Nigeria,
southern Nigeria, or both.*

_____*both*_____   6. In the Tropical Zone

_____*south*_____   7. Tropical rain forest

_____*both*_____   8. Warm climate year round

_____*north*_____   9. Savanna

_____*north*_____   10. Mud houses

_____*south*_____   11. Many oil wells

C. *Write the letter of the word that fits in each blank below. You will not use all the letters.*

a. equator	f. delta	k. French
b. coconut	g. Fulani	l. irrigation
c. dam	h. Asia	m. Abuja
d. cacao	i. English	n. Africa
e. Ibadan	j. Yoruba	o. generation

_m_   12. The capital city of Nigeria is ———.

_n_   13. Nigeria has the largest population of any country on the continent

of ———.

_i_   14. The official language of Nigeria is ———.

_g_   15. Many of the ——— people are herdsmen.

_a_   16. The sun rises and sets about the same time every day year round in

countries near the ———.

_d_   17. Chocolate products are made from the fruit of the ——— tree.

_c_   18. A ——— is a thick wall built across a river to control the flow of water.

_f_   19. A ——— forms at the mouth of some rivers.

_l_   20. When people in a dry land get water from a river to raise crops, they

are using ———.

D. *Match the letters on the map to the main tribes and rivers of Nigeria. You will not use all the letters.*

_E_   21. Yoruba tribe

_F_   22. Ibo tribe

_A_   23. Hausa and Fulani tribes

_C_   24. Niger River

_D_   25. Benue River

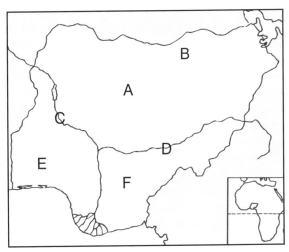

E. *Write the answers in complete sentences.*

26. What is the harmattan?   _a hot, dry wind from the Sahara_

27. What is the main difference between the northern and southern parts of

Nigeria? _Northern Nigeria has a much drier climate than southern Nigeria._

_____

28. Why are game reserves needed in Nigeria? _Game reserves protect_

animals that are in danger of dying off (because people kill too many of

them and destroy their habitat).

29. What is a natural resource? _something useful provided by God in nature_

_____

Homelands Around the World

Chapter 3 Test

Score _____

Name _____   Date _____

A. *Write* **true** *or* **false** *for each sentence.*

___true___   1. Most Filipinos live on the eleven main Philippine islands.

___true___   2. In the Philippines there are some small islands without names.

___false___   3. The Philippines are a part of the mainland of Asia.

___false___   4. The Philippines have cold winters.

___true___   5. Many Filipinos understand more than one language.

___false___   6. Sponges are grown in irrigated fields.

___false___   7. Narra trees have special roots that help keep the soil along the coast from washing away.

___false___   8. Dried abaca fibers are called copra.

___true___   9. Filipinos export lumber.

___true___ 10. Coconut oil can be used to make soap.

B. *Write the letter of the word that fits in each blank below. You will not use all the letters.*

a. stone	e. jeepney	i. Ifugao
b. volcano	f. Tropical	j. English
c. nipa	g. Luzon	k. Manila
d. typhoon	h. Temperate	l. Pilipino

___f___ 11. The Philippines is in the ——— Zone.

_j_ _l_ 12. The national languages of the Philippines are ——— and ———.

___c___ 13. Many Filipinos live in ——— huts.

___e___ 14. The ——— is widely used for public transportation in the Philippines.

___i___ 15. The ——— tribe built rice terraces on the mountains of northern
        Luzon.

___k___ 16. One of the best natural harbors in the world is ——— Bay.

___d___ 17. A——— is a tropical storm that brings strong winds and heavy rains.

C. *Match the letters on the map to the names below. You will not use all the letters.*

___G___ 18. Mindanao Island

___A___ 19. Luzon Island

___E___ 20. Mount Mayon

___C___ 21. South China Sea

___D___ 22. Pacific Ocean

___B___ 23. Manila

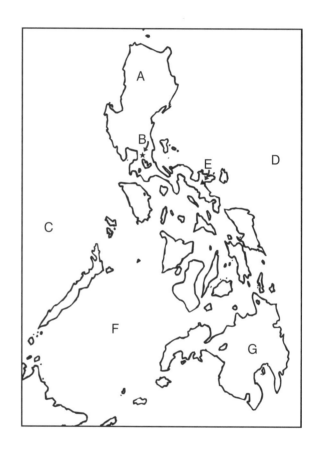

D. *Write the answers in complete sentences.*

24. Why are carabaos still used in the Philippines?   *Carabaos are less*
    expensive than tractors. (Carabaos also provide milk, meat, and new
    calves. Their broad feet work well in the muddy rice paddies.)

25. Why do some Filipinos have Spanish names?   *The Filipinos learned*
    some Spanish while the Spaniards ruled their country.

26. How have volcanoes helped the Filipinos?   _The ashes from volcanoes_

have enriched the soil.

27. Name two ways that rice paddies are used during the dry season. _____

to raise rice by using irrigation, to raise fish

28. Why do large ocean-going ships stop only at the largest Philippine ports? __

The water in smaller harbors is too shallow.

Homelands Around the World

Chapter 4 Test   Score _____

Name _____   Date _____

A. *Write* **true** *or* **false** *for each sentence.*

_____true_____   1. Northern Australia is in the Tropical Zone.

_____false_____   2. Australia has many large cities.

_____true_____   3. More people live in Sydney than on all the farms and stations of Australia.

_____false_____   4. Mount Kosciusko is higher than any mountain in North America.

_____false_____   5. Marsupials are mammals that lay eggs.

_____true_____   6. Eucalyptus trees shed their bark instead of their leaves.

_____false_____   7. The largest deserts of Australia are in the eastern half of the continent.

_____true_____   8. Australians raise sheep for both wool and meat.

_____true_____   9. Many of Australia's mines are in the west.

_____false_____   10. The Great Barrier Reef is near the city of Perth.

B. *Match these cities with their descriptions. You will not write all the names.*

Darwin   Perth   Sydney

Canberra   Melbourne

_____Canberra_____   11. The national capital of Australia.

_____Sydney_____   12. The largest city in Australia.

_____Perth_____   13. The largest city in western Australia.

_____Darwin_____   14. A city on the northern coast of Australia.

C. *Write the letter of the word that fits in each blank below. You will not use all the letters.*

a. aborigines	e. Northern	i. Indonesia
b. outback	f. Southern	j. Pacific
c. artistic	g. Murray	k. Indian
d. dingoes	h. artesian	l. Tasmania

_f_ 15. Australia is in the ——— Hemisphere.

_g_ 16. The ——— River and its tributaries provide some water for irrigation.

_a_ 17. The ——— were the first inhabitants of Australia.

_b_ 18. The ——— is the thinly settled inland area of Australia.

_h_ 19. An ——— well does not need a pump.

_d_ 20. The native wild dogs of Australia are called ———.

_l_ 21. The island of ——— is an Australian state.

_j_ 22. The ——— Ocean is east of Australia.

D. *Write the answers in complete sentences.*

23. Why is Australia called the "lonely continent"? ___Australia is separated from the other continents by great stretches of water.___

24. Why are the stations of Australia usually larger than the farms of North America? ___In Australia, cattle and sheep must graze large areas to find enough to eat. (Much pasture is needed because of the dry climate.)___

25. How are the seasons of Australia different from the seasons of North America? ___The seasons of Australia are opposite from the seasons of North America.___

26. Why is Australia's climate warmer than Canada's climate? ___Australia is closer to the equator than Canada is.___

27. Why is more land in Australia used for grazing than for growing farm crops? ___Most of the land in Australia is too dry for crops to grow.___

Homelands Around the World

Chapter 5 Test   Score _____

Name _____   Date _____

A. *Write **true** or **false** for each sentence.*

_____true_____ 1. Some of the highest mountains in Europe are the Alps.

_____true_____ 2. The Anabaptists and the Swiss Brethren were the same group

of people.

_____false_____ 3. A bannwald is a warm wind that causes snow to melt.

_____false_____ 4. Switzerland is blessed with many natural resources.

_____true_____ 5. Locks are needed so that boats can change to different water

levels in rivers and canals.

_____false_____ 6. Germany has many large farms.

_____false_____ 7. The castles along the Rhine River were built to protect the boats

on the river.

_____true_____ 8. The Netherlands are known for tulips, windmills, and wooden

shoes.

_____false_____ 9. All of the Netherlands may also be called Holland.

_____true_____ 10. Long ago, the Anabaptists and the Catholics were about the

only two churches in the Netherlands.

B. *Write the letter of the correct word before each meaning. You will not use all the letters.*

a. polder   d. tourist   g. sauerkraut

b. blizzard   e. avalanche   h. ancestor

c. delta   f. klompen   i. autobahn

__e__ 11. A huge mass of snow and ice that slides down a mountain.

__i__ 12. A big German highway with high-speed traffic.

__c__ 13. A triangle-shaped buildup of soil at the mouth of a river.

__g__ 14. A German food that came to America.

_a_ 15. Land claimed from the sea and protected by a dike.

_h_ 16. A person from whom one is descended, such as a great-grandfather.

C. *Write the letter of the correct name before each description. You will not use all the letters.*

a. Felix Manz   d. Black Forest   g. Ruhr

b. Pilgram Marpeck   e. Rotterdam   h. Paris

c. Johann Gutenberg   f. Palatinate   i. Cologne

_f_ 17. Area in Germany where persecuted Anabaptists lived for a time.

_c_ 18. Man who first used a printing press to produce a Bible.

_i_ 19. Largest city along the Rhine River, with a beautiful cathedral.

_g_ 20. Region with many factories along the Rhine.

_b_ 21. Anabaptist minister who had useful engineering skills.

_e_ 22. Busy port at the mouth of the Rhine River.

D. *Match the letters on the map to the names below. You will not use all the letters.*

_F_ 23. Germany

_H_ 24. France

_D_ 25. Netherlands

_I_ 26. Switzerland

_B_ 27. Great Britain

_G_ 28. Rhine River

_C_ 29. English Channel

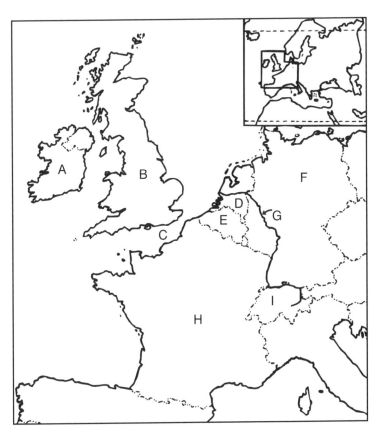

E. *Write the answers in complete sentences.*

30. What are two ways that you could get through the Alps from Switzerland to

    Italy?   *through a mountain pass, through a tunnel*

    _____

31. In what two ways is the Gulf Stream a benefit to Europe? _____

    The Gulf Stream causes a mild climate along the coast. Many fish can

    be caught in the Gulf Stream.

    _____

Homelands Around the World

Chapter 6 Test   Score _____

Name _____   Date _____

A. *Write* **true** *or* **false** *for each sentence.*

_____false_____   1. The islands of Japan lie off the coast of Australia.

_____true_____   2. Traditional houses in Japan have only a few pieces of furniture.

_____true_____   3. Farms in Japan are usually smaller than farms in North
                      America.

_____true_____   4. Most of the Japanese follow the Shinto and Buddhist religions.

_____false_____   5. A typhoon is caused by a volcano or an earthquake under the
                      sea.

_____false_____   6. Most of Japan's forests are crowded together along the coasts.

_____true_____   7. Japan has many earthquakes and active volcanoes.

B. *Write the letter of the word(s) that fits in each blank below. You will not use all the
letters.*

a. Tropical	f. lumber	k. bullet trains
b. seas	g. Asian	l. Fuji Mountains
c. subways	h. Tokyo	m. Temperate
d. four	i. pulp	n. Japanese Alps
e. seven	j. Japan	o. Honshu

___d___ 8. Japan has ——— large islands and more than 3,500 small islands.

___m___ 9. Japan is in the Northern ——— Zone.

___j___ 10. The ——— Current helps to warm the southern Japanese islands.

___b___ 11. The Japanese catch many fish in the ——— around their islands.

___k___ 12. Japan's ——— travel about 125 miles per hour.

___n___ 13. The highest mountain range in Japan is the ———.

___f___ ___i___ 14. The forests of Japan produce ——— for building and ——— for

making paper.

___h___ 15. About one-fourth of the people of Japan live in the city of ———

and the cities around it.

C. *Match the letters on the map to the names below. You will not use all the letters.*

___J___ 16. East China Sea   ___C___ 21. Sea of Japan

___D___ 17. Honshu   ___A___ 22. Sea of Okhotsk

___B___ 18. Hokkaido   ___F___ 23. Pacific Ocean

___G___ 19. Inland Sea   ___H___ 24. Shikoku

___I___ 20. Kyushu

Japan

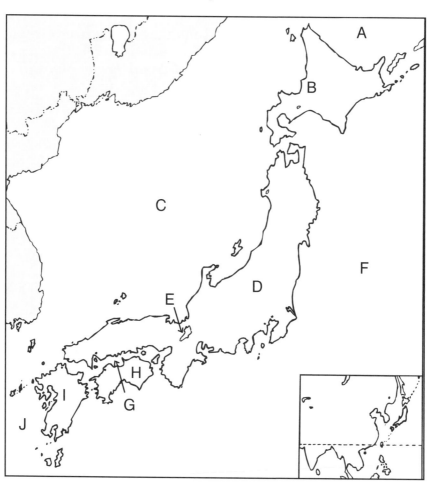

D. *Write the answers in complete sentences.*

25. What are two traditional Japanese customs that are different from American

    customs? __(Sample answers) bowing, removing shoes when entering a__

    house, sitting on floor cushions, eating with chopsticks, sleeping on floor

    mats, wearing kimonos

26. How are the crops of Hokkaido different from the crops of Shikoku and

    Kyushu? __Only cool-weather crops grow well on Hokkaido, but many__

    kinds of warm-weather crops can be raised on Shikoku and Kyushu.

27. What are two reasons that Japan has only a small amount of farmland?

    __Mountains or forests cover much of the islands, and cities have taken__

    over much of the good farmland.

28. What kind of products does Japan export? __Japan exports manufactured__

    goods.

Homelands Around the World

Chapter 7 Test

Name _____

Score _____

Date _____

A. *Write* **true** *or* **false** *for each sentence.*

   false   1. Antarctica is the largest island in the world.

   true   2. Greenland is colder than Iceland.

   false   3. A mineral is a kind of plant that grows in Antarctica.

   true   4. Most homes in Reykjavík are warmed by geothermal heat.

   true   5. Antarctica has winter while Greenland has summer.

   false   6. Permafrost lies under the steppes of Siberia.

   false   7. Vatnajökull is the only glacier on Iceland.

   true   8. Godthåb has an ice-free harbor year round.

B. *Match these clues with the cold lands they describe. Write* **G** *for Greenland,* **S** *for Siberia,* **I** *for Iceland, and* **A** *for Antarctica. Put one letter in each blank.*

  G   *S*   9. Eskimos live in the northern part.

     I   10. It has hot springs, geysers, and volcanoes.

    S   11. It is a large region in northern Asia.

  G   *I*   12. Fishing is an important industry.

     A   13. It has the coldest temperatures in the world.

    G   14. It belongs to the country of Denmark.

    A   15. Penguins live there.

    S   16. It has steppes, taiga, and tundra.

    G   17. It has land closest to the North Pole.

    A   18. No nation owns it.

     I   19. It has many greenhouses.

  G   *A*   20. It is almost entirely covered with an ice cap.

C. *Write the answers in complete sentences.*

21. How do icebergs form? ___*Icebergs form when glaciers slide into the sea,*___ *and great pieces of ice break off.*

22. What are the three main divisions of Siberia from west to east? ___ *a large plain in the west, a plateau in the central part, and a mountainous region in the east*

23. Where is Iceland? ___*between Europe and Greenland (just south of the Arctic Circle)*

24. How is most of the electricity generated in Iceland? ___*by waterpower*

25. Why do scientists travel to Antarctica? ___*to study the ice of Antarctica*

Homelands Around the World

Chapter 8 Test   Score _____

Name _____   Date _____

A. *Write* **true** *or* **false** *for each sentence.*

_____true_____ 1. The highest mountains in the world are in Asia.

_____false_____ 2. The equator is a line that can be seen from an airplane.

_____false_____ 3. Bananas are the most important crop in the highlands of Ecuador.

_____false_____ 4. The highlands of Ecuador have cool winters and hot summers.

_____true_____ 5. Ecuador has one of the highest active volcanoes in the world.

_____false_____ 6. Some deserts receive plenty of rainfall.

_____false_____ 7. All deserts are covered with sand dunes.

_____false_____ 8. The Gobi Desert is the largest desert in the world.

_____false_____ 9. The Sahara remains hot at night.

_____true_____ 10. Desert nomads move from place to place in search of food for their animals.

B. *Write the letter of the word that fits in each blank below. You will not use all the letters.*

a. altitude   f. caravan   k. Himalayas

b. equator   g. salt   l. Indians

c. tents   h. oasis   m. Quito

d. oil   i. camel   n. Andes

e. snow   j. mestizos   o. Guayaquil

_n_ 11. Longest mountain chain.

_a_ 12. The height above the level of the oceans.

_m_ 13. The capital city of Ecuador.

_o_ 14. A large city in the lowlands of Ecuador.

___l___ 15. People who live in the highlands of Ecuador.

___j___ 16. People who live in the lowlands of Ecuador.

___f___ 17. A large group of desert travelers.

___b___ 18. Quito is only a few miles from the ———.

___e___ 19. The high mountain peaks in Ecuador are covered with ——— the year round.

___i___ 20. God created the ——— with the special ability to go for days or weeks

without food or water.

___h___ 21. An ——— is a green, watered spot in a desert.

___c___ 22. Desert nomads live in ——— instead of houses.

___d___ 23. The men who work at ——— wells in the desert earn more money than

the nomads earn.

C. *Write the answers in complete sentences.*

24. What kind of climate do most lands near the equator have? _____

_____*a warm (tropical) climate*_____

_____

25. What kind of climate do the highlands of Ecuador have? _____

_____*a cool, pleasant climate year round*_____

_____

26. Why does a person sometimes get a strange feeling in his ears when he goes

up a mountain? ___*There is extra pressure inside the ears because the air*___

_*outside is becoming thinner.*_____

27. Why do crops and trees grow at only a few spots in the desert? _____

_____*There is water in only a few places.*_____

_____

28. Why are desert towns important to the nomads? ___*Nomads need a place*___

*to sell the products from their animals and to buy the supplies they need.*

_____

Homelands Around the World

Chapter 9 Test   Score _____

Name _____   Date _____

A. *Write* **true** *or* **false** *for each sentence.*

___false___   1. Most of the United States is in the Tropical Zone.

___true___   2. A coastal plain lies between the Appalachian Mountains and
                 the Atlantic Ocean.

___false___   3. The laws for the United States are made in Ottawa.

___false___   4. Most of the states are about the same size.

___true___   5. The states are divided into counties.

___false___   6. Canada is the largest country in the world.

___false___   7. Lake Michigan lies entirely within Canada.

___true___   8. The southern part of Canada is in the Northern Temperate
                 Zone.

___true___   9. The Atlantic provinces are the smallest provinces in Canada.

___false___ 10. English and Spanish are the two official languages of Canada.

B. *Write the letter of the word(s) that matches each description below. You will not use
all the letters.*

a. ten	d. president	g. Parliament
b. twelve	e. premier	h. Congress
c. forty	f. fifty	i. prime minister

___h___ 11. The group of people who make laws for the United States.

___g___ 12. The group of people who make laws for Canada.

___d___ 13. The highest leader in the United States.

___i___ 14. The highest leader in Canada.

___f___ 15. The number of states in the United States.

___a___ 16. The number of provinces in Canada.

C. *Match the letters on the map to the names below. You will not use all the letters.*

   D   17. Canadian Shield   **J**   22. Appalachian Mountains

   C   18. Rocky Mountains   **F**   23. St. Lawrence River

   A   19. Mackenzie River   **B**   24. Arctic islands

   H   20. Central Plains   **I**   25. Mississippi River

   E   21. Great Lakes

NORTH AMERICA

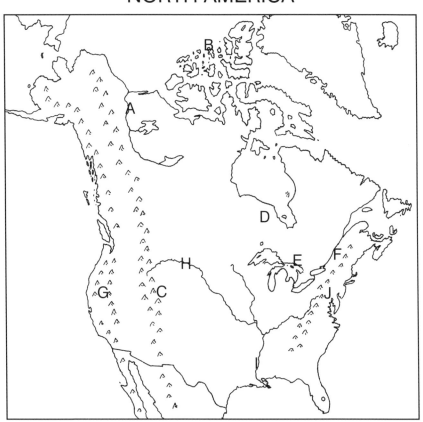

D. *Write the answers in complete sentences.*

26. What is the Continental Divide? *It is a ridge of mountains that separates the streams flowing into the Pacific Ocean from the streams flowing into the Atlantic Ocean.*

27. How are Alaska and Hawaii different from the other states? _Alaska and_
Hawaii are the only states that are separate from the rest. (They are also
the only states not entirely within the Northern Temperate Zone.)

28. Why do more people live in the heartland of Canada than on the Arctic islands?
The heartland of Canada is a mild region near the Great Lakes, but the
Arctic islands are in the cold Northern Frigid Zone.

29. How is the government of the Canadian territories different from the government of the provinces? _The territories are governed more directly by the_
national government than the provinces are. (The territories also do not
take part in the national government as the provinces do.)

E. *Bonus exercise for North American students.*

30. Write the name of your state or province. _____

31. Write the name of your capital city. _____

32. Write the name of your governor or premier. _____

(Answers depend on the home state or province.)

Homelands Around the World

Final Test   Score _____

Name _____ Date _____

A. *In the blank before each name, write the letter of the climate zone for that land.*

a. Northern Frigid Zone   d. Southern Temperate Zone

b. Northern Temperate Zone   e. Southern Frigid Zone

c. Tropical Zone

__b__ 1. Japan   _a, b_ 5. Canada (two zones)

__c__ 2. Nigeria   __c__ 6. Most of Brazil

__e__ 3. Antarctica   __b__ 7. Most of Europe

__b__ 4. United States   __a__ 8. Most of Greenland

B. *Write the letter of the correct name before each description. You will not use all the letters.*

a. Alps   e. Andes   i. Antarctica

b. Amazon   f. Gutenberg   j. Australia

c. Nigeria   g. Iceland   k. Manila Bay

d. Sahara   h. Greenland   l. Rhine River

__k__ 9. Excellent harbor in the Philippines.

__g__ 10. Land of hot springs, geysers, and volcanoes.

__f__ 11. Man who first used a printing press to produce a Bible.

__l__ 12. Switzerland's link to sea.

__j__ 13. Smallest continent in the world.

__h__ 14. Largest island in the world.

__b__ 15. Largest river in the world.

__d__ 16. Largest desert in the world.

__i__ 17. Coldest continent in the world.

__a__ 18. Some of the highest mountains in Europe.

C. *Write the letter of the correct word(s) before each description. You will not use all the letters.*

a. county   e. marsupial   i. harmattan

b. nomad   f. polder   j. natural resource

c. oasis   g. station   k. prime minister

d. dike   h. terrace   l. typhoon

_i_ 19. Hot, dry wind in northern Africa.

_j_ 20. Something useful provided by God in nature.

_l_ 21. A severe storm.

_e_ 22. Mammal that carries its young in a pouch.

_g_ 23. Sheep or cattle ranch in Australia.

_f_ 24. Land claimed from the sea.

_c_ 25. Green, watered spot in a desert.

_a_ 26. Division within a state of the United States.

_k_ 27. Highest leader in Canada.

_b_ 28. Person of a group that moves from place to place in search of food for animals.

D. *Write **true** or **false** for each sentence.*

true 29. When animals hibernate, they go into a deep sleep.

false 30. Jeepneys provide a popular way to travel in Nigeria.

false 31. Chocolate and cocoa come from the coconut tree.

true 32. There are many earthquakes along the Ring of Fire.

false 33. All of the Netherlands may also be called Holland.

true 34. Most farms in Japan are small.

true 35. An iceberg begins as part of a glacier.

E. *Write the answers in complete sentences.*

36. Why are there no trees in the frigid zones?   *It is too cold for trees to grow*

   there.

   _____

37. How have volcanoes helped the Filipinos?   *The ashes from volcanoes*

   have enriched the soil.

   _____

38. The Gulf Stream is a benefit to Europe in two ways. What is one of those ways?

   a mild climate along its coast, a good place for fishing

   _____

39. What do scientists do in Antarctica? *Scientists study the ice of Antarctica.*

   _____

   _____

40. The air on top of a high mountain is different from the air at the foot of the

   mountain. What is one way that it is different? *The air on top of a high*

   mountain is cooler (thinner).

   _____

F. *In the blank before each name, write the letter from the map that shows the loca-*
tion of that land. You will not use all the letters.

   J   41. Japan   *B*   46. United States

   D   42. Brazil   *K*   47. The Philippines

   H   43. Europe   *E*   48. Antarctica

   C   44. Ecuador   *F*   49. Greenland

   L   45. Australia   *A*   50. Canada

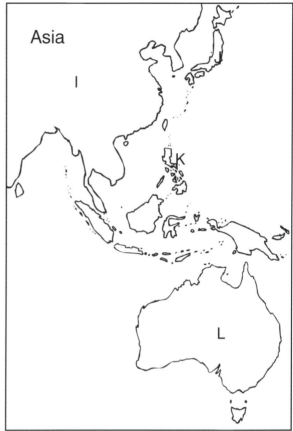

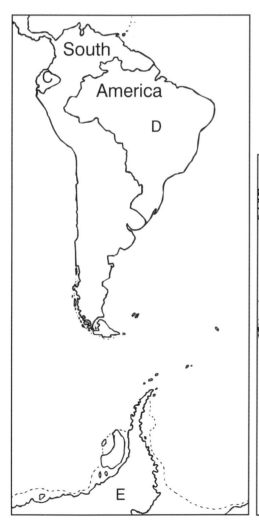

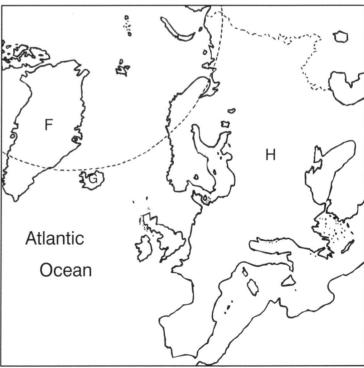

Glossary Word Index

The glossary words are listed alphabetically, with numbers showing in which lesson the word is introduced. The meanings and pronunciations of the glossary words are listed in the lessons.

The definitions tell only how the words are used in this book. Use a dictionary if you want to find other meanings for the words.

Most of the words have been respelled within parentheses to show how they are usually pronounced. Accented syllables are printed in capital letters.

abaca, 14
aborigine, 18
altitude, 36
Anabaptist, 21
ancestor, 21
Antarctic Circle, 1
antelope, 7
aqueduct, 23
archipelago, 11, 26
Arctic Circle, 1
artesian well, 17
atoll, 19
autobahn, 23
avalanche, 22
axis, 1

bannwald, 22
barge, 24
baron, 23
barrio, 11
blizzard, 34
brumby, 17
bullet train, 29

burnoose, 38
cacao, 6
Canadian Shield, 43
cannery, 13
carabao, 12
caravan, 38
cargo, 22
caribou, 4
cassava, 7
castle, 23
cathedral, 23
Catholic Church, 21
compound, 6
Congress, 42
continent, 1
Continental Divide, 41
copra, 14
coral, 19
county seat, 42
custom, 8

dam, 8
delta, 9

dike, 24
dingo, 17
dune, 38
engineer, 23
equator, 1
eucalyptus, 17
export, 14

fazenda, 2
ferment, 9
ferry, 28
fillet, 33
fiord, 31
fleece, 18
frigid, 4
frond, 11

game reserve, 7
game warden, 7
generate, 8
geothermal, 33
geyser, 33
glacier, 31

Map Index

(Pupil page numbers are given below, not Teacher page numbers.)

General Index
(Pupil page numbers are given below, not Teacher page numbers.)

farming in, 297–299
government of, 303–305
landforms of, 296–300
location and size of, 13, 116,
    150, 296
manufacturing in, 297, 298
Ural Mountains, 233

V

verandah, 116, 121
Victoria, 138
vineyards, 171
Virginia, 201, 305, 307
volcanoes, 87, 92, 93, 208, 215, 235,
    242, 250, 273, 274, 300

W

wallaby, 123, 127
Washington, D. C., 303, 305
weather, definition of, 10

weather stations, 229
weaving, 95, 273
Weddell Sea, 250
whales, 229, 237, 249
wheat, 202, 235, 237, 298, 303
White House, 303, 304
wildlife (See specific countries and
    animals.)
windmills, 175, 178
wool, 131, 135, 280

Y

yam, 53, 54
Yenisey River, 234
Yukon Territory, 318

Z

zebras, 64
Zeeland, 176
Zurich, 158, 159

Photo Credits
(Pupil page numbers are given below, not Teacher page numbers.)

Australian Overseas Information Service: 118, 124, 127, 130, 133, 138

Charaffi, Fabian/French Government Tourist Office: 169

Copyright © Corel Corporation: 1, back cover

Danish Tourist Board: 229, 231

Ecuadorian Foundation for the Promotion of Tourism: 264, 265

French Government Tourist Office: 170, 171

Frerck, Robert/Odyssey Productions/Chicago: 96, 97, 104, 119, 120

Georgia Department of Tourism: 297

Horst, Melvin G.: 50

Iceland Embassy: 242, 244

Iceland Tourist Board: 243

International Society for Educational Information, Tokyo, Inc.: 193, 199, 202, 207, 209, 213

Jackson, Rick/Travel Montana/Department of Commerce: 299

Japan National Tourist Organization: 188, 201, 206, 212, 215, 216

Kaschub, Norma: 44, 160, 163, 174 (bottom), 178, 313

Library of Congress: 83, 87, 194, 198

MacNeil, J./NWT Dept. of Economics Development and Tourism: 37

Martin, Michael S.: 312

McNeil, Crombie/NWT Dept. of Economics Development and Tourism: 35

Miller, Lester: 88, 91

Miller, Ray: 89, 106

Nations, James D./D. Donne Bryant Stock Photography: 271

Photri: 8, 18, 19, 27, 28, 48, 49, 57, 61, 63, 69, 70, 84, 103, 141 (bottom), 142, 148, 152, 154, 155, 167 (top), 180, 192, 196, 228, 235, 237, 238, 252, 260, 266, 267, 272, 273, 280, 281, 285 (M. Fantin), 286, 294, 298, 304, 305, 306, 311, 317, 318

Plett, Randall: 78, 95, 100, 107, 108

Schulz Global Travel Photos: front cover, 20, 21, 114, 131, 139, 141 (top), 224, 248, 249, 251, 278, 279

Stutzman, Grace: 167 (bottom), 176, 179

Thompson, Brian/NWT Dept. of Economics Development and Tourism: 319

Tourism British Columbia: 314

Weber, Wolfgang/NWT Dept. of Economics Development and Tourism: 36

Zurich Tourist Office: 159

ARCTIC

Beaufort Sea
Arctic
Islands
Baffin
Bay
Greenland
Iceland
Great Bear
Lake
Bering
Sea
Gulf of
Alaska
Great Slave
Lake
Hudson
Bay
Canadian Shield
Aleutian Islands
N O R T H
Central
Plains
Great Lakes
Appalachian Mts.
A M E R I C A
Coastal Plain
ATLANTIC
Canary
Islands
PACIFIC
Gulf
of
México
West
Indies
Cape
Verde
Hawaiian
Islands
Caribbean Sea
165°W   150°W   135°W   120°W   105°W   90°W
Guiana
Highlands
S O U T H
30°W   15°
Galápagos
Islands
Amazon Basin
O C E A N
A M E R I C A
Andes Mountains
Polynesia
Brazilian
Highlands
Gran
Chaco
O C E A N
Pampas
Bellingshausen Sea
Weddell Sea
Falkland
Islands
Ross Sea
A N T